THE
PENNSYLVANIA
MAGAZINE
OF HISTORY AND BIOGRAPHY

VOLUME CXLIII   *October 2019*   NO. 3

Editorial Advisory Committee

Editor

CHRISTINA LAROCCO

Editorial Interns

McKENNA BRITTON   OLIVIA ERRICO

THE PENNSYLVANIA MAGAZINE OF HISTORY AND BIOGRAPHY (ISSN 0031-4587, print; ISSN 2169-8546, online) is published in January, April, and October by THE UNIVERSITY OF PENNSYLVANIA PRESS, 3905 Spruce Street, Philadelphia, PA 19104-4112. Postage paid at Philadelphia, PA, and additional mailing offices. **Postmaster**: send address changes to PMHB, Historical Society of Pennslyvania, 1300 Locust Street, Philadelphia, PA 19107-5699. **Authorization for academic photocopying**: For permission to reuse material, please access http://www.copyright.com or contact the Copyright Clearance Center, Inc. (CCC), 222 Rosewood Drive, Danvers, MA 01923, 978-750-8400. CCC is a nonprofit organization that provides licenses and registration for a variety of uses. **Submission**: All communications should be addressed to the editor. Email may be sent to pmhb@hsp.org. Maunscripts should conform to *The Chicago Manual of Style*. Electronic submissions are welcome. For submission guidelines, visit the *PMHB* web page (http://hsp.org/publications/pennsylvania-magazine-of-history-biography). The editor does not assume responsibility for statements of fact or of opinion made by the contributors.

Contributors

ANNIE ANDERSON is the manager of research and public programming at Eastern State Penitentiary Historic Site in Philadelphia. She develops exhibits, audio stops, signage, and programs about the history of the building; the people who lived and worked there; and the evolving identity of the American criminal justice system. Anderson is a cultural historian who studies race, class, gender, sexuality, vice, crime, and morality. She has a decade of experience doing primary source research in archives big and small—authoring essays, a local history book, and exhibits along the way. She collaborates with academics, genealogists, front line interpreters, and museum visitors with an eye toward connecting the past to the present and revealing larger historical trends. Recent career highlights include researching and cowriting the exhibit *Prisons Today: Questions in the Age of Mass Incarceration* and serving as a contributor to MASS Action (Museum As Site For Social Action), a project promoting equity and inclusion in museums.

TAYLOR BAGWELL is a student at Christopher Newport University majoring in American Studies and finance. She has published two articles on Eastern State Penitentiary's blog and plans to attend law school.

CELIA CAUST-ELLENBOGEN is an archivist at the Friends Historical Library of Swarthmore College.

TAJAH EBRAM is a PhD candidate in the Department of English at the University of Pennsylvania. Her research is focused on twentieth and twenty-first century Black literature, history, and culture, with particular interests in Black feminism, prison writings, carceral studies, cultural geography, digital humanities, and Philadelphia Black radicalisms. She cofounded the Black Cultural Studies Collective, a reading and working group based in African diasporic studies at Penn. She is currently writing her dissertation, entitled *Black Urban Revolution: A Cultural History of MOVE and the Radical Everyday in West Philadelphia*.

BETH ENGLISH is director of the Project on Gender in the Global Community at the Liechtenstein Institute on Self-Determination at Princeton University. She is a lecturer in the Princeton Writing Program and an instructor with Princeton University's Prison Teaching Initiative. She received her PhD in history from the College of William and Mary, where she was a Glucksman Fellow and visiting assistant professor, and has taught at the University of Pennsylvania. Her research has been funded by the National Endowment for the Humanities. English's research and teaching focus primarily on gender, historical and contemporary labor and working-class issues, culture and society, global economy, and the US and Global Souths. She is the coeditor of *Global Women's Work: Perspectives on Gender and Work in the Global Economy* (with Mary E. Frederickson and Olga Sanmiguel-Valderrama); author of *A Common Thread: Labor, Politics, and Capital Mobility in the Textile Industry;* and a contributing author to several edited volumes focusing on gender and on the US South. Her article "'I . . . Have a Lot of Work to Do': Cotton Mill Work and Women's Culture in Matoaca, Virginia, 1888–1895" was recognized as one of the Organization of American Historians' *Best American History Essays of 2008* (David Roediger, ed.). She is the producer and host of the podcast *Working History.*

JEN MANION is associate professor of history at Amherst College and author of *Liberty's Prisoners: Carceral Culture in Early America* (University of Pennsylvania Press, 2015), which received the 2016 Mary Kelley Best Book Prize from the Society for Historians of the Early American Republic. Manion is coeditor of *Taking Back the Academy: History of Activism, History as Activism* (Routledge, 2004) and author of the forthcoming book *Female Husbands: A Trans History* (Cambridge, 2020).

STEVE MARTI is a historian of the First World War, based in Kingston, Ontario. He developed an interest in digital history while completing his PhD at the University of Western Ontario and had the opportunity to apply these skills as a digital humanities fellow with the Library of the American Philosophical Society in 2017.

JOHN McWILLIAMS is an American historian focusing on twentieth century social/political history. He has published a book and articles on federal drug control, the intelligence community and organized crime in the Cold War, black firefighters in Philadelphia, and the history of corrections in Pennsylvania. A book titled *Cultural Revolutions in the 1960s* is scheduled for publication in early 2020.

KRISTIN O'BRASSILL-KULFAN is a public historian and scholar of early American social history, teaching and working in the Department of History at Rutgers University in New Brunswick, New Jersey. She holds a

PhD in history from the University of Leicester and an MA in modern history from Queens University Belfast, and she researches poverty, labor, mobility, and crime and punishment in the early American Northeast, as well as public historical and commemorative representations of these subjects. O'Brassill-Kulfan is the author of *Vagrants and Vagabonds: Poverty and Mobility in the Early American Republic* (New York University Press, 2019).

ANNE E. PARSONS is associate professor of history and the director of public history at UNC Greensboro and the author of the book *From Asylum to Prison: Deinstitutionalization and the Rise of Mass Incarceration after 1945*.

DAN ROYLES is an assistant professor of history at Florida International University. He is currently working on a book about African American AIDS activism titled *To Make the Wounded Whole: African American Responses to HIV/AIDS*.

JONATHAN W. WHITE is an associate professor of American Studies at Christopher Newport University and is the author or editor of nine books, including *Midnight in America: Darkness, Sleep, and Dreams during the Civil War* (2017).

S. L. ZIEGLER is the head of digital programs and services at LSU Libraries in Baton Rouge, Louisiana, and is responsible for developing strategies for the libraries' digitization and preservation operations. Previously, Ziegler was the head of digital scholarship and technology at the American Philosophical Society and worked on a number of data-driven projects based on special collections material.

Editorial

ECENTLY, AS I EXPLAINED to an acquaintance where the Historical Society of Pennsylvania is located, she asked a question that surprised me: "Is that near the Daniel Faulkner plaque?" Indeed it is, though I had not realized it until recently. Every time I leave my office for a midday Target run or an Indian lunch buffet, I traverse the initial site of one of this state's most controversial pieces of carceral history.

In 1982, a jury convicted black civil rights activist and journalist Mumia Abu-Jamal of first-degree murder in the death of Faulkner, a white city police officer. Originally sentenced to death, Abu-Jamal is now serving a life sentence. Immediately, activists noted irregularities in the arrest, trial, and conviction, including possible connections to police abuse and corruption and a conflict of interest on the part of a state Supreme Court justice who heard the case on appeal. In 2019, Philadelphia district attorney Larry Krasner withdrew his objection to an opinion from the court of common pleas, clearing the way for a new appeal before the state Supreme Court. A case that began outside of HSP almost thirty-eight years ago will continue.[1]

Literally and symbolically surrounded by such stories, we have a responsibility to document their precursors. Thus this issue of the *Pennsylvania Magazine of History and Biography* is dedicated to exploring the history of incarceration in Pennsylvania. Due in large part to its Quaker heritage, Pennsylvania has long been a center of prison reform movements. At HSP, for example, researchers can find the papers of the Philadelphia Society for Alleviating the Miseries of Public Prisons (later the Pennsylvania Prison Society), founded in 1787. Yet today Pennsylvania stands out as the state with the largest population of incarcerated individuals in the Northeast and the fifth-largest in the nation. The racial disparities, too, are striking: the state incarcerates African Americans and Latinos at rates of 8.9 and 3.3 times that of whites, respectively.[2]

---

[1] On Krasner's withdrawn objection and a potential new appeal, see, for example, Chris Palmer, "Philly DA to Drop Challenge in Mumia Abu-Jamal Case, Clearing Appeal to Reach High Court," *Philadelphia Inquirer*, Apr. 17, 2019. As a journalist, Abu-Jamal supported MOVE members in their 1978 standoff with police; see Tajah Ebram's article in this volume, "'You Can't Jail the Revolution': Policing, Protest, and the MOVE Organization in Philadelphia's Carceral Landscape."

[2] ACLU Pennsylvania, "Ending Mass Incarceration in Pennsylvania," accessed Aug. 28, 2019, https://www.aclupa.org/our-work/current-campaigns/smart-justice-pa#sentencing.

THE PENNSYLVANIA MAGAZINE OF HISTORY AND BIOGRAPHY
Vol. CXLIII, No. 3 (October 2019)

The development of a mass incarceration infrastructure was a multi-decade, bipartisan project. As a younger and more diverse constituency holds politicians accountable for policies they advocated and/or implemented in the 1990s, this history haunts Democratic Party candidates in particular—including Hillary Clinton in 2016 and Pennsylvania native Joe Biden today. These issues are particularly important in Pennsylvania, not only because carceral control defines the lives of so many of our neighbors but also, and relatedly, because of the state's role as a fulcrum of national politics. As activists and scholars have pointed out for at least a decade, the prisons needed to house the burgeoning population of incarcerated individuals have overwhelmingly been built in rural areas. While incarcerated populations count toward congressional representation, these individuals cannot exercise the franchise. When racial disparities are taken into account, the carceral state thus echoes the Constitution's three-fifths clause. It also increases the political clout of overwhelmingly white, rural areas vis-à-vis that of cities, which lose representation when the criminal justice system sends community members to otherwise less populous portions of the state.[3]

Beginning with a review essay by guest editor Jen Manion, the articles in this issue ask, among other questions, how we got here. While historians are not equipped to chart a path forward alone, we also believe that looking back is a necessary prerequisite for doing so. Ending the crisis of mass incarceration is no exception.

Christina Larocco
Editor

---

[3] See Michelle Alexander, *The New Jim Crow: Mass Incarceration in the Age of Colorblindness* (New York, 2012); Peter Wagner and Elena Lavarreda, "Importing Constituents: Prisoners and Political Clout in Pennsylvania," June 26, 2009, Prison Policy Initiative, https://www.prisonersofthecensus.org/pennsylvania/importing.html; and Amaris Elliott-Engel, "Report: Census Prisoner Count Dilutes Urban Political Clout," *Philadelphia Legal Intelligencer*, June 26, 2009.

Carceral History in the Era of Mass Incarceration

THE US LEGAL SYSTEM is embedded with contradictions, perhaps none greater than the cherished promise of liberty and justice for all and the mass incarceration of the poorest among us, devastating African American and Latinx communities. It is now well established that the US carceral regime—especially at the state and local level—uses the denial of freedom as a tool of social control to devastating ends. Though making up just 5 percent of the world's population, the US is home to 25 percent of the world's inmates.

Mass incarceration is the greatest threat to justice, human rights, and democracy. Growing public awareness of this crisis has generated criticism of many dimensions of the carceral system, including the targeting of communities of color, the application of excessive fines and fees, the growth of the private prison industry, and the extension of surveillance through rigid parole practices. Evidence of racial bias in policing, convictions, detention, and incarceration are widely documented. How did we get here?

It is no exaggeration to say that one single book educated the entire nation about the fact of mass incarceration and its troubling legacy: Michelle Alexander's *The New Jim Crow: Mass Incarceration in the Age of Colorblindness*.[1] Alexander shows that the carceral state was a tool of racial segregation and discrimination, a backlash against civil rights era gains. While Alexander's book became a national bestseller, informing young readers, veteran activists, and policymakers alike, historians produced numerous works contemporaneously that further contextualized the issues raised.

Kali Gross and Cheryl Hicks, for example, examine how race, gender, and sexuality shaped attitudes toward and treatment of black women in the criminal justice systems of Philadelphia and New York, respectively.[2]

---

[1] Michelle Alexander, *The New Jim Crow: Mass Incarceration in the Age of Colorblindness* (New York, 2010).

[2] Kali Gross, *Colored Amazons: Crime, Violence, and Black Women in the City of Brotherly Love, 1880–1910* (Durham, NC, 2006); Cheryl D. Hicks, *Talk with You Like a Woman: African American Women, Justice, and Reform in New York, 1890–1935* (Chapel Hill, NC, 2010).

THE PENNSYLVANIA MAGAZINE OF HISTORY AND BIOGRAPHY
Vol. CXLIII, No. 3 (October 2019)

Khalil Gibrand Muhammad focuses on the same era, shedding light on social scientists who used the legitimacy of their professional field to advance racist theories of difference.[3] Charting these linkages has proven invaluable in exposing how racist views were justified and normalized. Important scholarship on the South reveals how quickly and easily state officials turned the carceral system into a new form of enslavement following the Civil War via the convict leasing system.[4] No sense of paternalism or chivalry protected black Americans, who faced excessive cruelties that were intensified when they resisted the violence aimed at them.[5]

Historians have shown that moments of potential and actual advancement for African American liberation and freedom—such as the abolition of slavery—were often stymied when white people characterized African Americans as a group not worthy or capable of handling the full rights of citizenship. This pattern of using crime/criminalization as a vehicle to deny black freedom and self-determination extends far beyond the Jim Crow era. Rather, it can be charted back to changes in colonial era slave patrols in the South. Slavery by definition criminalized black freedom. Changes to patrolling systems in Virginia and the Carolinas intensified the notion that all African Americans, by virtue of a desire for freedom, were lawbreakers. From the eighteenth century until the Civil War, the responsibility of patrolling shifted from local slaveholding families on a somewhat unregulated basis to full-time paid patrollers to a formal policing force.[6] These changes formalized what had long been an informal understanding: the principle job of the police was to protect the property of the elites; in this case, that meant capturing human beings who were by definition African American.

This pattern was not isolated to the South. In the colonial and early republican eras, local jails were known for detaining people suspected of being runaway slaves or servants, in North and South alike. The abolition of slavery was a gradual process that occurred over a century. As the

---

[3] Khalil Gibrand Muhammad, *The Condemnation of Blackness: Race, Crime, and the Making of Modern Urban America* (Cambridge, MA, 2010).

[4] David M. Oshinsky, *Worse than Slavery: Parchman Farm and the Ordeal of Jim Crow Justice* (New York, 1996); Douglas Blackmon, *Slavery by Another Name: The Re-Enslavement of Black Americans from the Civil War to World War II* (New York, 2008); Robert Perkinson, *Texas Tough: The Rise of America's Prison Empire* (New York, 2010).

[5] Talitha LeFlouria, *Chained in Silence: Black Women and Convict Labor in the New South* (Chapel Hill, NC, 2015); Sarah Haley, *No Mercy Here: Gender, Punishment, and the Making of Jim Crow Modernity* (Chapel Hill, NC, 2016).

[6] Sally E. Hadden, *Slave Patrols: Law and Violence in Virginia and the Carolinas* (Cambridge, MA, 2001).

northern states gradually embraced abolition in the 1780s and '90s, concerns about the place of free blacks in civil society grew.[7] Limited employment prospects and a series of economic crises left free blacks struggling and more likely to be homeless or unemployed vagrants—and thereby criminalized.[8] It should come as no surprise, then, that policing authorities, jailers, and judges—every arm of carceral authority—approached all African Americans with distrust and the suspicion that they had already done something wrong just by virtue of existing in freedom. For scholars of African American history, this is not news. Nearly fifty years ago, Mary Frances Berry argued that overt violence against African Americans was rampant in the colonial era, enshrined in the US Constitution, and continued largely unchanged until the 1940s.[9] While it would be inaccurate to argue a straight, unchanging perspective or experience across time, space, and person from eighteenth-century Virginia slave patrols to the Philadelphia police department of the 1970s, there are certainly underlying themes that resonate. Nowhere is this more evident than in the treatment of the MOVE family.

In her essay "'Can't Jail the Revolution': Policing, Protest and the MOVE Organization in Philadelphia's Carceral Landscape," Tajah Ebram argues that MOVE became a target of the Philadelphia police in the 1970s (the early years of the organization) because of its anticarceral politics and protests. Members became targets of policing authorities not because they were breaking laws but because, in freedom, they drew attention to the growing militarization of police forces and the growth of the prison industry. Health was at the heart of MOVE's founding philosophy, which inspired commitments to natural living, a rejection of all kinds of chemicals, and an avoidance of many forms of technology. As Ebram writes, "Theirs was revolutionary naturalism, combining environmentalism and self-governance with critiques of racist and capitalist exploitation of Black and poor people."

MOVE came into prominence in the wake of Lyndon B. Johnson's wars on poverty and crime. Its alternative kinship model was partly a response to the carceral state, which separated black families. Black urban

---

[7] Pennsylvania (1780), New Hampshire (1783), Massachusetts (1783), Connecticut (1784), Rhode Island (1784), New York (1799), and New Jersey (1804) abolished slavery after the revolution. Admitted to the nation in 1791, Vermont had abolished slavery in 1777.

[8] Brian Wagner, *Disturbing the Peace: Black Culture and the Police Power after Slavery* (Cambridge, MA, 2009).

[9] Mary Frances Berry, *Black Resistance / White Law: A History of Constitutional Racism in America* (New York, 1971).

communities were themselves subject to surveillance, making them part of a "carceral landscape" that was not very different from prison itself. The treatment of MOVE in this era highlights the limits of freedom and the legacy of criminalization that was a condition of freedom. In this way, Ebram's work builds on Leslie Patrick-Stamp's influential dissertation, which traced the association between blackness and criminality in Pennsylvania from the colonial era through the early republic, as well as Jeannine DeLombard's work.[10] But MOVE also embodied a confidence born of the civil rights era, using its numerous interactions with carceral authorities to spread its message and critique the system itself. Its rejection of the norms of modern life under white capitalist patriarchy (which included refusing the ritual deference granted to judges in legal proceedings) led to a standoff with the authorities that was only resolved when MOVE members agreed to leave their home in a quickly gentrifying neighborhood. Ebram's study offers new insights into MOVE's activism, including its use of carceral spaces to advance civil rights organizing, something Dan Berger illuminated so powerfully in his book *Captive Nation*.[11]

The criminalization of African Americans was a key dimension of mass incarceration, but it alone does not explain the vast expansion of the carceral state in the 1970s. Historians have also turned to postwar demographic trends, the political wars on poverty and drugs, the militarization of the police, and the emergence of a surplus workforce. Ruth Wilson Gilmore's pathbreaking *California Gulag* examines the movement in California in the 1980s to dramatically expand the size and capacity of carceral structures and to fill them with surplus workers.[12] Elizabeth Hinton turns back the clock even further, pointing to Johnson's War on Poverty, once thought of as linchpin of progressive liberal policymaking, as a key to igniting the war on crime, which decimated inner city communities.[13] Heather Ann Thompson makes the case for historians of the postwar era

[10] Leslie Patrick-Stamp, "Ideology and Punishment: The Crime of Being Black (Pennsylvania, 1639–1804)" (PhD diss., University of California, Santa Cruz, 1989); Jeannine Marie DeLombard, *In the Shadow of the Gallows: Race, Crime, and American Civic Identity* (Philadelphia, 2012).

[11] Dan Berger, *Captive Nation: Black Prison Organizing in the Civil Rights Era* (Chapel Hill, NC, 2014).

[12] Ruth Wilson Gilmore, *Golden Gulag: Prisons, Surplus, Crisis, and Opposition in Globalizing California* (Oakland, CA, 2007).

[13] Elizabeth Hinton, "'A War within our own boundaries': Lyndon Johnson's Great Society and the Rise of the Carceral State," *Journal of American History* 102 (2015): 100–112; Hinton, *From the War on Poverty to the War on Crime: The Making of Mass Incarceration in America* (Cambridge, MA, 2016).

to look more closely at the economic shifts that decimated inner cities, transformed labor, and ultimately set the conditions for the explosive growth of the prison industrial complex.[14] James Forman Jr. examines the role of black elites, politicians, and cops in supporting the "tough-on-crime" measures that escalated mass incarceration and devastated urban black neighborhoods in the 1970s, '80s, and '90s.[15] We have only just begun to learn how deinstitutionalization of psychiatric hospitals fueled the rise of incarceration for this vulnerable population.[16]

Long before mass incarceration reshaped the conversation and ensuing scholarship about punishment, scholars focused their attention on the origins and purpose of punishment in American life, with great emphasis given to the late eighteenth and early nineteenth centuries. David Rothman argued long ago that authorities used a vast array of carceral structures in the early decades of the nineteenth century to assert strength and order in a period of uncertainty and weakness. Michael Meranze asserted that carceral authority was nimbler and more forward-looking than that, as reformers used punishment, especially classification and segregation, to remake prisoners into model citizens for a liberal democracy. In my book, *Liberty's Prisoners,* I show how treatment of any given prisoner varied by crime, race, and gender. Punishment was used to stabilize a sexual division of labor and promote the ideal of the heterosexual family as an economic unit at the same time that it destroyed families and ensured women's economic dependency on men. Erica Rhodes Hayden's new book on women in the criminal justice system in antebellum Pennsylvania shifts our lens away from institutional reform back to the actions, dreams, and struggles of women who resisted the era's gender norms.[17] In this way, Hayden's work and my own build on Susan Branson's *Dangerous to Know*, an illuminating 2008 study of Ann Carson, early Philadelphia's most infamous women.[18] No one can deny that women committed crimes in sig-

[14] Heather Ann Thompson, "Why Mass Incarceration Matters: Rethinking Crisis, Decline, and Transformation in Postwar American History," *Journal of American History* 97 (2010): 703–34.

[15] James Forman Jr., *Locking Up Our Own: Crime and Punishment in Black America* (New York, 2017).

[16] Anne E. Parsons, *From Asylum to Prison: Deinstitutionalization and the Rise of Mass Incarceration after 1945* (Chapel Hill, NC, 2018).

[17] Erica Rhodes Hayden, *Troublesome Women: Gender, Crime, and Punishment in Antebellum Pennsylvania* (State College, PA, 2019). See also Hayden and Theresa R. Jach, eds., *Incarcerated Women: A History of Struggles, Oppression, and Resistance in American Prisons* (Lanham, MD, 2017).

[18] Susan Branson, *Dangerous to Know: Women, Crime, and Notoriety in the Early Republic* (Philadelphia, 2008).

nificant numbers and were punished for them in highly racialized and gendered ways in the early republican and antebellum eras.

Reformers designed the penitentiary to be self-sustaining, with forced labor by inmates at its heart—sort of. In *Reading Prisoners,* Jodi Schorb illuminates the often-overlooked moment in penal history when reformers believed that literacy and reading were valued components of punishment and reform. Instead, this tradition was abandoned in favor of labor.[19] The purpose of this labor varied over time and place—it could be reformative, exploitive, or punitive. While the centrality of labor in American punishment has long been established, the role of profit making as a founding and continuing legacy is not well understood. Scholars long argued against the idea that early penitentiaries were motivated by profit because they were so expensive to build and generally functioned at great deficit to the state. Prison labor in workshops was sporadic, unpredictable, often not profitable, and greatly resisted by inmates—especially men.[20] Rebecca McLennan challenges this view when she asserts that contract penal servitude was central to defining and stabilizing the penitentiary in the antebellum period as a "system of punishment founded on the sale of prisoners' labor power to private business interests."[21] In rural white communities, prisons became driving engines of economic growth and employment for many, though not without controversy.[22] While the institutions themselves provided some jobs, they also were seen as a threat to free market labor, leading various unions to lobby against prison labor.

The penitentiary and other carceral structures served numerous functions in early American life. They were celebrated tourist destinations for genteel visitors. They were sites of authority and order, which for some encapsulated an American national identity.[23] Longstanding beliefs about

---

[19] Jodi Schorb, *Reading Prisoners: Literature, Literacy, and the Transformation of American Punishment, 1700–1845* (New Brunswick, NJ, 2014).

[20] Michael Meranze, *Laboratories of Virtue: Punishment, Revolution, and Authority in Philadelphia, 1760–1835* (Chapel Hill, NC, 1996), 226–27; Jen Manion, *Liberty's Prisoners: Carceral Culture in Early America* (Philadelphia, 2015), 33–47.

[21] Rebecca M. McLennan, *The Crisis of Imprisonment: Protest, Politics, and the Making of the American Penal State, 1770–1941* (Cambridge, 2008), introduction.

[22] Judah Schept, *Progressive Punishment: Job Loss, Jail Growth, and the Neoliberal Logic of Carceral Expansion* (New York, 2015); Heather Ann Thompson, *Blood in the Water: The Attica Prison Uprising of 1971 and Its Legacy* (New York, 2016).

[23] Peter Okun, *Crime and the Nation: Prison Reform and Popular Fiction in Philadelphia, 1786–1800* (New York, 2002); Mark E. Kann, *Punishment, Prisons, and Patriarchy: Liberty and Power in the Early American Republic* (New York, 2005); Caleb Smith, *The Prison and the American Imagination* (New Haven, CT, 2009); Tamara Plakins Thornton, "Capitalist Aesthetics," in *Capitalism Takes Command: The Social Transformation of Nineteenth-Century America,* ed. Michael Zakim and Gary J. Kornblith (Chicago, 2012).

American punishment have followed a disparate trajectory defined by region and period. Despite a robust historiography of punishment in American history, it has not led to a significant conceptual payoff. Mary Ellen Curtin describes the historiography as rich, varied, and fragmented, stating, "It fails to give a national picture. It rarely addresses change over long periods of time. . . . It has focused on racism and forced labor in the South but ignored comparable trends elsewhere"[24] This pattern is partly born of fact—the intense regionalism that has and continues to define punishment practices. But there are also longstanding gaps in what we know, which newer work has begun to address. There is reason to be optimistic that we are well on our way to having this complete national picture of the role of carceral authority in American history. Two exciting essay collections, *Buried Lives: Incarcerated in Early America* and *Crime and Punishment in the Jim Crow South*, contribute to this shift.[25]

A wave of important and exciting scholarship has vastly expanded our knowledge of carceral practices—especially policing, a much lesser known arm of the carceral state.[26] These three new studies by Max Felker-Kantor, Marisol LeBron, and Adam Malka together allow us to compare the role of policing in three distinct regions: Baltimore, Maryland, Los Angeles, California, and Puerto Rico. The intense focus on the post–World War II carceral state has given way to scholarship by those aiming to situate carceral practices within a longer durée of punishment. This is great news. Punishment has changed dramatically in degree but little in kind. It would be a great mistake to only look at modern American life to understand the unique, vast, and persistent role of authority and punishment in American life. Two books whose authors have anchored their research in the revolutionary era include *Discretionary Justice: Pardon and Parole in New York from the Revolution to the Depression* by Carolyn Strange and Kelly Lytle Hernandez's *City of Inmates: Conquest, Rebellion,*

---

[24] Mary Ellen Curtin, "State of the Art: The New Prison History," *Labor: Studies in Working-Class History of the Americas* 8, no. 3 (2011): 97–108, 99. A rare early study spanned North and South: Michael Hindus, *Prison and Plantation: Crime, Justice, and Authority in Massachusetts and South Carolina, 1767–1787* (Chapel Hill, NC, 1980).

[25] Michele Lise Tarter and Richard Bell, eds., *Buried Lives: Incarcerated in Early America* (Athens, GA, 2012); Amy Wood and Natalie Ring, eds., *Crime and Punishment in the Jim Crow South* (Champaign, IL, 2019).

[26] Adam Malka, *The Men of Mobtown: Policing Baltimore in the Age of Slavery and Emancipation* (Chapel Hill, NC, 2018); Max Felker-Kantor, *Policing Los Angeles: Race, Resistance, and the Rise of the LAPD* (Chapel Hill, NC, 2018); Marisol LeBron, *Policing Life and Death: Race, Violence, and Resistance in Puerto Rico* (Oakland, CA, 2019).

and the Rise of Human Caging in Los Angeles, 1771–1965.[27] Hernandez situates mass incarceration as an extension and outgrowth of settler colonialism, including Native American erasure and anti-immigrant sentiment and practices, while Strange's volume charts how and when the state offers forgiveness and to what end.

In this special issue of the *Pennsylvania Magazine of History and Biography,* we bring together scholars working on Pennsylvania's unique legacy in the history of punishment in the US. The essays speak to a range of urgent questions in the field of carceral studies, including modes of resistance to carceral authorities, the tremendous and often unfettered violence of carceral authorities against people, the role of whiteness in granting a degree of protection for some inmates, and the persistent attempt to classify, organize, and segregate people as a form of punishment. The essays featured here take a fresh look at topics that have long engaged scholars of Pennsylvania's legendary carceral practices. Of special interest is the focus on institutions that we simply know less about: Arch Street Prison, Western State Penitentiary, Pennsylvania Industrial Reformatory, and Rockview.

Pennsylvania plays an important role in the nation's history of incarceration, from its designation of the nation's first penitentiary in 1790 to its twentieth and twenty-first century status as a state with one of the highest rates of institutionalization.[28] Pennsylvania has incarcerated people longer than any other state and more often than most.[29] What does this say about a state that boasts "Virtue, Liberty, and Independence," as its official motto? Carceral authorities have been quick to declare the poorest among us as *not worthy of freedom,* that is for sure. To what end? Pennsylvania has long enjoyed a legacy as one of the more meritocratic places in colonial and early America—"the best poor man's country," as one prize-winning history book declared.[30] Not all poor people fared as well as those men featured in Lemon's book. This picture is greatly complicated when

[27] Carolyn Strange, *Discretionary Justice: Pardon and Parole in New York from the Revolution to the Depression* (New York, 2016); Kelly Lytle Hernandez, *City of Inmates: Conquest, Rebellion, and the Rise of Human Caging in Los Angeles, 1771–1965* (Chapel Hill, NC, 2017).

[28] Anne E. Parsons, *From Asylum to Prison: Deinstitutionalization and the Rise of Mass Incarceration after 1945* (Chapel Hill, NC, 2018), introduction.

[29] The authoritative study of colonial crime and punishment remains Jack D. Marietta and G. S. Rowe, *Troubled Experiment: Crime and Justice in Pennsylvania, 1682–1800* (Philadelphia, 2006).

[30] James T. Lemon, *The Best Poor Man's Country: Early Southeastern Pennsylvania* (Baltimore, MD, 1972).

examined through the lens of race and gender, as Clare Lyons shows in her study of how the regulation of sexuality shaped the lives, opportunities, and limitations of poor people in Philadelphia.[31]

There was a fine—and at times nonexistent—line between poverty and crime in early America. In her essay " 'Severe punishment for their misfortunes and poverty': Philadelphia's Arch Street Prison, 1804–37," Kristin O'Brassill-Kulfan examines the imprisonment of poor people in antebellum Philadelphia to better understand broader developments in the Pennsylvania carceral landscape beyond the penitentiary. Building on Simon Newman's influential *Embodied History: The Lives of the Poor in Early Philadelphia*, O'Brassill-Kulfan shows that the treatment of poor people was sometimes punitive and other times "welfare-based."[32] The poor moved and were moved between the almshouse and the numerous prisons in early Philadelphia. Arch Street Prison was the least known of the city's carceral structures in this era—at least until it was hit with the cholera epidemic of 1832. Arch Street Prison was emblematic of the "intensifying criminalization of poverty" and offers important lessons for this development.

Though vagrants had not committed actual crimes of note, their treatment was often worse than that of individuals who had been convicted of significant crimes (theft was the most common). Members of the latter group were deemed more intelligent and of a higher class, and they were granted greater provisions than vagrants. This hierarchy had consequences. The poor were largely cast aside, forced to live in a filthy state and then condemned for being dirty. A woman incarcerated in Arch Street was blamed for the cholera outbreak that swept through the city. Even in the face of evidence that degraded conditions in the institution contributed to the epidemic, reformers and managers had a very narrow vision as to the solution. Now inmates were to be bathed and their clothing replaced or fumigated. No attempt was made to minimize the numbers of those admitted in the first place. For those featured in O'Brassill-Kulfan's account, poverty itself was a carceral experience.

Given the fixation of historians and the public alike on the origins of the penitentiary and those housed behinds its great walls, we have not given enough attention to the other carceral spaces. O'Brassill-Kulfan's

---

[31] Clare A. Lyons, *Sex among the Rabble: An Intimate History of Gender and Power in the Age of Revolution, Philadelphia, 1730–1830* (Chapel Hill, NC, 2006).

[32] Simon P. Newman, *Embodied History: The Lives of the Poor in Early Philadelphia* (Philadelphia, 2003).

work—both here and in her new book, *Vagrants and Vagabonds*—puts Arch Street Prison and the poor more generally at the heart of the story, which is where they belong.[33] Another essay in the volume follows this trend by highlighting the experiences of a different vulnerable group: children. In her essay "'Not Model Children': Culture and Contested Control at the Pennsylvania Industrial Reformatory," Beth English charts a culture of abuse in an institution created to provide leniency in punishment by virtue of the age of its residents. Here we see theory and practice clash—not an unusual development in carceral studies but particularly distressing in this "reformatory prison," which the second generation of prison reformers founded in response to the violence and hypocrisy of the first wave. Residents of the Northeast and Midwest, where more of the inmates were white, widely embraced these reformatories. By contrast, the convict-lease system of the South predominantly detained black people. The architects of the Pennsylvania Industrial Reformatory embraced rigid classification, dividing inmates into three grades with resultant privileges and dress. In this regard, many of the same practices existed across the carceral landscape.

English's study shows that white men from stable homes were not exempt from punishment for their wrongdoings by virtue of their race or sex, but they could leverage certain advantages if their families were respected and persistent. In this case, the father of one such inmate blew the whistle on a culture of violence and abuse of the inmates, who were predominantly young adults from ages seventeen to twenty and 90 percent white. The details of the abuse are horrific, including torture of those involved in consensual sexual intimacies or masturbation. By contrast, monitors who abused their authority and assaulted inmates were not punished. This new research reveals an old story: despite a very public investigation and hearing, the institution and its workers did not assume responsibility for the conditions.[34]

Like the Pennsylvania Industrial Reformatory, Rockview prison was built to offer a more benign and relaxed carceral experience for those deemed worthy. Despite its intense investment in classification and the

---

[33] Kristin O'Brassill-Kulfan, *Vagrants and Vagabonds: Poverty and Mobility in the Early American Republic* (New York, 2019).

[34] Two recent and relevant books on this subject are Karin L. Zipf, *Bad Girls at Samarcand: Sexuality and Sterilization in a Southern Juvenile Reformatory* (Baton Rouge, LA, 2016); and Tera Eva Agyepong, *The Criminalization of Black Children: Race, Gender, and Delinquency in Chicago's Juvenile Justice System, 1899–1945* (Chapel Hill, NC, 2018).

establishment of an elaborate, seemingly nuanced scale of treatment from the harshest conditions to the nearly bucolic, it scarcely worked in practice. In fact, reading of practices, systems, and controversies that unfolded in Pennsylvania's many carceral spaces over a two-hundred-year span, one is struck by the similarities, not the differences. John McWilliams powerfully illustrates this principle in his essay "Shining A Light in a Dark House: Riots, Rebellion, and the Politics of Penal Reform in Pennsylvania." McWilliams charts the prison riots of the 1950s in Pennsylvania's lesser known penitentiary, Western State Penitentiary, and Rockview, the "honor prison" organized around agricultural "activities" on thousands of acres. Both institutions were sites of riots in the 1950s.

The mostly white inmates in both places suffered degraded conditions that were typical of such institutions. But when they turned against the guards in a riot, the authorities (including Pennsylvania Republican governor John S. Fine) recognized their humanity and the value of their lives. McWilliams notes a strategy for quelling the riot in Western State was devised particularly "to prevent—or at least minimize—possible bloodshed." Anyone familiar with other prison riots—and Attica in particular—will find such remarks startling. There is no denying that whiteness was a powerful defense against the blunt force of state violence. When New York authorities were faced with a similar circumstance in the prison riot at Attica, they acted without regard for the lives of the largely black and brown people inside.

We must pause for a moment and consider the significance of race in carceral spaces that are dominated by white people, which is the case in several of the essays in this issue. What are the ethical and political implications of research into historically white carceral spaces *in this moment* of the mass incarceration of predominantly black and brown people? Does this distract from the racial dimensions of punishment, weakening a critique of the race-based nature of carceral authorities? I think this work is very important in offering a fuller picture of punishment generally and in particular helping us to understand how carceral spaces shaped race. We can compare policies and practices of punishment across racial and geographic lines in more nuanced ways. It is instructive to understand when and why whiteness was a buffer from the full violence of the carceral state—and when and why it wasn't. As Dan Berger powerfully argued, prisons are still fundamentally racist institutions even when they detain white people. In his words, "prisons do not just *house* victims of racism.

Rather, they *produce* racism."[35] The fact that carceral institutions targeting predominantly white communities were often designed to be more benign and humane in their treatment of inmates is just one of the many manifestations of this concept.

There is no denying that the present and future of carceral studies are propelled by questions of how race, gender, and sexuality have factored into both criminalization and punishment. Regina Kunzel forged this association in 2008, showing that while sex and sexuality were central to modern punishment, so too was the prison instrumental in defining sexuality.[36] Stephen Dillon's *Fugitive Life* centers the struggle of queer and feminist antiracist activists in the 1970s and '80s who saw and challenged the neoliberal carceral state as it emerged.[37] Many of the "Hidden Gems" featured in this issue take up similar questions in new and exciting ways. Annie Anderson of Eastern State Penitentiary reflects on its new interpretive project to center the lives of the formerly enslaved as well as those charged with sodomy. In "Working at the Margins: Unearthing and Interpreting New Research at Eastern State Penitentiary," Anderson highlights the newly unearthed records about two prisoners, Isaac Hall and Charlotte Hilton. The records reveal cultural norms and biases, shedding light on the anxieties that officials expressed about race, gender, religion, and rehabilitation. For instance, warden Michael Cassidy observed that Hall "was convicted in Philad. of sodomy & buggery. [Hall] was known in the locality where he resided as Lady Washington and is no doubt of the kind who are addicted to that crime." Hall served six years and six months of an eight-year sentence before being released early for good behavior. Dan Royles highlights the criminalization of people with HIV in his gem, entitled "Tales from Behind the Wall: ACT UP/Philadelphia and HIV in Prisons." Royles recounts the story of Greg Smith, an HIV positive man incarcerated in New Jersey's Camden County Jail, who in 1989 was charged with attempted murder for biting someone. He was found guilty and later died in prison in 2003 while serving this sentence. There is much historical research to be done about how racism intertwined with homophobia and transphobia shaped the

---

[35] Dan Berger, "Rise in White Prisoners Doesn't Change Innate Racism of Prisons," *Truthout.org*, Apr. 28, 2019, https://truthout.org/articles/rise-in-white-prisoners-shows-prison-racism-goes-be yond-disparities/.

[36] Regina Kunzel, *Criminal Intimacy: Prison and the Uneven History of Modern America* (Chicago, 2008).

[37] Stephen Dillon, *Fugitive Life: The Queer Politics of the Prison State* (Durham, NC, 2018).

treatment of people like Hall and Smith both before and during their incarceration.

We seldom learn about people who were imprisoned in their own words—especially prior to the 1900s. A notable recent exception to this pattern is the discovery and authentication of the 1833 memoir by Austin Reed, published in 2016 by Caleb Smith as *The Life and the Adventures of a Haunted Convict*.[38] The memoir is now the oldest known record by an African American convict. Several hidden gems take up the issue of expanding the available archive through which we can learn about the past. Celia Caust-Ellenbogen draws our attention to the Anna Wharton Morris Papers as a window into the prison reform movement, quoting Morris from 1915, "Let us abandon the outworn method of secrecy in prison affairs! Let us take every opportunity to bring them and to keep them openly before the public, so that all may understand the vast waste of human material that has been practiced." The records include a series of drawings by Eastern State Penitentiary inmate Frederick Funk from the 1920s. Pardon records provide another window into personal experiences of inmates and their families. Jonathan W. White and Taylor Bagwell's gem, "Prison Life at Eastern State Penitentiary as Seen through Pardon Records," provides a window into the very personal and daily experiences of ordinary people who suffered during the separation caused by incarceration.

Official institutional and government records are still those best preserved, but even here there are gaps in preservation and access. Anne Parsons notes the paucity of Record Group 58 at the Pennsylvania State Archives in "Preserving the Recent Past of Prisons." I recall noticing that myself when working with the record group about fifteen years ago. It is rather startling for the collection of official state prison records at the state archives to be so spare. Historians and archivists are seeking to remedy this. One such effort is the acquisition of the Press Secretary Papers, an extensive collection that documents the prison system from 1970 to 2010. Finally, the American Philosophical Society is engaging exciting digital methods to make new means of old records. The "Historic Prison Admission Books and Data-Driven Digital Projects" opens up a new window into pattern recognition in approaching the logbooks by visualizing the dataset for users.

As much of the new scholarship suggests, there has been a great effort

---

[38] Caleb Smith, *The Life and the Adventures of a Haunted Convict* (New York, 2016).

to expand our study of the carceral state beyond the founding generations in Pennsylvania and New York and the Jim Crow era of the South. Such work is sorely needed and long overdue. But what does that mean about current and future work on Pennsylvania? The new scholarship featured in this issue powerfully illustrates the enduring significance of new work on Pennsylvania that looks beyond Eastern State Penitentiary. By recasting the history of MOVE, shining a light on rural prison riots of the 1950s, centering the experiences of incarcerated youths, and marking the early origins of the criminalization of poverty, each essay provides a unique and important contribution to the field of carceral studies. Pennsylvania carceral histories will always matter because the state embraced carceral structures with abandon for so long, using Quaker-led penal reform principles to justify its expansion. Early American reformers never questioned the value of prisons but instead focused on tweaking the rules for and treatment of the incarcerated. A new twenty-first century movement advocates ending mass incarceration. A vast grassroots campaign in Pennsylvania, known as Decarcerate PA, aims to keep people out of prison, stop the construction of new prisons, and use precious resources for community enrichment rather than punishment. Its members hope to write a new ending to Pennsylvania's excessive and violent history of punishment. The new research presented here is an important contribution to that effort.

Amherst College   JEN MANION

"Severe punishment for their misfortunes and poverty": Philadelphia's Arch Street Prison, 1804–37

ABSTRACT: This article is a case study of the intersections between poverty, disease, and nineteenth-century criminal justice and penal policy, focusing on the Arch Street Prison, which operated in Philadelphia from the 1810s until the 1830s. In this prison, poor "strangers," "wanderers," and people experiencing homelessness were incarcerated for vagrancy, alongside debtors and untried prisoners. Philadelphia prison managers classified prisoners according to their socioeconomic class, which they viewed as linked to the crimes that these prisoners committed, distinguishing inmate populations across the carceral facilities in the city. During the 1832 cholera epidemic, approximately a third of the prison's inmates died. Records documenting the epidemic reveal the experiences of Arch Street's inmates, contemporaries' perception of links between poverty, race, and disease, and the unique position of this prison in Philadelphia's carceral history.

VAGRANTS AND THE POOR posed an especial challenge to early republican Philadelphia's carceral system. Between the 1790s and 1840s, the city incarcerated these groups in a variety of different institutions, some ostensibly welfare-based and others expressly punitive. It even constructed one bespoke building, the Arch Street Prison, to incarcerate vagrants, but it was "never considered sufficiently safe or well constructed to house prisoners."[1] While criminal convicts were on the receiving end of reform-driven experiments with solitary confinement in the north of Philadelphia at Eastern State Penitentiary, across the city, vagrants, debtors, and prisoners awaiting trial were sharing common rooms filled with hundreds of other people at Arch Street. City watchmen

---

[1] Samuel Hazard, ed., *The Register of Pennsylvania* (Philadelphia, 1831), 100; Hazard, *Hazard's Register of Pennsylvania* (Philadelphia, 1836), 160; John F. Watson, *Annals of Philadelphia and Pennsylvania, in the Olden Time* (Philadelphia, 1879), 181–82. Arch Street's place in Philadelphia's prison history is addressed partially in Negley K. Teeters, *The Cradle of the Penitentiary: The Walnut Street Jail at Philadelphia, 1773–1835* (Philadelphia, 1955), 104–8, 113–14.

THE PENNSYLVANIA MAGAZINE OF HISTORY AND BIOGRAPHY
Vol. CXLIII, No. 3 (October 2019)

sentenced thousands of people to Arch Street each year under the state's vagrancy law, for sleeping outdoors, begging, and being unemployed. Debtors were housed in a separate apartment, but the rest of the people incarcerated in the jail occupied one shared room, leading to the much-decried practice of "reputed pirate[s] and murderer[s]" being "seated beside . . . youth[s] confined for a drunken brawl."[2] The fact that prisoners of all types were housed in the same space concerned authorities, who had condemned this mixing at the facilities that preceded Arch Street—indeed, the Walnut Street Prison was meant to prevent this very problem. At both of these institutions, the prisoners' proximity to one another had so concerned prison inspectors and reformers that it led to the adoption of the "separate system," or solitary confinement of prisoners, and construction of the penitentiary, so that their influence upon each other could not breed further crime.[3] Arguably, a more realistic concern was the spread of communicable diseases, a serious threat in such close quarters with limited medical care available. This led to great loss of life, most notably, at Arch Street during the 1832 cholera epidemic.

The justices of the peace and city watchmen who comprised the proto-police force in the early nineteenth century wielded the judiciary power to monitor and punish vagrants summarily. In particular, they independently determined whether vagrants and paupers should be incarcerated in jails or almshouses. Countless people vacillated between these two institutions in early national Philadelphia. Scholars still have only a limited understanding of the mechanisms that governed vagrants' incarceration, in part because there are so few extant sources documenting the internal operations of jails like Arch Street, or the experiences of the people who occupied them.[4] In fact, the sources that best provide a sense of what the people incarcerated at Arch Street experienced are those generated following the devastation of the inmate population during the 1832 cholera epidemic, when intensive investigations were made into the conditions in which prisoners there were held. The state legislature published a detailed report on the facility and its operations after a committee investigated

---

[2] "The Prison on Arch Street, Philadelphia," *Reports of the Prison Discipline Society, Boston, 1826–1835* (Boston, 1855), 363.

[3] David J. Rothman, *The Discovery of the Asylum: Social Order and Disorder in the New Republic* (1971; rev. ed., New Brunswick, NJ, 2009); Michael Meranze, *Laboratories of Virtue: Punishment, Revolution, and Authority in Philadelphia, 1760–1835* (Chapel Hill, NC, 1996).

[4] Mark E. Kann, *Punishment, Prisons, and Patriarchy: Liberty and Power in the Early American Republic* (New York, 2005), 208–9; Jen Manion, *Liberty's Prisoners: Carceral Culture in Early America* (Philadelphia, 2015), 86–93.

"the local causes of cholera in the Arch Street Prison" and "the sufficiency of the legal provisions for the maintenance of untried prisoners and debtors" held there.[5] Newspapers chimed in with estimates of the death toll and editorials claiming to pinpoint its causes. A local pamphleteer even printed an exposé after the epidemic, titled *A Tale of Horror! Giving an authentic account of the dreadful scenes that took place in the Arch Street Prison On that ever memorable Sunday when The Cholera destroyed nearly 100 of the Prisoners: to which is added, life As it Exists, in that institution, being a faithful sketch of the manners, mode of living, and discipline of the prisoners.* Philadelphia's public memory of the epidemic centered on the jail: in an 1839 illustrated *History of Philadelphia*, the brief entry on epidemic cholera described the experiences of "the vagrants and prisoners in the Arch Street prison," where "a large number died."[6] These sources reveal how insulated smaller jails often were from the effects of the prison reform movement, as conditions remained dire in institutions like Arch Street throughout the Jacksonian Era.

Despite its dominant presence in the city arguably most central to the development of the penitentiary and penal reform, Arch Street only intermittently and briefly appears in the historiography, perhaps because of the intense focus paid to facilities more closely tied to the penitentiary revolution in this period.[7] It stood behind a tall stone wall at the corner of Arch and Broad Streets within sight of City Hall, where thousands of poor Philadelphians, and others passing through the city, walked through its gates. Referred to by contemporaries as a prison, it actually functioned as a jail, holding various misdemeanants and untried prisoners. This article argues for Arch Street's significance as an institution in shaping Philadelphia prison officials' understandings of the limitations of incarceration as a penal or reform tool and acting as an integral link, alongside the Philadelphia Almshouse, in the chain tying together poverty and crime in the early American republic. On paper, individuals sentenced to serve time in the jail versus the almshouse are scarcely distinguishable, and indeed, many individuals spent time in both institutions. The identities and experiences of those incarcerated at Arch Street, alongside the investigations

---

[5] "Report of the Committee appointed to investigate the Local Causes of Cholera in the Arch Street Prison, in the City of Philadelphia," *Reports of the Prison Discipline Society, Boston, 1826–1835* (Boston, 1855), 119–27.

[6] Daniel Bowen, *A History of Philadelphia* (Philadelphia, 1839), 135–37.

[7] Teeters, *Cradle of the Penitentiary*; Manion, *Liberty's Prisoners*; H. E. Barnes, *Evolution of Penology in Pennsylvania: A Study in American Social History* (Indianapolis, IN, 1927).

undertaken by prison inspectors and reformers in the early nineteenth century, reveal clear similarities among individuals—and clear differences of management and material conditions—across the city's carceral system based on the socioeconomic class of the incarcerated.

The story of the Arch Street Jail is the story of the intensifying criminalization of poverty during the early American republic: poor "strangers" and "wanderers" were subject to punishment as vagrants as a result of their mobility and subsistence activities and were forced into jails and almshouses. Two thirds of Arch Street's inmates arrived there following a vagrancy conviction, which frequently targeted peripatetic behaviors listed under Pennsylvania's vagrancy law: "being destitute of a home," "wandering," "strolling," and "having no residence."[8] This mobility and general lack of stability not only prompted their arrest and punishment but also signaled to city officials the level of physical comfort due such persons while incarcerated. Philadelphia prison managers classified prisoners according to their socioeconomic class, which they viewed as linked to the crimes that these prisoners committed and thus the conditions in the facilities where they were held. These distinctions were paramount in determining the experiences of poor people within the carceral system in early nineteenth century Philadelphia.[9] Contemporaries were aware of these disparities, particularly as they contributed to high mortality rates due to disease, especially during the 1832 cholera epidemic. Arch Street's short life span provides a discrete case study to examine the experiences of the inmates it was designed to hold and how the contemporary perception of the links between poverty and health shaped the experiences of the people incarcerated at Arch Street, as well as those responsible for their care. The investigations that followed the 1832 epidemic created a paper trail that facilitates an exploration of the intersection of disease,

[8] "Poor" [1782], *A Digest of the Laws of Pennsylvania* (Philadelphia, 1818); Vagrant Dockets, 1809–1844, Philadelphia Prisons System, Philadelphia City Archives, Philadelphia, PA.

[9] Scholars have documented the criminalization of poverty in varying degrees from the colonial period through the mid-nineteenth century in works such as Priscilla Ferguson Clement, "The Transformation of the Wandering Poor in Nineteenth-Century Philadelphia," in *Walking to Work: Tramps in America, 1790–1935*, ed. Eric H. Monkkonen (Lincoln, NE, 1984); Clement, *Welfare and the Poor in the Nineteenth-Century City* (Cranbury, NJ, 1985); Billy G. Smith, *The "Lower Sort": Philadelphia's Laboring People, 1750–1800* (Ithaca, NY, 1990); Smith, *Down and Out in Early America* (University Park, PA, 2010); Smith and Simon Middleton, *Class Matters: Early North America and the Atlantic World* (Philadelphia, 2008); Manion, *Liberty's Prisoners*; Simon Newman, *Embodied History: The Lives of the Poor in Early Philadelphia* (Philadelphia, 2003); Newman and Smith, "Incarcerated Innocents," in *Buried Lives: Incarcerated in Early America*, ed. Michelle Lise Tarter and Richard Bell (Athens, GA, 2012), 60–84; and Meranze, *Laboratories of Virtue*.

class, and the carceral system in this period. The experience of this devastating epidemic led to profound realizations by prison authorities about the impact of incarceration on the poor, prompting them to suggest significant policy changes for how vagrants and other poor prisoners should be treated. This marked an important chapter in Philadelphia's penal legacy that offers a glimpse at how people incarcerated in the city's jails survived, and did not survive, one especially dark episode in its history.

After holding virtually all of Philadelphia's prisoners since its opening in 1776, by the turn of the nineteenth century, the city's infamous Walnut Street Prison was overflowing. In 1803, Philadelphia prison inspectors petitioned the state legislature for funds to open a new jail that would make it possible to divide prisoners by "grades of crimes." By separating more serious criminals from the ubiquitous "fugatives [*sic*] from service, vagrants, servants, and apprentices" who filled the prison, they hoped to ensure that the "novice" criminal inmate would not be "mingled together in a common crowd" with "adepts in crime and come . . . out of prison prepared to follow the instructions and examples which have been given him."[10] The impetus to separate prisoners in order to offer them the space and solitude in which to reform themselves through inner contemplation was a hallmark of the penitentiary movement, and it led to the creation of the Eastern State Penitentiary not long after. But the goal behind building Arch Street was not to force criminals to reflect on their actions but to effectively protect petty criminals from becoming hardened.

The Pennsylvania legislature allocated the requested funds and in 1804 began erecting a jail at the intersection of Broad and Arch Streets, the Arch Street Prison. The construction of the prison, fraught by budgetary and bureaucratic issues, dragged on. As contemporary observer Samuel Wood, in a letter to Thomas Kittera, chairman of a Joint Committee of Councils on the Subject of the Walnut Street Prison, observed in 1831, the Board of Inspectors had been "anxious to relieve" the pressure at Walnut Street and quickly spent "$25,000 in building the yard walls, and in partially finishing the house" of the new facility at Arch Street. But "the sum was not sufficient to finish the edifice, and it was apparent that the building was not at all calculated for the confinement of convicts." Rather, Arch Street was constructed, as Wood argued, to hold "untried prisoners

---

[10] "Sale of Walnut Street Prison," *Hazard's Register of Pennsylvania*, vol. 7 (Philadelphia, 1831), 99; Samuel R. Wood, *Letter from Samuel R. Wood to Thomas Kittera, Esq. Chairman of the Committee of Councils, on the Subject of the Walnut-Street Prison* (Philadelphia, 1831), 1–2, 5.

and vagrants (to relieve the Walnut-street Prison from this class of persons)."[11] This distinction was important, as reformers believed that legitimate criminals were appropriate targets for reform and thus deserved to be housed in circumstances that would facilitate their penitence, while vagrants and debtors, whose poverty had led them to the jail, were viewed almost as hopeless causes, merely to be kept away from the general population for a time, so as not to become a negative influence.[12]

Inspectors and the state legislature planned to continue to hold those convicted of crimes at Walnut Street, while the "denomination of prisoners for trial, vagrants, runaway or disorderly servants and apprentices, and all other descriptions of persons (except convicts)" would be transferred to Arch Street.[13] After 1816, debtors and witnesses were held at Arch Street, as construction on the building continued. Around this time, Philadelphia's prison inspectors began to negotiate an arrangement with the Philadelphia Guardians of the Poor, who managed the city's almshouse, about whether vagrants could also be held at the latter facility in order to lower the jail population. This discretionary practice, which allowed city police and almshouse officials to determine subjectively whether vagrants should be sent to the almshouse or the jail, continued for decades.[14] While Arch Street was under construction, the vagrants that were normally incarcerated at Walnut Street were sent to the nearby Prune Street Apartment at Sixth and Prune Streets and to the almshouse. Over the next eight years, more than two hundred vagrants and prisoners awaiting trial per month were sentenced to serve their time at Prune Street; dozens more were sent to the almshouse.[15] Arch Street Prison received the first of the prisoners it was built to house in April of 1823, when 176 vagrants and untried prisoners, both men and women, were transferred from Walnut Street.[16] The jail's inmate population rose steadily; by 1824, extant documents suggest, as many as eight thousand vagrants had passed through Arch Street's gates. Many of these were likely recidivists, as individuals were frequently arrested for vagrancy repeatedly, serving month-long sentence after month-long sentence, but this number still indicates a

[11] Wood.

[12] Meranze, *Laboratories of Virtue*, 125.

[13] "Sale of Walnut Street Prison," 99.

[14] "Sale of Walnut Street Prison."

[15] Minutes of the Board of Inspectors of the County Prison, 1812–1821, Guardians of the Poor, Philadelphia City Archives.

[16] Minutes of the Board of Inspectors of the County Prison, 1821–1827, Guardians of the Poor, Philadelphia City Archives.

huge swath of the population of Philadelphia.[17] Nearly a thousand debtors were also held at Arch Street each year.[18] All told, during the first full year of Arch Street's operation, "vagrants, disorderly persons, and disturbers of the peace" comprised "two thirds" of those held within its walls, while the rest were debtors.[19]

Though Arch Street was built to alleviate the poor conditions of Philadelphia's carceral facilities, it was overwhelmed as soon as it opened. This was due in part to the timing of its opening, which coincided with the long fallout of the Panic of 1819, which significantly raised the populations of the poor and homeless in the United States. According to prison inspectors, the "vagrants and untried prisoners" within Arch Street's high walls were held there "with privations so great as to form a severe punishment for their misfortunes and poverty."[20] Contemporary observers noted that the people incarcerated in this prison were sentenced summarily, not as "convicts," but as "men whom the law holds as innocent, they not having received a trial by a jury of their peers."[21] Prison inspectors also noted this distinction between the vagrants and debtors incarcerated at Arch Street and those who had been convicted of crimes, now held at Walnut Street, and they raised concerns over whether the poor and unfortunate, as they described Arch Street's prisoners, deserved to be held in such poor conditions. The authors of an 1824 investigation argued that "the arrangements made for the safety and health of the convicts [at Walnut Street Prison] are as well calculated for those objects as the extreme scarcity of room in the . . . apartments of the vagrants and untried prisoners" at Arch Street, where prisoners were kept "nearly naked."[22] Arch Street was divided up into a women's and a men's wing, with "nine locking-up rooms on the men's side, and four for the women." Each of these rooms was roughly twenty square feet in size, and prisoners were locked inside each night. During the day, the prisoners were brought into "two large apartments." Arch Street had a reputation for mixing the sexes

[17] "Sale of Walnut Street Prison," 99; Barnes, *Evolution of Penology in Pennsylvania*, 137; Vagrant Dockets, 1809–1844, Philadelphia Prison System, Philadelphia City Archives.

[18] Minutes of the Board of Prison Inspectors of the County Prison, 1827–1835, Guardians of the Poor, Philadelphia City Archives.

[19] H. Niles, "Sept. 29, 1832—Cholera in Arch Street Prison," *Niles' Weekly Register* (Baltimore, 1833), 71.

[20] Niles.

[21] *A Tale of Horror! Giving an Authentic Account of the Dreadful Scenes that took place in the Arch Street Prison* (Philadelphia, 1832), 10.

[22] Manion, *Liberty's Prisoners*, 181–82.

and the races within its walls, though jail keepers claimed that, in these day rooms, "the blacks are allotted one side, and the whites the other," while "the sexes" were also "in different divisions of the prison."[23] At the time the epidemic struck in 1832, there were four keepers, by the names of Reakirt, Black, Leuellen, and McDaniels, charged with managing the prison.[24] During their incarceration, most vagrants were put to work "picking hair or moss for the upholsters, taking the burrs from wool, and shearing sheep-skins" to keep them occupied and to generate some income for the jail keepers to offset the costs of incarceration.[25]

One former inmate described the jail as an "instrument of revenge and iniquity."[26] "The fare of the prisoners," one report claimed, was "of the most wretched description immaginable [sic]," consisting of meagre portions of molasses water, and rye bread, broth thickened with "Indian meal," and periodically potatoes. "The inmates of the Arch street prison" received "no supper," but rather were left "hungry and weary" on their way to bed, with one blanket to sleep upon and one to sleep under.[27] Prisoners were given "liberty to provide themselves with bedding, food and other necessaries, during their imprisonment," but as inspectors of the prison reported, "a great majority" were "too destitute to derive any benefit from the permission."[28] To some prison officials, legislators, and other city and state officials, this lack of comfort was meant to send a clear message to the incarcerated to take whatever steps would be necessary to ensure they would not return in future. Given that poverty and its attendant misfortunes were the primary impetus behind most admissions to Arch Street, however, such admonitions had little effect.[29] Convicts at Philadelphia's new model prison, Eastern State Penitentiary, were viewed as being "of a different class" than the prisoners at Arch Street and were provided with somewhat greater human comforts in their solitary cells. The convicts were thought to possess "higher intelligence," to be more aware of societal expectations, and to be healthier and cleaner than Arch

[23] "Report of the Committee appointed to investigate the Local Causes of Cholera in the Arch Street Prison," 120.

[24] *Tale of Horror*, 7.

[25] "Report of the Committee appointed to investigate the Local Causes of Cholera in the Arch Street Prison," 124.

[26] *Tale of Horror*, 11.

[27] *Tale of Horror*, 10–11.

[28] "Report of the Committee appointed to investigate the Local Causes of Cholera in the Arch Street Prison," 121.

[29] *Annual Report of the Board of Managers of the Prison Discipline Society*, vol. 5, 363.

Street's "miserable vagrant[s]."[30] In 1833, the state legislature warned against the provision of comforts to vagrants, lest they slip into idleness and profligacy.[31] The conditions in which people were incarcerated at Arch Street—as the city's facility built expressly to hold vagrants—clearly reflect the punishment many contemporaries thought vagrants deserved.

The Philadelphia Almshouse also housed its share of the city's vagrant population during the 1820s and '30s, as a result of almshouse and jail officials lending discretionary power for the sentencing of the poor and transient to city watchmen and justices of the peace. In some cases, vagrants were sent directly to the almshouse after their arrest, while others would be sent to the almshouse after serving part or all of their sentence at Arch Street. About one tenth of the people held in the Philadelphia Almshouse from 1827–33 were held in the "vagrant's cellars" in the basement of the facility; during these years, the population in the cellars appears to have peaked at 125.[32] Many also moved between the two institutions repeatedly. Catharine Morrison, for example, was a homeless widow who had lived in New York with her husband before he died "of the Yellow Fever," and her house later burnt to the ground, leading her to travel to Philadelphia in 1822 in search of work. She was arrested later that year for being a "strolling vagrant" and was sentenced to serve "one month" in either the county jail or the almshouse.[33] Similarly, Mary Porter served numerous terms for vagrancy in the Philadelphia Almshouse and Arch Street Prison. An Irish immigrant, she had lived in Delaware and central Pennsylvania with family and independently before she was arrested for "having no residence" in 1823 and sentenced to serve her term in the almshouse. She refused to remain there, however, and "eloped," but she was arrested again for vagrancy just two weeks later.[34] This process was repeated—with more arrests and more almshouse admissions—over the next couple of years.[35] Ann Stewart, an African American woman

[30] *Philadelphia Inquirer,* Nov. 9, 1832.

[31] "On the apartment for Criminals and untried Prisoners, in the Arch Street Jail," Hazard's Register of Pennsylvania (Philadelphia, 1833).

[32] Clement, *Welfare and the Poor,* 110–11.

[33] Examination of Catharine Morrison, Examinations of Paupers, 1822–1827, Guardians of the Poor, Philadelphia City Archives; Commitment of Catharine Morrison, Vagrant Dockets, 1822–1827, Philadelphia Prisons System, Philadelphia City Archives.

[34] Examinations of Mary Porter, Examinations of Paupers, 1822–1827, Guardians of the Poor, Philadelphia City Archives.

[35] Jeremiah Peirsol to Directors of the Poor of Lancaster, Jan. 10, 1827, Letter Book, Guardians of the Poor, Philadelphia City Archives; Commitments of Mary Porter, Vagrant Dockets, 1822–1827, Philadelphia Prisons System, Philadelphia City Archives.

whose husband had "left her," was making ends meet by "going out to work by the day, for different people" before she entered the Philadelphia Almshouse. Not long after leaving the almshouse, she was convicted of vagrancy and committed to Arch Street.[36]

Catherine Morrison, Mary Porter, and Ann Stewart's poverty and homelessness (which was often, for women, compounded by low wages and limited employment opportunities) led to their repeated stints in the almshouse and jail. For many African Americans like Ann Stewart in Philadelphia and beyond, their mere presence within the city could lead to their arrest, despite the city's large population of free people of color. Vagrancy was commonly viewed as a racial attribute in the nineteenth century, leading authorities to view the mobility of African Americans as innately criminal, and, in many cases, transient people of color were presumed to be runaways and targeted accordingly. In 1820, Pennsylvania made it illegal for individuals to bring into the state African Americans who might be unable to give an acceptable "account of themselves," in order to "prevent the increase in pauperism in the Commonwealth." Any African Americans found to have entered the state in such a condition were to be arrested for vagrancy.[37] The mobility of African Americans was viewed as highly suspect, with some early nineteenth-century Pennsylvanians advocating to restrict the movement of people of color into the state, imposing strict punishments on "black criminals and vagrants," whom they argued comprised "half the expenses of our criminal business and our paupers," despite substantial evidence to the contrary.[38] Fugitive slaves were often incarcerated either as punishment for running away, and were held along with some non-fugitive enslaved people who were temporarily placed at Arch Street by their masters, or while awaiting transportation back to their place of enslavement, though there is little evidence of this happening at Arch Street after 1820.[39] In Philadelphia's prisons as well as its almshouse, the proportion of African Americans in these institutional populations exceeded their representation in the overall city population significantly. In Philadelphia in the 1820s, African

[36] Examination of Ann Stewart, Examinations of Paupers, 1826–1831, Guardians of the Poor, Philadelphia City Archives; Commitment of Ann Stewart, Vagrant Dockets, 1822–1827, Philadelphia Prisons System, Philadelphia City Archives.

[37] "Law to prevent the increase in pauperism in the Commonwealth," *Laws of the Commonwealth of Pennsylvania* (Philadelphia, 1822), 480.

[38] Beverly C. Tomek, *Colonization and Its Discontents: Emancipation, Emigration, and Antislavery in Antebellum Pennsylvania* (New York, 2011), 176–77.

[39] Vagrant Dockets, 1809-1836, Philadelphia Prisons System, Philadelphia City Archives.

Americans were about 20 percent of the almshouse population, double the population in the city at large.[40] The imbalance was more significant at Arch Street, where, in the 1820s, African Americans composed nearly half (2,325 of 4,848) of those sentenced for vagrancy, representing more than five times their population in the city.[41] This disproportionate representation is likely due to the documented tendency of watchmen and justices to view people of color as criminal.[42]

There was substantial convergence in the purpose of, as well as people held within, the Philadelphia Almshouse and Arch Street Prison. One local official even proposed that the city ought "to erect a suitable edifice near the Alms-House on the Schuylkill, for all the vagrants," because so many of the people he described as "poor miserable creatures" were "constantly passing from the Poor-House to the Prison, and from the Prison to the Poor-House."[43] The people held in both of these facilities shared much of their status before the law and society, as well as the corporeal experiences within these institutions. Their poverty increased their vulnerability to arrest as well as illness, in part because so many people lived in overcrowded conditions with contaminated water sources outside the jail, which compounded contemporaries' view of vagrants as vectors of disease. The lower classes, especially poor African Americans and the Irish, were viewed as "inherently dirty," a belief that became entrenched as newspapers reported the highest mortality rates in poor neighborhoods during epidemics.[44] Poorly dressed, conspicuously destitute-looking vagrants were taken as symbols of the lower classes and targeted with the public's fears of the spread of disease through their mobility. Authorities marshalled vagrancy laws, which had been used for centuries to circumscribe the movement and subsistence activities of the poor, to prevent epidemics. During the 1832 epidemic, the first act many cities in in the United States and Britain took to prevent their residents from contracting cholera was to "arrest . . . all beggars and vagrants" in

[40] Kenneth Kusmer, *Down and Out, on the Road: The Homeless in American History* (New York, 2002), 24.

[41] Vagrant Dockets, 1822–1827, Philadelphia Prisons System, and Examinations of Paupers, 1822–1831, Philadelphia Guardians of the Poor, Philadelphia City Archives; "Report on Punishments and Prison Discipline," *Register of Pennsylvania*, Apr. 19, 1828, 244.

[42] Kusmer, *Down and Out*, 24.

[43] Wood, *Letter from Samuel R. Wood to Thomas Kittera, Esq. Chairman of the Committee of Councils, on the Subject of the Walnut-Street Prison*, 11.

[44] Charles Rosenberg, *The Cholera Years: The United States in 1832, 1849, and 1866* (Chicago, 1962); Kathleen M. Brown, *Foul Bodies: Cleanliness in Early America* (New Haven, CT, 2009).

order to contain their perceived contagion. Some contemporaries believed that "wandering companies of . . . vagrants" could "originate" and "operate as quick conductors" of cholera, because they believed that "the march of the epidemic" was "dependent mainly on human intercourse," through "the bodies of troops, dirty vagrants, and foul clothes."[45] In the absence of knowledge about germ theory, which was not discovered for nearly two more decades, poverty and vagrancy were pathologized in ways that played out in the punishment and incarceration of vagrants.[46] Destitute people were more likely to contract diseases like cholera and to die from lack of treatment, in part because of the cramped and unsanitary conditions in which their poverty forced them to live.

Because cholera was understood to spread through physical proximity and bad air (or "miasma") in the early nineteenth century, the movement of individuals who may have come in contact with it was viewed as especially threatening. Documentation from the carceral and philanthropic institutions that housed vagrants in 1832 and the official reports created by inspectors and others following the epidemic illustrate this association between class, morality, and health. News reports were filled with descriptions of the demand for gravediggers, the need for whose services was being outpaced by the rate at which people were dying. The epidemic, which had spread from India through Europe and Canada, traveled south to New York in the spring of 1832 and took four thousand lives in Montreal and nearly three thousand in New York City. New York City officials had released all residents from the city almshouse and petty criminals from the jails, but Philadelphia was slow to act, and hundreds had died before the decision was made to open Arch Street's gates.[47] Though Philadelphia had one of the lowest death tolls of cities in the Northeast that year, with just shy of 1 percent of the city's population dying during the epidemic, the mortality rate at Arch Street Prison was closer to 36 percent.[48] The number of deaths was investigated carefully by a number of parties immediately following the epidemic, but it was considered "impos-

[45] William Baly, *Reports on Epidemic Cholera* (London, 1854), 228.

[46] Brown, *Foul Bodies*, 10.

[47] Rosenberg, *The Cholera Years*, 29; Alan Kraut, *Silent Travelers: Germs, Genes, and the Immigrant Menace* (Baltimore, 1995).

[48] John B. Osborne, "Preparing for the Pandemic: City Boards of Health and the Arrival of Cholera in Montreal, New York, and Philadelphia in 1832," *Urban History Review / Revue d'histoire urbaine* 2, vol. 36 (2008): 37; C. Reynolds, *Albany Chronicles* (Albany, 1906); Buckler, *A History of Epidemic Cholera at the Baltimore City and County Almshouse*, 5; *Tale of Horror*; Rosenberg, *Cholera Years*, 133; Brown, *Foul Bodies*, 284.

sible to decide the exact number who died ... during this terrible catastrophe."[49] Meanwhile, across the city, the Walnut Street Prison, the House of Refuge, and Eastern State Penitentiary almost completely avoided the epidemic. According to some reports, "the principle means of exemption" from the epidemic at these institutions was "the improved diet" and "habits of cleanliness" of the prisoners there, as well as the "purer air" inside these facilities. The safety of the air in confined spaces was of particular concern because contemporaries believed that diseases could be transmitted by miasma. To some contemporaries, this distinction between prisoners and the facilities where they were incarcerated affirmed perceptions of how poverty affected an individual's susceptibility to disease.[50]

Philadelphia prison officials had long viewed incarcerated vagrants as unique among the city's incarcerated population due to their social class and the environments in which they lived. When a yellow fever epidemic struck the city in 1798, Philadelphia's prison inspectors were concerned that the vagrants held in the Walnut Street Prison were a danger to "the health of the Prisoners" and took precautions to separate them.[51] 1832 was not the first time that cholera struck Arch Street, either—an 1823 epidemic took 265 lives in Philadelphia, a large number of them from the jail.[52] The high "quantum of disease" at Arch Street was explained by the city's prison inspectors in a report issued the following year as the result of the presence of so many vagrants among the population of inmates.[53] This assessment was repeated after the epidemic in the following decade, rooting officials' understandings of the links between vagrancy and disease susceptibility and transmissibility.[54]

The arrival of cholera in Philadelphia in 1832 was blamed upon a vagrant woman who became sick on July 13, just "a day or two" after entering the Arch Street Prison. Around this time, a number of "old vagrants, who were constantly in and out of the jail" were admitted; according to authorities, these individuals were thought to have "suffered the most" during the epidemic.[55] In mid-July, Arch Street held just shy of

[49] "Report of the Committee appointed to investigate the Local Causes of Cholera in the Arch Street Prison," 120.

[50] Brown, *Foul Bodies*, 126–27.

[51] Minutes of the Board of Inspectors, Nov. 21, 1798, Philadelphia Prisons System, Philadelphia City Archives.

[52] "American Intelligence," *The Philadelphia Journal of the Medical and Physical Sciences* (Philadelphia, 1824), 245.

[53] "American Intelligence."

[54] Rosenberg, *Cholera Years*, 95.

[55] "On the apartment for Criminals and untried Prisoners, in the Arch Street Jail," 177.

three hundred prisoners, 43 percent of whom were women.[56] The wardens later told prison inspectors that, "a few days before the disease appeared, an attempt was made to induce all who entered to wash themselves," but "many, who were the most miserable, resisted this rule."[57] Seven women sentenced for vagrancy during the few days preceding this first recorded illness may have been the one held responsible for bringing the disease to the prison. Just one of them, Eliza Gray, who was arrested on July 12, died as a result, on August 4, during the week when the greatest number of deaths was recorded in the prison.[58] During her stay, an investigative committee reported that "the epidemic cholera" had broken out "decidedly in the Arch street jail." One of the jail keepers reported that the spread of the disease throughout the jail was "like a shock of electricity."[59] By the end of July, the board of inspectors recommended that "one or more resident physicians be appointed for Arch Street Prison during the existence of the cholera" in addition to the usual visiting physician, Dr. Buck, in order to nurse sick prisoners.[60] Dr. Richard Harlan, a local physician, wrote in a letter to his friend John James Audubon about his experience caring for sick prisoners at Arch Street that he felt "usefully, at least, if not profitably employed, night and day," because of "cholera, cholera, cholera!!!!" At least "60 were sick at one time," and "the suffering and agony of the dying wretches was an awful sight." He reported that dozens were dying each day in early August, and, as he finished his duties on August 6, he knew there would "be more [deaths] tomorrow."[61]

Prison inspectors recommended restricting the interaction of prisoners to limit the communication of the disease, altering "the workshops of the Arch Street Prison, or other rooms as may be necessary" so that "as few prisoners as possible may sleep together during the . . . prevailing sickness."[62] The inspectors worried about designating "a suitable place for the

[56] Minutes of the Board of Prison Inspectors of the County Prison, 1827–1835, Guardians of the Poor, Philadelphia City Archives.

[57] "Report of the Committee appointed to investigate the Local Causes of Cholera in the Arch Street Prison," 122.

[58] "On the apartment for Criminals and untried Prisoners, in the Arch Street Jail," 177.

[59] "Report of the Committee appointed to investigate the Local Causes of Cholera in the Arch Street Prison," 120.

[60] Minutes of the Board of Inspectors of the County Prison, 1827–1835, Guardians of the Poor, Philadelphia City Archives.

[61] Richard Harlan to John James Audubon, Aug. 1832, cited in Richard Rhodes, *John James Audubon: The Making of an American* (New York, 2004), 368–70.

[62] Minutes of the Board of Inspectors of the County Prison, 1827–1835, Guardians of the Poor, Philadelphia City Archives.

reception of vagrants committed by the legal authorities" and enlisted the aid of "police officers" to "use the necessary means to keep the prisoners in confinement in the City Watch house" in order to limit the admission of any new prisoners.[63] For those who were already in the prison, "a requisition for an increase of food" was made on August 2 in hopes of allowing prisoners to shore up strength to fight off cholera. This requisition consisted of "half a pound of meat for each person daily . . . a pint of coffee for each person at breakfast, and for supper a pint of black tea, sweetened with molasses, without milk." "Ginger tea" was also "prepared for the prisoners." This offering was a marked improvement in the inmates' ordinary rations, which consisted of "five gills of molasses and water, and half a pound of bread, made of rye and Indian meal" for breakfast, and "for dinner, one pound of rye bread each, and five gills of soup." To supplement these meals, each day, eighteen pounds of beef were cooked to be divided up among the inmates evenly, averaging out to about one ounce per person, along with a few pieces of boiled potato. The extra rations offered during the epidemic were accompanied by an attempt to improve external bodily comfort, too, in the form of "straw . . . to be made into beds with coarse linen," so that prisoners might have some cushion between themselves and the hard floor upon which they slept.[64] Being offered slightly more food and thin beds of straw could not stymie the spread of the disease, but these changes do reflect the views of prison officials on how they might spare the lives of some of their wards, as common advice during the epidemic suggested ensuring sufficient intake of food while avoiding raw vegetables and fruits.[65]

The death toll at Arch Street rose steadily through late July and early August. The situation was desperate; according to one of the keepers, "the diseased were so numerous upon the floors of the extensive halls, that [they] had difficulty to avoid treading upon them, as they performed their duties." The night of August 4, "about eighty persons were lying dead, dying or suffering." The keepers were so concerned about keeping the prisoners contained that "the dead . . . were kept all night in the Jail, because the keepers feared to open the doors, lest the prisoners, for whose security they were responsible, should attempt to escape." Come morning, according to one report, "the sleeping rooms of the prisoners were not

[63] Minutes of the Board of Inspectors of the County Prison, 1827–1835.

[64] "Report of the Committee appointed to investigate the Local Causes of Cholera in the Arch Street Prison," 122.

[65] Rosenberg, *Cholera Years*, 30.

unlocked until near nine o'clock . . . instead of being opened at five, as usual," which left "the prisoners . . . immured for upwards of four hours longer than was customary, breathing the noxious air caused by so many persons being confined in one apartment." Miasma theory stimulated tremendous fear among the prisoners, who, when they were "released from the rooms" and into "the yard," were "surrounded by a dense, and truly contagious atmosphere." The keepers claimed that "the air of the prison" was so "highly impregnated . . . with disease . . . that the meat which was left there on Saturday, for the Sunday use, was during the night rendered completely putrid and unfit for use." The air, they reported, "was so dense and thick" because of the "very high wall which surrounds the apartments in which [the prisoners] are contained" that "it hung like a canopy over the yard" and "might have been cut with a knife."[66]

The "truly dismaying" scene must have been traumatic to those trapped within Arch Street's walls.[67] By this point, the prisoners had staged two pseudo-insurrections. "Twice, in a furious and mutinous manner," they had rushed toward the keeper to inquire "if they were to be kept to die there?" Their actions encouraged the keepers to pursue arrangements for their release, though the inmates' requests were not met until after August 5.[68] Word of the situation inside the prison had begun to "spread over the city," raising "a general alarm." A "mob . . . collected outside of the walls" of the jail, "so numerous, as to render it necessary to remove the dead bodies from the prison through a back gate." Because, as one report described it, "death continued to make such continual havoc" that the keepers could not keep up with the necessary burials, they elected instead to "dispos[e]" of "the coffins (or wide boxes) . . . into a large ditch or trench in the potters field."[69] On August 5, Arch Street's wardens requested permission from the county prison inspectors to release "as many from the criminal side, as their powers would admit of." The inspectors determined that "the urgency of the case" warranted this course of action, following the model of prison officials in New York City the month before. Joel Barlow Sutherland, a Philadelphia attorney and recorder of deeds, released most vagrants and untried prisoners. He also contacted wealthy "medical gentlemen and others, private citizens, as well

---

[66] *Tale of Horror*, 4–5.

[67] *Tale of Horror*, 4.

[68] "Report of the Committee appointed to investigate the Local Causes of Cholera in the Arch Street Prison," 120.

[69] *Tale of Horror*, 4.

as the county commissioners" to put up "sums of money to release the debtors."[70] He was hailed for this "humane conduct" and credited with ensuring that no one died "in the debtor's appartment [*sic*]."[71]

According to eyewitnesses, the prisoners' desire to escape the diseased prison did not prevent them from nursing the sick, unflinchingly aiding their colleagues at risk to their own health. One keeper attested that he had "never heard an instance of refusal by a prisoner, during this period, to assist the sick when requested to do so." Some even acquiesced to keepers' and physicians' requests that they stay on to continue caring for the victims in the prison and helping to remove the bodies of the dead "upon a promise of compensation." Most were offered five dollars, some ten; these amounts were viewed as "trifling remuneration" to some, but many inmates were compelled "by their want" to accept it. Contemporaries found it "surprising" that the vagrants, drunkards, and petty larcenists "still possessed humanity" to a "degree . . . great" enough to assist their fellow prisoners. One of these prisoners turned nurses, among the few violent criminals who had been awaiting trial at Arch Street, was enticed to "help out with the dead" with the possibility of a pardon.[72]

Meanwhile, in early August, the Philadelphia Almshouse had opened its doors to all, regardless of residence, in response to the epidemic. Eighty-nine cholera deaths were reported out of the almshouse's 1,140 residents that summer; many more fell ill but survived. The institution faced so many cholera-stricken residents that all other administrative tasks were placed on hold; as the situation began to improve, one of the almshouse agents wrote that he was so behind on his correspondence because of "the great press of business . . . attributable in a great measure to the prevalence of the epidemic which mired itself over our city."[73]

Three hundred and ten people were incarcerated at Arch Street when the epidemic first struck in mid-July, thirty of whom were debtors, held in the wing reserved for them, while 110 women and 170 men were divided into female and male apartments.[74] Many of the individuals whose

[70] *Tale of Horror*, 5; "On the apartment for Criminals and untried Prisoners, in the Arch Street Jail," 177–78.

[71] *Tale of Horror*, 5.

[72] "Report of the Committee appointed to investigate the Local Causes of Cholera in the Arch Street Prison," 121.

[73] Jeremiah Peirsol to Directors of Poor of Lancaster County, Oct. 18, 1832, Guardians of the Poor, Philadelphia City Archives.

[74] Bruce H. Mann, *Republic of Debtors: Bankruptcy in the Age of American Independence* (Cambridge, MA, 2009).

names appear on the vagrancy docket at this time had spent time in the prison previously, as well as in the almshouse, making it possible to trace their life experiences through documentation created by both facilities. Because of these documents—arrest records, physician's reports, and settlement examinations—we can piece together more information about some of the victims of the cholera epidemic at Arch Street. An Irish immigrant named Patrick Cane had traveled around New York and New Jersey looking for work before he settled in Philadelphia as a day laborer. After having been admitted to the Philadelphia Almshouse, he was later sentenced to Arch Street for "being [an] idle vagrant." He was about halfway through his one-month sentence when he contracted cholera and died in the prison.[75] Susan Hunter had been jailed at Arch Street for being an "idle vagrant" at least three times before she died on August 5, not long before inspectors discharged most prisoners to spare them from the death toll of what was later described as "that ever memorable Sunday."[76]

Some of the prisoners released from Arch Street were blamed for infecting communities around the city upon being discharged. One member of the Society for Alleviating the Miseries of Public Prisons "investigated" the death toll "carefully," reporting that "two . . . were found dead on the roads some distance from the city, having sunk under the disease after being discharged from the Jail."[77] The Philadelphia *National Gazette* reported that some had spread out across "the neighborhood . . . fell sick, and died . . . on the road," while others made it just outside the city, to "the Lancaster turnpike not far from the town," or succumbed to the disease "on the commons."[78] Newspapers reported alarmist fears of releasing prisoners or moving sick almshouse inmates lest they contribute to "spreading the contagion." Vagrants in particular were expected to return to their itinerancy and "burst away, and spread around the country, going into the farm houses."[79] One man who was reported to have been released

[75] Examination of Patrick Cane, Examinations of Paupers, 1822–1825, Guardians of the Poor, Philadelphia City Archives; Commitment of Patrick Cane, Vagrant Dockets, 1827–1833, Philadelphia Prisons System, Philadelphia City Archives.

[76] Commitments of Susan Hunter, Vagrant Dockets, 1827–1833, Philadelphia Prisons System, Philadelphia City Archives; "On the apartment for Criminals and untried Prisoners, in the Arch Street Jail," 177.

[77] "Report of the Committee appointed to investigate the Local Causes of Cholera in the Arch Street Prison," 120.

[78] "For the *National Gazette*," *Philadelphia National Gazette*, Oct. 25, 1832.

[79] William E. Watson et al., *The Ghosts of Duffy's Cut: The Irish Who Died Building America's Most Dangerous Stretch of Railroad* (Westport, CT, 2006), 91.

from Arch Street immediately found work at the Plymouth Locks on the Schuylkill River as far west as Montgomery County and was blamed for bringing cholera to fifteen other people on the crew, nine of whom died.[80] Word of the fate that befell prisoners at Arch Street traveled quickly. Baltimore's *Niles' Weekly Register* blamed the high death toll on the African American population, claiming that "in the places where persons of color abound, the disease has affected them most severely . . . because of their own imprudence," as well as "the want of attention and necessaries when sick."[81] Others claimed that it was the lack of cleanliness among vagrants that precipitated the great loss of life, and if each prisoner had been forced to "take a bath," like "the first act imposed upon a convict as obligatory" at the state penitentiary, lives could have been saved. Some believed that the prison itself had contributed to this level of uncleanliness; one editorial argued that prisoners were "sometimes ejected from the prison in a state of more abject filth and destitution" than that in which they arrived.[82] The blame for these conditions fell on the wardens and managers, who, as a 1790 law stipulated, were tasked with guaranteeing that "every person who shall be ordered to hard labor shall be separately lodged, washed and cleansed," and "if such person be a convict, the clothes in which he or she shall then be clothed, shall either be burnt, or at the discretion of two of the inspectors be baked, fumigated, and carefully laid by, until the expiration of the term for which such offender shall be sentenced to hard labor, to be then returned to him or her."[83] The Philadelphia Society for Alleviating the Miseries of Public Prisons was especially concerned with ensuring that these processes were carefully followed because of the skyrocketing "population of the city and its suburbs" that found itself "as vagrant and untried prisoners" at Arch Street. Those imprisoned at Arch Street suffered more than those held at Eastern State, reformers argued, in part because of the cramped quarters in the prison, which made it difficult for "the vagrants to be suitably classed" before being "compelled to hard labor."[84] A *Philadelphia Inquirer* editorial claimed that the poor condition of the building itself at Arch Street—and

[80] Watson, *The Ghosts of Duffy's Cut*, 91; "The Cholera," *Hazard's Register of Pennsylvania*, vol. 10 (Philadelphia, 1832), 299.

[81] "Progress of the Cholera," *Niles' Weekly Register*, Sept. 29, 1832; Rosenberg, *Cholera Years*, 59.

[82] *Philadelphia Inquirer*, Nov. 9, 1832.

[83] "Report of the Committee appointed to investigate the Local Causes of Cholera in the Arch Street Prison in the City of Philadelphia."

[84] Roberts Vaux, *Notices of the Original, and successive efforts, to improve the discipline of the prison at Philadelphia, and to reform the criminal code of Pennsylvania* (Philadelphia, 1826), 37.

the resulting internal environment—was responsible for the high death toll. Officials claimed the contrary, though: Visiting Inspector of Arch Street Prison Dr. J. R. Burden described the prison as being in "in fine order," asserting that "few private dwellings equalled, none exceeded it in cleanliness." Burden insisted that it was the vagrants' bodies themselves that had caused the excessive mortality at Arch Street. According to him, it could be blamed upon "the character of the inmates, most of whom are vagrants of dissolute habits and of broken down constitutions, victims of unwholesome and scanty diet, and destitute of proper clothing."[85]

In the months after the epidemic, a special committee ordered by the state legislature to "investigate the local causes of cholera in the Arch Street Prison" considered these claims. The committee's visit to the facility troubled its members deeply: "none of the committee, or . . . other members of the legislature who accompanied them to the Arch Street Jail, entered the apartment in which the untried prisoners and vagrants were confined during the day, without the most marked disgust at the filth, destitution, and personal misery in which the majority of the prisoners were found." Committee members used cigar smoke to mask the distinct odor within the jail. During the visit, they wrote, the "general sensation was one of desire to escape."[86] The report that they issued to the state House of Representatives on February 21, 1833, carefully documented the experiences that prisoners faced at Arch Street, arguing that the high number of deaths in the prison may have been due, in part, to insufficient "legal provisions for the maintenance of untried prisoners and debtors." The report, which was authored by J. H. Gibbon, a legislator and physician, suggested a dramatic change in the management of penal facilities within the state, even those operated by city and county governments. Vagrants and other non-criminal prisoners held in penal facilities such as Arch Street should be treated, committee members argued, at "least upon an equal position with the convicts."[87] Though the author acknowledged that no law could eliminate poverty, the committee's report admitted that "the character of some of our laws, as well as in their mode of administra-

---

[85] Minutes of the Board of County Prison Inspectors, 1827–1835, Guardians of the Poor, Philadelphia City Archives.

[86] "Report of the Committee appointed to investigate the Local Causes of Cholera in the Arch Street Prison in the City of Philadelphia."

[87] "Report relative to the Cholera and untried Prisoners in the Arch-street prison," *Journal of the Forty Third House of Representatives of the Commonwealth of Pennsylvania* (Harrisburg, 1833), 588.

tion . . . disadvantageously" impacted "the poorer portions of the community," which changed policies could work toward addressing.[88]

In particular, the committee worried about the rates of illness among the vagrants and other poor people incarcerated at Arch Street, arguing that their class, as well as the policies governing and people policing these populations, "peculiarly expose[d] them at all times to the influences of epidemic disease, and unduly increase[d] the number who tenant the jails." The report admitted that the laws of the state had contributed to the destitution of some of its population, leading to the high numbers of poor people being incarcerated, especially as debtors. But these acknowledgments were not accompanied by proposed policy changes either in the form of revised vagrancy laws or the abolition of debt imprisonment, despite the fact that many surrounding states had already phased out this archaic punishment by the time this report was issued in 1833. Rather than finding ways to ensure that fewer poor people and vagrants found their way into prisons, the committee focused on suggestions for improving their conditions within prisons so that they more closely matched the conditions of convicts.[89] But no substantive change followed these suggestions.

In 1849, when another cholera epidemic plagued Philadelphia, prison inspectors reported that "the experience gained in 1832 was of some avail" and yet again assessed the challenges vagrants posed during epidemics, issuing more suggestions for their management.[90] In particular, they argued that the best way to prevent the spread of disease in future epidemics was by instituting more effective policing and punishment. "The want of a house of industry" to complement the city's prisons and almshouse, they argued, "was very apparent during the prevalence of the epidemic." Such a facility might stanch the spread of disease among vagrants and would also serve a philanthropic role, creating a place "where the houseless vagrant might be fed, clothed, worked, and kept the proper length of time." These were the primary needs of vagrants, they argued, who were identified by the prison inspectors as "victims of unwholesome diet, and destitute of proper clothing."[91] A common nineteenth-century belief held

[88] "On the apartment for Criminals and untried Prisoners, in the Arch Street Jail," 182–83.

[89] S. Laurence Shaiman, "The History of Imprisonment for Debt and Insolvency Laws in Pennsylvania as They Evolved from the Common Law," *American Journal of Legal History*, 4 no. 3 (1960): 205–25.

[90] *Third Annual Report of the Board of Inspectors of the Philadelphia County Prison* (Harrisburg, 1850), 441.

[91] *Third Annual Report of the Board of Inspectors of the Philadelphia County Prison*, 441–70; Clement, *Welfare and the Poor*.

that hard labor was a panacea for the idle and indigent vagrant's criminal tendencies. Though vagrants were not convicts, the inspectors argued, if they were treated more similarly to convicts, particularly through longer periods of incarceration, they might benefit more fully from the reformative potential of imprisonment. "The vagrant," the inspectors argued, "is not imprisoned long enough to make that change in his physical constitution by diet, comfort, and work, as will enable him to resist disease."[92] If vagrants served longer terms in an institution designed to offer them sufficient physical provisions as well as to reform their destitute and idle constitutions, they argued, they might maintain their health. Vagrants, according to the inspectors, experienced greater vulnerability to cholera than did real criminals; they considered it "fair to presume" that some of the cholera victims at Arch Street might have survived "beyond the atmosphere of a vagrant prison."[93]

The distinct constitutions of vagrants' bodies rendered the facilities where they were held weak: "At the approach of an epidemic," the inspectors asserted in their 1849 report, "the vagrant prison is always the cause of deep anxiety; it is the nucleus of diseases. In the time of the cholera in 1832, the mortality was dreadful; whilst at the convict prison, situated at a distance, there was but a solitary case." Meanwhile, during an epidemic in 1848, "the influence of the vagrant male apartment operated on the convict apartment; and in the female prison, where convicts and vagrants are under the same roof, the mortality was the greatest."[94] To the prison inspectors, the distinctions between convicts and vagrants and the ways in which they experienced disease were so profound as to necessitate physical separation in different facilities. Having seen the dark scenes inside of the Arch Street Prison, the inspectors viewed vagrants more as casualties of their economic and social standing, while criminals supposedly possessed more control over their lives and health.

The state legislature's special committee to investigate the high death toll at Arch Street in 1832 argued that Pennsylvania could minimize rates of vagrancy by providing the poor with financial and social aid. Because "certain physical comforts are essential to morality," they admitted, "crimes *do* originate from the misery, the distresses . . . of the poor." As a result, in order to prevent even the minimal criminality associated with vagrants,

---

[92] "Fourth Annual Report of the Board of Inspectors of the Philadelphia County Prison," *Journal of the Senate of Pennsylvania*, vol. 2 (1851), 421.

[93] *Third Annual Report of the Board of Inspectors of the Philadelphia County Prison*, 440.

[94] "Fourth Annual Report of the Board of Inspectors of the Philadelphia County Prison," 421.

"there must be an improvement in their condition." Committee members realized that poverty was the root of vagrants' so-called degradation: "the very sight of the prisoners in the Arch Street Jail, gives an opinion of the operation of such causes. We fear that too frequently the combined influences of ignorance and of want have more effect in causing their offences, than the voluntary desire to outrage the regulations of society."[95] This was a significant admission in the midst of the nineteenth century's tendency to view class as an indicator of morality. The severe consequences of criminalizing poverty by incarcerating vagrants and debtors had led the inspectors to realize that "there can now be no doubt" that "the physical condition affects the moral character . . . as well as of the reverse reaction."[96] Having investigated the conditions at the prison in 1832, the legislative committee was persuaded that, in the words of "one of the admired writers of our country," William Ellery Channing, "a new feeling of what is due to the ignorant, poor and depraved has sprung up," and policy changes needed to be enacted to improve the lot of the destitute.[97]

Arch Street's inadequacies, and larger developments in carceral practice in the Philadelphia region, led to its demolition by 1837. The class of prisoners it had housed was subsequently sent to Moyamensing Prison, which had opened in 1835.[98] Pennsylvania's defining contribution to the prison reform movement, the separate system, was designed expressly to solve the problems posed by facilities like the Arch Street Prison, where prisoners were confined close together in tight quarters and offered little by way of physical sustenance and comfort. Its predecessor, the Walnut Street Prison, has long figured in the historiography as a significant site where arguments over carceral practice played out. Many of the same issues around the population and conditions in Walnut Street defined Arch Street, but it has received far less attention from historians. Documenting the experiences of those incarcerated at Arch Street amid the 1832 epidemic can begin to fill this gap.

Rutgers University   KRISTIN O'BRASSILL-KULFAN

[95] "Report of the Committee appointed to investigate the Local Causes of Cholera in the Arch Street Prison," 126.

[96] "Report of the Committee appointed to investigate the Local Causes of Cholera in the Arch Street Prison."

[97] "Report of the Committee appointed to investigate the Local Causes of Cholera in the Arch Street Prison."

[98] Teeters, *Cradle of the Penitentiary*, 123–27.

"Not Model Children": Culture and Contested Control at the Pennsylvania Industrial Reformatory

ABSTRACT: The Pennsylvania Industrial Reformatory (PIR) at Huntington, established on the principles of rehabilitative incarceration that underpinned the new penology of the late nineteenth century, was supposed to be one of the most modern, humane, and enlightened prisons of its day. Yet sensational charges of abuse and mistreatment of inmates within three years of the prison's opening spurred a months-long investigation in 1892 that attracted national attention. This investigation uncovered the details of daily interactions between inmates, administrators, and guards at PIR, revealing the existence of an inmate culture rooted in institutionalization and state policies gone awry and exposing a wide gap between the theory and the practice of the era's new penology. The results of the PIR investigation, however, ultimately circumscribed the possibility of systemic reform and helped to further entrench and normalize a punitive punishment regime that prioritized discipline over rehabilitation.

EIGHTEEN-YEAR-OLD EDWARD JOSEPH CONLAN JR. was Pennsylvania Industrial Reformatory inmate number 159, "the boy who . . . started this." Eddie, as he was known, arrived at the reformatory on October 5, 1889, sentenced from Philadelphia County to a term of up to three years on a larceny charge. But his arrest, incarceration, and subsequent appeal for release unleashed an improbable and revelatory chain of events. By early 1892, reports began appearing in the Philadelphia press detailing lurid accounts of abuse inmates suffered at the hands of prison officials while incarcerated at the Pennsylvania Industrial Reformatory (PIR) in Huntingdon—beatings, being strung-up by their wrists for weeks in "the solitary," starvation diets. "The stories that some of them tell of their treatment while in that institution . . . are astounding," reported the Philadelphia Inquirer, "horrors too lightly painted." The sensational charges against the administrators and guards at PIR, which was

Research support for this article was provided in part by a Samuel W. Pennypacker Fellowship, awarded to the author by the Pennsylvania Historical and Museum Commission.

supposed to be one of the most modern, humane, and enlightened prisons of its day, spurred a months-long investigation that garnered national attention and also revealed a complex culture that functioned among the prison's largely urban poor and working-class inmates. As revealed by the 1892 investigation, these incarcerated men shaped and were shaped not only by their own inmate-defined culture but also by the often arbitrary, often vicious enforcement of prison rules and discipline by prison officials and guards. This inmate culture, based on norms of masculinity, reciprocity, and solidarity, blended acquiescence and resistance to the prison's rules and punishment regime and made the reformatory a contested space. The day-to-day interactions between inmates, administrators, and guards at PIR called into high relief an inmate culture rooted in institutionalization and state policies gone awry. Bad behavior and rule breaking by PIR inmates took on another level of meaning within the context of an ongoing struggle over power and prerogatives and revealed a wide gap between the theory and the fact of the era's "new penology."[1]

Eddie Conlan's path to PIR was a common one for many of his fellow inmates. By some measures, he was well-positioned within Philadelphia's larger white working class. His father, Edward J. Conlan Sr., was an Irish-born cooper, a skilled craftsman who owned the family's home; his American-born mother, Mary, was a housewife and homemaker for Eddie and his four siblings. They were, in a neighbor's estimation, "honest, industrious people, and good citizens." Eddie could read and write and was proficient in intermediate mathematics. He had apprenticed in blacksmithing.[2] Yet Eddie's youth had not been without problems. The Conlan family lived in hardscrabble Fishtown, a densely populated

[1] Huntingdon is located approximately two hundred miles west of Philadelphia and 125 miles east of Pittsburgh. Edward Conlan (#159), Biographical Register, Biographical and Descriptive Registers, 1889–1932, series 87, Pennsylvania Industrial Reformatory, Department of Justice, RG 15, Pennsylvania State Archives, Harrisburg, PA (Pennsylvania Industrial Reformatory, Department of Justice Records hereafter cited as PIR Records). "The 'Solitary' and the 'Lashes,'" *Philadelphia Inquirer*, Mar. 11, 1892; "The Punishment at Huntingdon," *Philadelphia Inquirer*, Mar. 12, 1892; "The Treatment at Huntingdon," *Philadelphia Inquirer*, Mar. 14, 1892. The analysis in this article is informed by Michel Foucault's *Discipline and Punish: The Birth of the Prison* (New York, 1977), specifically an understanding of punishment as a system of power and regulation imposed on a population and how the internal structures of penal institutions function to exercise control.

[2] Report of the General Superintendent to the Board of Managers, Mar. 8, 1892, Reports, 1889–1950, series 87, PIR Records, Pennsylvania State Archives; Edward Conlan (#159), Biographical Register, PIR Records, Pennsylvania State Archives; U.S. Federal Census, 1880, Philadelphia County, Philadelphia City, 18th Ward, Ancestry.com; John Virdin to Francis A. Osbourn, Feb. 25, 1891, Prison Administration Records, Reports and Testimony in Relation to Investigations, vol. 1 (1892), series 88, PIR Records, Pennsylvania State Archives (hereafter cited as Investigation Report).

working-class Philadelphia neighborhood stretching along the Delaware River northeast of Center City. By 1880, the roughly one and a half square miles that Fishtown comprised was home to over two hundred mills, factories, breweries, distilleries, and other industrial establishments. But as the turn of the century approached, Fishtown had become as well-known for its abundance of prostitutes and disreputable types as for its waterfront factories and cheap wood-frame row houses that many first- and second-generation German and Irish immigrants called home. By the time he was sixteen, Eddie Conlan was running with what his father called "a rough crowd." A year and a half before the September 1889 arrest that would send him to PIR, he spent the seven months between December 1887 and June 1888 in the Philadelphia House of Refuge, a juvenile detention center, confined for vagrancy and incorrigibility.[3]

At the time of his September 1889 arrest, Eddie Conlan had been employed for eight months as a die maker at Rowland's Rolling Mill, located on the waterfront. He was arrested when a revolver stolen from a boat docked nearby in the Delaware River was found in his possession. But according to Eddie, a man known to him as "Hoosher" gave him the gun in the mill yard during a break at work, not telling him that it was stolen. Following the arrest, the owner of the pistol declined to press charges, and the apprehending officer, Edward Coffin, told Eddie's father that he would not testify against him, saying, "he was very sorry he had had Conlan arrested and would not appear against him." In spite of this, the case against Eddie moved forward and three days later came before Judge Samuel W. Pennypacker. Edward Conlan Sr. had not hired legal counsel for his son and did not appear at court to testify on his behalf, "thinking it would not be necessary as there was no one to appear against the boy, and supposed the judge would only give him a good talking to." But at trial, Judge Pennypacker called Officer Coffin to testify. Coffin told the judge that he did not "know anything personally about the facts of said taking [of the revolver] and was not aware of who had taken the pistol," but he confirmed that he found the stolen gun in Eddie's possession. On this testimony alone, as his mother watched from the court

---

[3] Edward Conlan (#159), Biographical Register; Affidavit of Edward Conlan Sr., Apr. 6, 1891, Investigation Report, PIR Records, Pennsylvania State Archives; Lorin Blodget, *Census of Manufactures of Philadelphia: A Census of Industrial Establishments, and of Persons of Each Class Employed Therein, in the City of Philadelphia* (Philadelphia, 1883), 64–75; John J. Macfarlane, *Manufacturing in Philadelphia, 1683–1912, with Photographs of Some of the Leading Industrial Establishments* (Philadelphia, 1912).

gallery, Edward Conlan Jr. was sentenced to a one- to three-year term at PIR.[4]

This likely would have been the end of the story for many, but at the start of Eddie's incarceration at PIR his parents set into motion an appeal on his behalf to their state senator, Francis A. Osbourn. The Honorable Francis Osbourn, a Republican and Civil War veteran who lost his right arm at the Battle of Petersburg, was first elected to the Pennsylvania General Assembly as a state representative in 1876. Having been a member of the Pennsylvania Bar since 1869, he then served a six-year stint as assistant solicitor for the City of Philadelphia until his election as a state senator in 1884 representing Philadelphia's Eighteenth Ward. On behalf of his constituents the Conlans, Osbourn took up Eddie's case, marshaling the support of Judge Pennypacker—a future governor of Pennsylvania—for the cause. Yet Osbourn's letters to PIR's general superintendent requesting Eddie's release, threats to block the passage of appropriations bills that funded the reformatory, and affidavits submitted by Judge Pennypacker testifying to what Pennypacker now thought was Conlan's innocence failed to sway the prison's Board of Managers to release him. "I beg to say," PIR's then–general superintendent, R. W. McClaughry, responded after months of Osbourn's and Pennypacker's efforts, "that Conlan has only himself to blame for his long detention in the institution." Promising to bring the matter before the Board of Managers but portending a negative outcome, McClaughry—somewhat ironically, given the political patronage that had positioned him as PIR's general superintendent in the first place—added, "If a young man can escape the results of his wrong doing through importunities of friends, however worthy they may be, it will . . . be detrimental to the very person for whom this favor is asked."[5]

The campaign for Eddie Conlan's release took a more insidious turn a

[4] Affidavits of Edward Conlan Sr., Edward Coffin, and Mary Conlan, Apr. 6, 1891, Investigation Report, PIR Records, Pennsylvania State Archives. In Edward Conlan's testimony to the PIR investigating committee, he referred to the arresting officer as Officer Kauffman, not Coffin. Edward Conlan Testimony, "Transcript of Stenographic Notes of Testimony Taken During the Investigation of the Pennsylvania Industrial Reformatory at Huntingdon, Beginning Wednesday, March 22, 1892," 683, series 88, PIR Records, Pennsylvania State Archives (hereafter cited as Investigation Transcript).

[5] Francis A. Osbourn to R. W. McClaughry, Feb. 26 and Mar. 24, 1891; McClaughry to Osbourn, Feb. 28 and Mar. 25, 1891; Samuel W. Pennypacker to McClaughry, Dec. 17, 1890, Apr. 3, 1891, and Apr. 20, 1891; W. McKay Williamson to McClaughry, Mar. 24 and Apr. 16, 1891; McClaughry to Williamson, Mar. 25, 1891, all in series 88, PIR Records, Pennsylvania State Archives.

month later. In March 1891, Conlan Sr. visited the prison for the first time to meet with Eddie and update him on the progress, or lack thereof, in securing his release. Eddie arrived at this meeting visibly bruised, and the senior Conlan learned from his son what inmates' letters home— letters that had to pass through institutional review before being sent— and those not sent at all were unable to reveal: that Conlan was one of many inmates at PIR who had been routinely subjected to corporal punishment ranging from "the lashes"—whipping with large leather paddles—to strikes on the head with blackjacks, to solitary confinement. "I wrote two letters, and Mr. McClaughry tore 'em up; —and I asked why I was to be hit here . . . and he said 'You have no right to write two letters like this,'" PIR inmate John Miller later testified. "He licked me, and after he licked me I wrote these letters, to see whether I would be allowed to be licked; and instead, he tore the letters up." Upon his return to Phila- delphia, Edward Conlan Sr. pressed Senator Osbourn to make further inquiries into his son's claims of abuse. As part of his investigation, in early 1892 Osbourn met ten inmates recently transferred to the Moya- mensing Prison in Philadelphia from PIR. They confirmed Eddie's accusations.[6]

After nearly a year of informal fact-finding, Osbourn was convinced that Eddie Conlan's story was both true and only part of a much larger problem. Osbourn took his case to Governor Robert Pattison, who imme- diately ordered the state Board of Public Charities to undertake a full investigation. The 1892 investigation into these allegations of systemic abuse and negligence at PIR revealed that what inmates experienced dur- ing their incarceration there was a far cry from the rational program of the new penology touted by prison reformers, which was supposed to have made corporal punishment a relic of the past. Under the new system, punishment exacted by guards and administrators was to be based on rewards and demerits rather than corporal and retributive punishment, regardless of the levels of bad or rebellious behavior. Inmates instead faced beatings and solitary confinement. They found themselves at the whim of prison administrators, guards, and inmate monitors, who often meted out these punishments randomly and acted with virtual impunity within an

---

[6] Affidavit of Edward Conlan Sr., Investigation Report, PIR Records, Pennsylvania State Archives; John Miller Testimony, Investigation Transcript, 296, PIR Records, Pennsylvania State Archives; "The 'Solitary' and the 'Lashes'"; "The Boys in Moyamensing"; "The Punishment at Hun- tingdon"; "The Treatment at Huntingdon."

institution where reform fell by the wayside in the larger interest of maintaining order and discipline.[7]

Reformatory prisons like PIR in Huntingdon were an institutional response to the disillusionment with and failures of the penitentiary system of the early nineteenth century. In Pennsylvania specifically, this related to Western State Penitentiary and Eastern State Penitentiary, which opened in 1826 and 1829, respectively. At Eastern State, a "separate system" model of punishment was put into place to instill self-discipline and "form habits of industry." It would "make the life of the prisoner hard and laborious, thus punishing him more severely and making him repent more quickly."[8] Through the 1830s, 1840s, and 1850s, prison reformers and others recognized that penitentiaries were largely ineffective in stemming crime and criminality. According to legal scholar Lawrence M. Friedman, "[D]ecay set in almost immediately in most prisons—almost as soon as the last brick was laid and the prison opened for business." Cruelty and corruption within were common, overcrowding meant that Pennsylvania's separate system devolved into disorder, the use of convict labor and sale of convict-made goods covered only a fraction of

[7] A. W. Scott (Board of Public Charities Chairman) Statement, Investigation Transcript, 601, PIR Records, Pennsylvania State Archives; Edward Conlan Testimony, Investigation Transcript, 717, PIR Records, Pennsylvania State Archives; "The Punishment at Huntingdon."

[8] Pennsylvania Prison Society, *Memorial of the Philadelphia Society for Alleviating the Miseries of Public Prisons, to the Legislature of Pennsylvania* (1881), 2; Harry Elmer Barnes, *The Story of Punishment: A Record of Man's Inhumanity to Man* (Boston, 1930), 219. During the penitentiary era of the early nineteenth century, Pennsylvania's separate system competed with the New York system, first used at Auburn Prison and commonly known as the Auburn system. The Pennsylvania system was a model of confinement based on inmates' complete isolation and the theory that solitude fostered repentance and reformation. Within the separate system, inmates lived and labored at handicraft production within the small, confined spaces of individual cells. Rules banned communication of any kind among inmates and dictated that they wear hoods that completely covered their heads and faces to maintain silence and anonymity when moving about the prison. The Auburn system dictated complete silence and isolation of prisoners in their cells at night, but by day inmates worked in large groups, which therefore lent itself more readily to factory-style labor within prison walls, and prisons throughout the country implemented it more widely. On the early nineteenth-century penitentiary era in Pennsylvania and nationwide, see Harry Elmer Barnes, *The Evolution of Penology in Pennsylvania: A Study in American Social History* (Indianapolis, 1927); Adam Hirsch, *The Rise of the Penitentiary: Prisons and Punishment in Early America* (New Haven, CT, 1992); Blake McKelvey, *American Prisons: A History of Good Intentions* (Montclair, NJ, 1997), 1–63; Rebecca McLennan, *The Crisis of Imprisonment: Protest, Politics, and the Making of the American Penal State, 1776–1941* (New York, 2008), 1–86; David J. Rothman, "Perfecting the Prison: The United States, 1789–1865," in *The Oxford History of the Prison: The Practice of Punishment in Western Society*, ed. Norval Morris and David J. Rothman (New York, 1998), 100–116; David J. Rothman, *The Discovery of the Asylum: Social Order and Disorder in the New Republic* (1971; repr., Boston, 1990); Negley Teeters, *The Cradle of the Penitentiary: The Walnut Street Jail at Philadelphia, 1773–1835* (Philadelphia, 1955); and Frederick H. Wines, *Punishment and Reformation: A Study of the Penitentiary System* (New York, 1919).

prison operation costs while arousing the ire of organized labor, and the overarching goal of prisoner rehabilitation had largely fallen by the way-side. As the country grappled with reuniting the nation after the Civil War, prison reformers declared the experiment of the penitentiary an abject failure. "There is not a state prison in America in which the refor-mation of the convicts is the one supreme object of the discipline," wrote prison reformers Enoch C. Wines and Theodore Dwight in a scathing 1867 report detailing their nationwide investigation into the conditions of state prisons. These prisons, Wines and Dwight concluded, "needed careful and judicious revision."[9]

In the decades that followed, states throughout the country fundamen-tally reassessed their goals and strategies for the punishment and reform of criminal offenders, underpinned by new theories of punishment and by the realities of a society facing radical changes arising from rapid indus-trial development, immigration, and urbanization. Across the nation through the 1870s and 1880s, there was a surge in the creation of state prison inspection boards, paralleled by the establishment and robust growth of national and international prison reform associations. By the mid-1870s, states attempted to implement what contemporaries called the "new penology" in completely new institutions—reformatory prisons.[10]

According to the tenets of the new penology, the reformatory prison would inculcate obedience and discipline through regimented work, while also socializing criminal offenders and teaching vocational skills that would smooth their transitions back into society upon release as law-abiding citizens. "The penitentiary says to the prisoner, 'Be good'; it asks

[9] Lawrence M. Friedman, *Crime and Punishment in American History* (New York, 1993), 155; Enoch C. Wines and Theodore Dwight, *Report on the Prisons and Reformatories of the United States and Canada* (Albany, 1867), 287, 1. For a detailed examination of criticisms leveled against the Pennsylvania system, and Eastern State in particular, see Barnes, *The Evolution of Penology in Pennsyl-vania*, chap. 6. For a more general examination of the penitentiary system, especially connections to the developing market and industrial economy, see McLennan, *The Crisis of Imprisonment*, 107–59.

[10] Edgardo Rotman, "The Failure of Reform: The United States, 1865–1965" in Morris and Rothman, *The Oxford History of the Prison*, 151–77; Alexander W. Pisciotta, *Benevolent Repression: Social Control and the American Reformatory-Prison Movement* (New York, 1994); McLennan, *The Crisis of Imprisonment*, 155–63; Mark Colvin, *Penitentiaries, Reformatories, and Chain Gangs: Social Theory and the History of Punishment in Nineteenth-Century America* (New York, 1997); McKelvey, *American Prisons*, 64–196; Rothman, *The Discovery of the Asylum*; Robert G. Waite, "From Peniten-tiary to Reformatory: Alexander Machonochie, Walter Crofton, Zebulon Brockway, and the Road to Prison Reform—New South Wales, Ireland, and Elmira, New York, 1840–1970," in *Criminal Justice History: An International Annual*, ed. Louis Knafla (Westport, CT, 1993), 85–105; Zebulon R. Brockway, *Fifty Years of Prison Service: An Autobiography* (1912; repr., Montclair, NJ, 1969).

him to be submissive. The reformatory system says, 'Be good,' but also 'Be good for something,'" prison reformer S. J. Barrows explained at the turn of the century. "It trains his capacities and fits him to go out into life and earn an honest living. It . . . puts him through a course of ethical gymnastics."[11] In theory, the reformatory program would work to build up rather than break down the inmate, and prison administrators would implement individualized daily routines meant to approximate life on the "outside." Individual and group socialization and recreation through reading, music, and exercise in the prison yard would replace the silence and isolation imposed within antebellum penitentiaries. Academic and vocational training programs would supplant the arduous labor regimens of the past. Corporal punishment as the primary tool to shape obedience would become obsolete within a graded system wherein demonstrated positive behavior earned prisoners rewards and advancement toward release, while infractions meant lost privileges and time added to minimum sentences. Ongoing monitoring of reformatory prisoners' behavior during periods of parole after release, which required parolees to remain gainfully employed, would prepare and help ease them from the standing of prisoner to productive member of society.[12]

Based on this new penology, the nation's first reformatory prison opened in Elmira, New York, in 1876. While states throughout the US South embraced the convict-lease system, states from New England to the Midwest over the next four decades followed the Elmira example. These reformatory prisons functioned within a growing late nineteenth- and early twentieth-century state criminal justice system that came to include penitentiaries, juvenile reform schools, and adult reformatories. In these reformatories, states sought to incarcerate first-time offenders, generally between the ages of sixteen and twenty-five, who, though considered adults, were presumably not hardened, habitual criminals and thus were those with the highest potential for reformation. Pennsylvania's

---

[11] S. J. Barrows, "Introduction," in *The Reformatory System in the United States: Reports Prepared for the International Prison Commission* (Washington, DC, 1900), 10.

[12] On the reformatory model generally, and parole as an extension of state social control, see Pisciotta, *Benevolent Repression.* On state policy development, prisons, and social control during the late nineteenth and early twentieth centuries, see also Morton Keller, *Regulating a New Society: Public Policy and Social Change in America, 1900–1933* (Cambridge, 1994); David J. Rothman, *Conscience and Convenience: The Asylum and Its Alternatives in Progressive America* (Boston, 1980); Jonathan Simon, *Poor Discipline: Parole and Social Control of the Underclass, 1890–1990* (Chicago, 1993); and William G. Staples, *Castles of Our Conscience: Social Control and the American State, 1800–1985* (Cambridge, 1990).

General Assembly enacted legislation in June 1878 to create a new "middle" penitentiary district with the intent of building a third state penitentiary, which would intake inmates from twenty-seven counties in the central part of the state and relieve overcrowding at Eastern State and Western State. But two years later, in 1880, the legislature tasked a special commission with visiting the reformatory at Elmira and determining the feasibility and desirability of opening a prison in Pennsylvania along the Elmira model instead. In June 1881, the legislature approved a supplementary act to the 1878 one creating the middle penitentiary district for "the purposes of a State Industrial Reformatory" that could house up to five hundred inmates from all parts of the state. "The giving of a chance to reform . . . the showing to him that upon his own exertions depends his future, and that he may become a useful and respected citizen," asserted the legislative committee studying the feasibility of constructing a reformatory in Pennsylvania, "is certainly a great advance in penology." On February 15, 1889, the Pennsylvania Industrial Reformatory in Huntingdon recorded entrance of its first inmate, twenty-one-year-old John G. Moore, admitted into custody from Huntingdon County on a larceny conviction.[13]

Through the Huntingdon reformatory, then, Pennsylvania intended to pursue a more holistic approach to crime and crime prevention. "The object the [Pennsylvania] Reformatory has in view," its administrators asserted, "is to repair, remodel, to rehabilitate for the full duties of male citizenship."[14] What inmates experienced during their incarceration at PIR, however, was a vast departure from these objectives and from a rational, individualized program of reform. The prison's superintendent, deputy superintendent, and guards occupied the gray space between the creation of policy and its implementation, where the rhetoric of reform was supposed to become reality but often did not. For inmates, a group identity developed by virtue of their common backgrounds, physical

---

[13] Commonwealth of Pennsylvania, *Report of the Committee Appointed by the Governor to Inquire into the Expediency of Establishing a State Industrial Reformatory, Made to the Legislature of Pennsylvania, May 10, 1881* (Harrisburg, 1881), 10–11; Pennsylvania Industrial Reformatory, *Biennial Report of the Managers of the Pennsylvania Industrial Reformatory, at Huntingdon, Pa., from January 1, 1891, to December 31, 1892* (Huntingdon, PA, 1893). Until 1931 PIR operated as a reformatory prison for men between the ages of sixteen and thirty, when it became a prison exclusively for juvenile "defective delinquents." The Huntingdon prison incarcerated juvenile offenders from 1931 to 1960, when it became a maximum-security prison for men. Since 1995, State Correctional Institution–Huntingdon has been a close-security prison.

[14] Pennsylvania Industrial Reformatory, *Biennial Report of the Board of Managers*.

incarceration, and the demeaning treatment they experienced within an institution that defined them not as men worthy of respect, but at best deviant children and at worst brutes. As revealed by the 1892 investigation of PIR, it was within this gap that the institution's inmates exerted a level of agency through their particular identity and culture.[15]

The formal State Board of Charities inquired into conditions at PIR in March 1892. Three of the Moyamensing Ten, as they became known in the press, and twenty-one other PIR inmates who testified or had family members or family physicians testify on their behalf at the inquiry, paralleled the familial, economic, and criminal backgrounds of the wider prison population at PIR at the time of the investigation. Between February 1889 and March 1892, PIR received over nine hundred inmates, largely between the ages of seventeen and twenty, from counties throughout the state. The majority of admittances to PIR came from courts in the state's urban-industrial centers. Some 42 percent of PIR's inmate population was admitted from Philadelphia County, 9 percent from Pittsburgh's Allegheny County, and 4 percent each from Erie County and Harrisburg's Dauphin County. Taken together, inmates from these counties, and counties immediately adjacent, represented 75 percent of the reformatory's population. The vast majority of PIR's inmates, 89 percent, were white, compared to 11 percent categorized in official intake records as "negro" or "mulatto." Collectively, most PIR inmates were born in Pennsylvania, though some 20 percent of inmates claimed seventeen other states and nine countries as their places of birth. Their work histories

---

[15] Studies of late nineteenth- and early twentieth-century prison cultures, written from the perspectives of convicted individuals themselves rather than from the perspectives of journalists or prison reformers as part of "undercover" investigations, are scant. The current analysis is informed by recent studies of late nineteenth- and early twentieth-century inmate cultures and cultural expression, as well as by works that analyze cultural mores and norms of marginalized groups, and juxtapose these norms with those of the hegemonic society. See, for example, George Chauncey, *Gay New York: Gender, Urban Culture, and the Making of the Gay Male World, 1890–1940* (New York, 1994); H. Bruce Franklin, *Prison Writing in 20th Century America* (New York, 1998); Timothy J. Gilfoyle, *A Pickpocket's Tale: The Underworld of Nineteenth-Century New York* (New York, 2006); Talitha LeFlouria, *Chained in Silence: Black Women and Convict Labor in the New South* (Chapel Hill, NC, 2015); Peter Linebaugh, *The London Hanged: Crime and Civil Society in the Eighteenth Century* (New York, 1991); Scott Reynolds Nelson, *Steel Drivin' Man: John Henry—The Untold Story of an American Legend* (New York, 2006); and James C. Scott, *Domination and the Arts of Resistance: Hidden Transcripts* (New Haven, CT, 1990). For examples of analyses of inmate cultures that existed in the 1960s and 1970s, see especially Heather Ann Thompson, *Blood in the Water: The Attica Prison Uprising of 1971 and Its Legacy* (New York, 2016); and Robert T. Chase, "Civil Rights on the Cell Block: Race, Reform, and Violence in Texas Prisons and the Nation, 1945–1990," (PhD diss., University of Maryland, College Park, 2009).

reflected their urban-industrial backgrounds, with most engaged at or near the time of their arrests in factory and industrial craft work ranging from shoemaking and bottle manufacturing to blacksmithing and carpentry, or in heavy labor on farms, in mines, and on the docks. These young men served terms at PIR most commonly for crimes against property—top among them larceny, as well as burglary, robbery, receiving stolen goods, breaking and entering, and false pretenses—sentenced most commonly to maximum sentences of three years.[16]

Reflective of this wider population, the average age of the twenty-four inmates testifying or represented at the inquiry was 18.5 years, and all but one were white. They were serving, on average, three-year prison terms for crimes ranging from receiving stolen goods to aggravated assault and battery to one case of attempted sodomy and buggery, and, most frequently, as in Eddie Conlan's case, larceny. The twenty-four inmates involved in the investigation came largely from families where both parents were native born in Pennsylvania, but in the case of nine inmates, including Eddie Conlan, at least one parent was foreign born. The young men lived overwhelmingly in urban areas, and prison officials categorized the majority of their economic status as "poor" or "renters." Seventeen of the inmates claimed a religious affiliation—eleven Catholic, three Episcopalian, two Methodist, and one Jewish. Others noted that they attended church irregularly. Eleven members of the group, like Eddie Conlan, lived at home with their families at the time of their arrests. Though only eight of the twenty-four inmates indicated that they were gainfully employed at the time they committed their crimes, as a group they had histories working as common and odd-job laborers, wagon drivers and delivery men, factory, foundry, and mill workers, shoemakers' and seamen's apprentices, bricklayer, typesetter, railroad yardman, wood and ivory carver, leather worker, cigar maker, clerk, and baker's helper. The bulk of the inmates had some, albeit limited, education. Twenty-three of the

[16] Prisoners' Record, 1889–1932, vol. 1, series 93, PIR Records, Pennsylvania State Archives; Biographical Registers, Biographical and Descriptive Registers, 1889–1932, vols. 1–2, series 90, PIR Records, Pennsylvania State Archives. Data analyzed for 923 inmates, from the first intake record at PIR on February 15, 1889, through the first month of the investigation to March 29, 1892. This is the same number of inmates and time frame used for data about punishments at PIR presented to the Investigating Committee. Adjacent counties to Philadelphia County include Delaware, Montgomery, and Bucks Counties; to Allegheny include Westmoreland, Washington, Beaver, and Butler; to Dauphin include Lancaster, Lebanon, York, Schuylkill, and Northumberland; and to Erie include Crawford and Warren.

twenty-four could read and write, in four cases though only "barely" or "poorly," and twelve could do basic math.[17]

Recognized by offenders, family members, and sentencing judges alike, PIR was officially positioned within the state's carceral apparatus as an alternative for young though not juvenile first-time offenders to the punitive justice meted out at state penitentiaries. Prior to the 1892 investigation, the perception of PIR was that incarceration there would be a more lenient and far easier sentence than time at Eastern State or Western State. Though documentation elucidating the thinking behind judges' individual sentencing decisions is scant, racial and ethnic bias, as well as preconceptions about groups prone to vice and criminality were certainly at play, contributing to the creation of the overwhelmingly white and native-born inmate population in PIR's early years. Further, where proof of criminal wrongdoing was lacking but family connections to politicians were in play, there is evidence of favoritism in sentencing to PIR. Although Eddie Conlan had spent time as a juvenile offender in the Philadelphia House of Refuge, George Smith, the reformatory's deputy superintendent, presumed that because of his family's relationship with Senator Osbourn, "he had plenty of influence behind him that enabled him to do as he pleased." In inmate Edward Creasy's case, at the urging of his father, a Philadelphia constable, the "weak minded" nineteen-year-old was sentenced to a three-year term for larceny at PIR in October 1889 rather than to Eastern State Penitentiary. "[W]ith the admission of his father[,] . . . [t]hey were going to send him to the penitentiary, and wanted him to come here."[18]

In spite of interventions and personal connections like these, prison officials and reformatory defenders attempted to use the backgrounds of the inmates to cast doubt on their testimony from the outset of the

---

[17] Biographical Registers, Biographical and Descriptive Registers, 1889–1932, PIR Records, Pennsylvania State Archives. Prison officials obtained the information contained in the biographic registers as part of the inmate intake process into PIR. In addition to the categories analyzed above, for which most (though not all) inmates have recorded information, other information in the registers includes the county from which the inmate was sentenced, family history of insanity or epilepsy, parental information including alcohol use, education, occupation, and criminal history, non-familial associations of the inmate, physical, mental, and moral categorization of the inmate, whether the inmate used alcohol or tobacco, and whether the inmate frequented prostitutes. Some register entries include even more extensive information, including information about siblings and extended family, past criminal history, and aliases.

[18] George Smith Testimony, Investigation Transcript, 768, PIR Records, Pennsylvania State Archives; David Miller Testimony, Investigation Transcript, 400–401, PIR Records, Pennsylvania State Archives.

inquiry, and they invoked the prisoners' upbringing, limited education, and "idleness" at the time of their arrests as reasons to discount their testimony.[19] A reporter attending the 1892 hearings described one of the inmates who "exposed a large scar on his head . . . received from an official, who beat him with a black-jack" as "[a] well-dressed youth of favorable appearance, who seemed to have good breeding." But prison officials aggressively asserted that the testifying inmates could not be trusted and used their backgrounds, especially past criminal activity, as supporting evidence. "The stories come from men who are criminals and who have spoken falsely concerning their treatment here," bluntly stated Samuel McCamant, member of the PIR Board of Managers, about the charges brought against the prison. Many of PIR's inmates "have served terms in Houses of Refuge or other institutions for juvenile criminals, where they were deemed more or less incorrigible," PIR's first superintendent, R. W. McClaughry, claimed, "so that, although dealing with what are technically known as 'first offenders' we have a large proportion of inmates who are as thoroughly schooled in crime as if they were old offenders." For McClaughry, a former warden of Illinois' Joliet Penitentiary, the first-time offender categorization, regardless of past incarceration, was irrelevant because of their perceived questionable upbringings. "[M]any of these boys . . . are as thoroughly committed to criminal ways as if they had served a whole term in the penitentiary, and the majority of them are far more rash,—more ready to take risks,—more ready to do desperate things, to escape, or to wreak vengeance." In fact, over one-third of the twenty-four inmates testifying or represented at the hearing had prior records, having served sentences as juveniles in the Philadelphia House of Refuge, in the Philadelphia County Jail, or, in one case each, Eastern State Penitentiary and the Iowa State Penitentiary.[20]

Prison administrators further attempted to challenge the veracity of the

[19] Certainly, sworn testimony is not always a completely reliable source, as fabrications, elaborations, and omissions are common. In the case of the PIR investigation, inmate testimonies often corroborated one another, but commonly with variations in details that indicate vagaries of individual memories of events rather than outright perjury or a collusion to fabricate events and experiences at the prison. Testimony from similar, subsequent investigations at other reformatories further shows that while there was a certain performative nature to testimony given at these inquiries, inmates suffered similar and widespread abuse at the hands of prison officials across a number of institutions.

[20] T. H. Nevin, "The Model Prison," in *Proceedings of the Eighth Annual Conference of Charities and Correction* (1881), 252; "What the Managers Say," *Philadelphia Inquirer*, Mar. 12, 1892; "The 'Solitary' and the 'Lashes'"; R. W. McClaughry to the Board of Managers, Pennsylvania Industrial Reformatory, Feb. 10, 1890, series 88, PIR Records, Pennsylvania State Archives; R. W. McClaughry Testimony, Investigation Transcript, 564, PIR Records, Pennsylvania State Archives.

inmates' testimony by characterizing and often referring to the reformatory's inmates as children—wards of the state with limited rights—by virtue of their lawbreaking and lack of self-control. As such, administrators used small personal comforts and obvious marks of rank to demarcate the men, classifying inmates by their general behavior and performance at school and work, and creating a hierarchy of first, second, and third grades. All cells at PIR were eight feet long and eight feet wide, each furnished with a straw tick mattress, blanket, and one copy each of the reformatory rules and a bible. First- and second-grade inmates, however, also received a bedstead, sheets, blanket, pillow, wooden table, stool, comb, toothbrush, molasses can, vinegar bottle, pepper box, knife, fork, spoon, and a dust brush and dust pan to keep their cells clean. First-grade inmates wore uniforms of a solid gray, and second-grade inmates wore a gray uniform with a black stripe running through it. Third-grade inmates wore "the red garb of disgrace," a gray uniform with a red stripe running through it, and were deprived of additional comforts such as coffee or tea at meals, light in their cells at night, access to library books and newspapers, and receiving letters or visitors.[21]

The men incarcerated at PIR were already bound by many commonalities of life before arrest and the process of conviction, incarceration, and ranking, and the reformatory's administrative and disciplinary regimes worked to further strengthen these bonds. Rather than reining in inmate resistance to authority and halting pervasive rule-breaking, this apparatus often had the opposite effect. The use of "special punishments," namely paddlings and solitary confinement, was pervasive. From April 1889 through the spring 1892 investigation, administrators logged nearly one thousand offenses for which inmates received these special punishments. Close to one-third of the 923 inmates incarcerated at PIR received solitary and/or physical punishments, with almost three-fourths of these inmates punished multiple times for serious infractions that included disorderly conduct in the cell houses, threatening an officer, fighting with other inmates, and attempting to escape. Though punishments were meted out for "crookedness," "feigning sickness," and "fooling" at school or chapel, paddlings and solitary confinement were also the response to what the Philadelphia press described as "trifling" infractions resulting in charges of insolence, disobedience, and refusing to obey an officer: "hair

---

[21] Prison guards wore a solid, dark navy blue suit. T. B. Patton Testimony, Investigation Transcript, 129–30, PIR Records, Pennsylvania State Archives.

not combed, hands in pockets, dirty wash-basin, dusty wall in cell, dusty floor in cell, out of step in line and arms not folded." This was a perversion of the reformatory approach to punishment as set out by post–Civil War prison reformers. "The rigorously coercive systems, by whatever names known or under whatever forms existing, viewed as reformatory agencies, are based on an essentially wrong principle. . . . they subdue, but do not reclaim," leading prison reformer Enoch C. Wines wrote in 1871. "Its tendency is to crush the weak, irritate the strong, and indispose all to submission and reform."[22]

Only fifty of the 923 inmates made what administrators characterized as "perfect records" with "no demerits of any kind" while at the prison. The reformatory's official record of special punishments includes nearly twenty separate infractions for which inmates were punished with the paddle or solitary confinement: obscene or vile language, profanity, swearing; cell house disorderly conduct or disturbance; insolence, disobedience or refusing to obey an officer; threatening or attempted assault on an officer; fighting with other inmates; refusal to work; gross indecency, defiling the cell house and exposure of person; attempted sodomy and licentious intercourse. The most common infraction was insolence, disobedience, or refusing to obey an officer, accounting for nearly 20 percent of all infractions and typically paired with an additional charge. Less commonly used categories included mutinous conduct, crookedness, stealing, smoking or possession of tobacco, lying or feigning sickness or insanity, laughing or fooling, destroying prison property, attempted escape, general "bad conduct," and circulating obscene pictures or notes. After October 1891, administrators began using "continued disobedience" as a catchall infraction for many of the recorded punishments. By January 1892 nearly all recorded special punishments were noted as being for continued disobedience or for the generic "loss of marks" against an inmate's conduct record.

Prison officials, especially Superintendent Patton and Deputy Superintendent Smith, never denied that they used corporal punishment or soli-

---

[22] Summary of Huntingdon Hearings, Investigation Transcript, 602–3, PIR Records, Pennsylvania State Archives; Record of Special Punishments, 1889–1925, 1931, vol. 1, series 96, PIR Records, Pennsylvania State Archives; "The Treatment at Huntington"; "Huntingdon's Reformatory Cruelties," *Philadelphia Inquirer*, Mar. 21, 1892; Enoch C. Wines, "Alexander Maconochie and His Principles of Prison Discipline," in *International Prison Congress on the Prevention and Repression of Crime, Including Penal and Reformatory Treatment: Preliminary Report of the Commissioner Appointed by the President to Represent the United States in the Congress, in Compliance with a Joint Resolution of March 7, 1871* (Washington, DC, 1872), 177, 187.

tary confinement at PIR. In fact, Patton's predecessor, R. W. McClaughry, made it known to PIR's Board of Managers within a year of the prison's opening that he had begun using corporal punishments and solitary confinement. "About the first of September last," he wrote in February 1890, "when the disorderly element became so strong and defiant, encouraged by continually increasing numbers, that I was compelled to resort, in extreme cases, to corporal punishment," with solitary confinement "a last resort to secure obedience." McClaughry later justified his actions further, asserting, "[I]n the formative days of an institution, you have to do some things that you would not have to do after you get the discipline settled. . . . The moment you lose your grip on the discipline in an institution of this kind, it is gone."[23]

By letting this use of corporal punishment and solitary confinement go unchecked, PIR's Board of Managers—political appointees who oversaw PIR's general operations—within a year of the institution's opening gave the state's tacit consent to punishments that ran counter to the most basic thinking behind reformatory prison discipline. Nor did the Board of Managers challenge attempts to minimize the impact of these severe punishments by PIR's administrators, who framed them as discipline meted out from a caring parent to a child. In the case of what prison officials called the "paddle" but inmates called the "lash," of the 389 times administrators paddled inmates, Superintendent Patton said the use of this physical punishment was no more severe than a parent spanking a child. "How was he punished then," Senator Osbourn asked Patton about one of the Moyamensing Ten during questioning at the 1892 inquiry:

A. By spanking.
Q. Whipped, was he?
A. Spanked, yes sir.[24]

Samuel McCamant, a member of PIR's Board of Managers, described the paddle to the press as a leather strap "of the same shape as that used by boys in playing ball," though former superintendent McClaughry was more explicit to the managers behind closed doors, admitting that "corporal punishment . . . has been administered by a strap or paddle of sole leather, soaked in water, 15 inches long and 4½ inches broad." When paddlings began in spring 1889, four to six "spanks" were the punishment

---

[23] McClaughry to the Board of Managers; McClaughry Testimony, Investigation Transcript, 567.
[24] Patton Testimony, Investigation Transcript, 37.

norm. By July 1890, this number had increased to between eight and twelve, and by September 1891, ten to fifteen strikes were common.[25]

"[T]here is something in the idea of punishment beyond the mere infliction of it," Deputy Superintendent George Smith postulated. "On the contrary, the application of a paddle . . . is directly in the line of paternal harmoniousness, and is more like the paternal application of a member of the family."[26] But according to PIR inmates, beatings with the paddle were not the benign spankings that prison administrators claimed them to be, and they told of the severe physical and mental toll the whippings took.[27] Inmate Sol Foster, reported by the mess hall steward for "carrying on," received "12 cracks." With his hands pinned by the steward, Smith whipped Foster in "the small of the back, a little above; and that left a good many marks behind." The beating left injuries, both physical and psychological. Hurt and humiliated, Foster went back to work in the chair shop, where "Mr. Pullard . . . seen me crying and asked me what was the matter; and I said 'I am black and blue all over.' And he started to laugh."[28]

As horrific as the "spankings" could be, many inmates thought them preferable to time in solitary confinement. "I was licked with a strap. . . . Every time it went off, it sounded like a dozen soda water bottles cracking," Harry Levis said of his twenty-five lashes:

Q. Were you ever in the solitary?
A. No sir, I had that good fortune.[29]

When constructed, PIR had no solitary cells incorporated into the prison, reflecting the notion that discipline at the reformatory would be maintained through the system of rewards and demerits, not punishments traditionally found in penitentiaries. Within a year of opening, however, then-superintendent McClaughry began using empty cells in the upper tier of cell house B for solitary confinement, with Joseph Zurita, a

[25] Record of Special Punishments. "What the Managers Say"; McClaughry to the Board of Managers; McClaughry Testimony, Investigation Transcript, 556–57.

[26] Smith Testimony, Investigation Transcript, 17, 557.

[27] William Steiner said of the paddle, "This had brass rivets on it, and after a few blows it began to draw blood." Superintendent Patton denied the claims that the paddles had rivets in them. See summary of Steiner's testimony in "Huntingdon Reformatory Cruelties"; Patton Testimony, Investigation Transcript, 16, 41.

[28] Sol Foster Testimony, Investigation Transcript, 247.

[29] Harry Levis Testimony, Investigation Transcript, 748.

seventeen-year-old cigar maker serving a three-year sentence for receiving stolen goods, holding the inauspicious distinction of being the first inmate to be punished by solitary confinement at PIR. While in solitary, inmates' diets consisted of "some bread and water,—about six inches to two and a half thick, and one cup of water." Fastened during daytime hours by the wrists to a neck-level ring in the wall, or to a diagonal bar fastened to the wall along which they could slide their shackles to stand or sit, inmates had little freedom of movement. While in this restrained position inmates received their meals, which they consumed standing up. Solitary cells had no bed or other furniture, instead only a wooden plank on which to sleep and a "hopper" for relieving themselves. According to McClaughry these conditions were far from inhumane. Though "three or four blows upon the boy's bare buttocks" were "better than three or four days in solitary, and . . . better for him physically and mentally," he insisted "[t]hey had been so accustomed to sleeping on sidewalks, in coal pits, and cellar ways that a plank bed in a dry warm cell was to them a luxury." Conditions in solitary aside, prison officials maintained that "one sent to 'solitary' could free himself at any time when he should choose to give promise of proper behavior and obedience to the rules of the Institution."[30]

At PIR solitary confinement was a tool meant to break an individual's will to rebel against rules of the institution. But as a shared—though individually experienced—potential or actual punishment, it further bound inmates to one another. For infractions large and small inmates could spend days, weeks, or even months in isolation, chained in a standing position, on a bread and water diet. "The cell had on a blind door and I could not see out at all. The keeper never came around, except to put in the bread," Jacob Johnson told of his nearly three-week stint in solitary. "It was entirely dark in the room and there was no ventilation at all. I was not allowed to have any communication with the outside world for those twenty days."[31] For inmate Harry Anderson, his three months in solitary began when he could not perform his work in one of the prison workshops because of his foot, which had been maimed in a rolling mill accident prior to his incarceration. "The man was not able to do his task," Eddie

[30] McClaughry to the Board of Managers; McClaughry Testimony, Investigation Transcript, 567; A. B. Kennedy Testimony, Investigation Transcript, 202; Smith Testimony, Investigation Transcript, 481; Patton Testimony, Investigation Transcript, 34; Foster Testimony, Investigation Transcript, 250; Investigation Report, 6–7.

[31] "The Sworn Testimony," *Philadelphia Inquirer*, Mar. 17, 1892. Johnson gave his sworn testimony at the law office of Senator Osbourn in Philadelphia before the hearings in Huntingdon and Philadelphia.

Conlan explained. When pressed by the investigating committee to confirm that Anderson "was put in solitary, because he would not do his task," Eddie reiterated, "No, sir, because he *couldn't*." Countering the administrators' claims that if inmates were repentant and asked to be let out of solitary they would be released, Eddie stated bluntly, "They put you up there until *they* think you had enough."[32]

The revelations reported in the press about these punishments at PIR shocked the public, especially in the context of the reformatory's purported humane punishment systems, but not more so than the pervasiveness of violence beyond the paddle and solitary confinement used to maintain order. In fact, what motivated prison administrators and guards was intimidating, imparting fear, and exerting power as much as instilling a healthy respect for PIR rules. "I very frequently got hold of a boy, and shook him," George Smith told the investigating committee, ". . . [b]ecause I thought I would give them to understand that I had more power than they did." Smith added, "I can do almost anything."[33] Deputy Superintendent Smith and other guards often used whatever tools— whether canes or blackjacks, hands or hammers—that were at their disposal. When Henry Albertis heckled the band director during a parade rehearsal, Smith was swift with his punishment. "Smith called me out . . . and when he met me in the office, he caught and pushed me around in his office . . . he hit me over the face; and he hit me over the ear. . . . I can't hear pretty good in that ear yet," Albertis told the investigating panel. "He got his hands around my neck, and choked me . . . you could see the finger marks."[34] Indeed, the investigation revealed that Smith regularly punched and choked inmates for minor infractions, resulting in injuries including black eyes, bloodied noses, and lacerations.[35]

The very unpredictability of punishments at PIR, meted out by poorly trained guards and inmate monitors, spoke to the wide gap between the theory and practice of the new penology. The indeterminate sentence and rational marks system was supposed to encourage inmates to understand that the "only avenue of escape from the grim reality of his maximum

[32] Conlan Testimony, Investigation Transcript, 653, 684, 689; Harry Anderson Testimony, Investigation Transcript, 801, 808–9. Italics added to both Conlan quotations for emphasis. "Edward Conlan's Story," *Philadelphia Inquirer*, Mar. 17, 1892; "The Sworn Testimony."

[33] Smith Testimony, Investigation Transcript, 505, 512, 576.

[34] Henry Albertis Testimony, Investigation Transcript, 224–25. See also testimonies of Samuel Levi, John Harvey, William Fred Strum, A. B. Kennedy, and Edward Conlan.

[35] See, for example, Harry Levis Testimony, Investigation Transcript, 746–47; Frank Cole testimony, Investigation Transcript, 753, 759; and Conlan Testimony, Investigation Transcript, 693.

sentence is through *improvement*, improvement of hand, heart and brain." But the often random and excessive use of extreme punishments for "trifling" and "trivial" offenses diminished this ideal.[36] It ran counter to inmates' expectations and a collective notion among them that even though they were convicted criminals, they still had the right to decent treatment, basic care, and predictability in the system. On a very basic level, inmates thus felt compelled to stand up for one another, whether to demand better treatment, prove abuse, or for mutual protection. In response to questions about whether or not he was lying when he claimed Deputy Superintendent Smith punched and choked him, Henry Albertis claimed, "I can prove it by the gang that I was working with," who could see the bruises left "for three or four weeks."[37]

Beyond identifying themselves as a group against the guards, accepted standards of behavior within the group also shaped the culture and identity among PIR inmates. They determined their good standing within the group by largely unspoken but expected standards of comportment with one another and against prison officials. Even if it was posturing, one's pre-prison backstory was an important way that prisoners defined themselves and exuded a toughness that inmates expected of each other and respected. In his testimony about inmate John Ward, sentenced to PIR for ten years on a charge of burglary and larceny, Deputy Superintendent Smith said Ward's influence on other inmates was "very bad," owing to his boastfulness about a previous stint in the Iowa Penitentiary for burglary and a purported attack he made on a guard there:

Q. Was he looked upon as a leader by any?
A. A great many, because he was giving the story out that he was.
Q. Do you know that he told the other boys of his past career, or that they knew of it?
A. I don't know what he told them, but they knew of it. At least they knew that he was there; at least they told me.[38]

Standing up to guards and Smith, who had started his career at PIR as a rank-and-file guard, likewise solidified one's standing within the group.

---

[36] Pennsylvania Industrial Reformatory, *Biennial Report of the Board of Managers*, 21; "The Treatment at Huntingdon"; "Huntingdon's Reformatory Cruelties."

[37] Henry Albertis Testimony, Investigation Transcript, 225.

[38] George Smith Testimony, Investigation Transcript, 767. Ward denied the previous arrest when questioned as part of his PIR intake interview. He served the Iowa sentence under the name James Harris, and PIR officials later indicated in his record that his real name was not John Ward but James McKenna.

When questioned about whether he "expressed contrition, and asked to be forgiven" by Smith during his time in solitary, inmate John Marlin scoffed, "I wouldn't give him the satisfaction of asking him."[39]

Among inmates, one's larger identity within the group was also a product of rule breaking. Case after case of rule-breaking and violence appeared in PIR's records—from hiding contraband items in cells, to various verbal and physical attacks on guards, to attempting to escape. But prisoners revealed in their testimony to the 1892 investigating committee that while rule breaking for rule breaking's sake was common, it was frequently a product of standing one's ground as an individual or a group in the face of actual or perceived injustices or slights, even knowing that punishment would follow.[40] Henry Albertis, for instance, recalled a time when the prison band refused to play in retaliation for events of the previous day. "One Sunday afternoon we had an overture, and Professor Reudenberg, he was supposed to lead us. He could not play the piece himself and so we played it that we were tired out, and couldn't play any more; and we wanted him to relieve us, and he wouldn't do it," Albertis recounted. "So the next day we didn't play the piece and so he gave us a blue ticket, and that is the way of it."[41]

Solidarity among inmates also developed by virtue of prisoners' "us versus them" attitude toward PIR's guards. Among the guards this feeling was mutual, as observed by prison reformer Frank Tannenbaum. "After all *he* is a keeper, an official, a good man (at least in his own judgment). Whereas a convict is a criminal. For his own clear conscience sake the keeper must, and does, instinctively, make a sharp distinction between himself and the man whom he guards," Tannenbaum wrote. "The keeper succeeds in making a gap between himself and the prisoner, and the gap is filled by contempt." In a letter to the guards at PIR, superintendent T. B. Patton shared the contents of an article he read, written by a guard at another reformatory. He conveyed to the officers that it "impressed me

[39] John Marlin Testimony, Investigation Transcript, 893. George Smith previously worked at a prison in Lancaster, Pennsylvania, and at the time of his promotion to deputy superintendent was "principal keeper" at PIR. See Smith Testimony, Investigation Transcript, 467, 536. Chad Gregory, "Among the Dockhands: Another Look at Working-Class Male Culture," *Men and Masculinities* 9 (2006): 252–60.

[40] As noted in PIR's conduct ledgers and the journals of the superintendent, violent attacks on guards by inmates were frequent. See Conduct Ledgers, series 91, PIR Records, Pennsylvania State Archives; Record of Special Punishments, series 96, PIR Records, Pennsylvania State Archives; Journals of the General Superintendent, series 84, PIR Records, Pennsylvania State Archives. See also Pisciotta, *Benevolent Repression*, 97–99.

[41] Albertis Testimony, Investigation Transcript, 234.

. . . containing as it did the quiet suggestion that after all a Reformatory was to a certain extent what the officers of the Institution made it" but adding, "[n]aturally reformatory life is divided into two sides: the officers on one side and the inmates on the other."[42]

At PIR and prisons throughout the country, guards were by and large poorly paid state workers with backgrounds—excepting for age and the commission of a crime—surprisingly similar to the inmates in their charge.[43] At the time of the 1892 investigation, PIR guards received pay of one dollar per day plus meals and worked six and a half day weeks of eight hour shifts. "While standing on one of the main streets in the evening I saw a delegation or bucket brigade of uniformed men, about fifty in all . . . going to their homes. They told me they were officers from the Reformatory . . . and that the pittance of $1.00 per day was what they received for their pay," a Huntingdon resident recounted. "This to me seems shameful." Guards ate the same food as inmates and, until the enactment of Pennsylvania's 1891 law limiting labor in prisons to eight hours a day, boarded at the institution. These conditions were far different from those that would have allowed for the recruitment of the educated, specially trained, and well-compensated professional reformatory guards envisioned by the new penology. "The guards are an ignorant set," the *Philadelphia Inquirer* candidly stated in the days leading up to the 1892 investigation. "The keeper too is a prisoner . . . for him there is little beyond the exercise of power."[44]

The widespread antagonism inmates felt and displayed toward the guards extended to PIR's inmate monitors—inmates at the institution

---

[42] Frank Tannenbaum, "The Psychology of Prison Cruelty," *Prison Labor Leaflets* 59 (New York, 1920), 7, italics in original; T. B. Patton to "Officers Only," n.d., Pennsylvania Industrial Reformatory, Scrapbook, 1889–1929, series 89, PIR Records, Pennsylvania State Archives.

[43] Prison guards, beyond their role in maintaining order or meting out discipline, are largely overlooked in the existing literature on late nineteenth- and early twentieth-century prison systems, and, more generally, on the late nineteenth- and early twentieth-century working class.

[44] Patton Testimony, Investigation Transcript, 167–69; "Young Victims of Huntingdon," *Philadelphia Inquirer*, Mar. 15, 1892; Frank Nalder, "The American State Reformatory with Special Reference to Its Educational Aspects," *University of California Publications in Education*, Mar. 10, 1920, 323, 325–26. "Huntingdon's Reformatory Cruelties." Guards' meals varied from those served to inmates in that they could have as much as they wanted rather than a set portion, had the option of tea and coffee with each meal, and usually had a dessert of pie, cake, or pudding with the main midday dinner. The passage in 1891 of a prison labor law in Pennsylvania impacted both inmates and guards. This law regulated an individual's labor in prisons to a maximum of eight hours per day. Prior to this, guards typically worked ten- to twelve-hour shifts and sometimes boarded at the prison. See Blake McKelvey, "The Prison Labor Problem: 1875–1900" *Journal of Criminal Law and Criminology* 25 (1934): 259.

who acted as an additional guard force. These men, Superintendent Patton explained, were in the first or second grade, "who show the qualifications to be safely entrusted with men" by virtue of their good behavior at the reformatory, irrespective of the crime that brought them there in the first place. This group of roughly twenty inmates supplemented the regular guard force of sixty officers, which was limited by a lack of state appropriations.[45] Physically set apart by special blue and white-striped uniforms and ostracized from the dominant inmate culture, the monitors used their positions to gain favor from regular guards and the prison administrators, often at the expense of the rest of the inmate population.[46]

"There appears to be a decided repugnance on the part of the average prisoner to any seeming authority on the part of a fellow prisoner," the 1892 investigating committee observed, especially because the monitors "had very much to do with affecting the grade of standing of the prisoners." Infractions reported by monitors frequently resulted in inmates' demotions to the third grade. Inmates Harry Angel and Sol Foster, who worked together in the chair shop, entered into a pact to keep a monitor from falsely accusing them of acting up at work. After monitor Thompson reported the men "four or five times" for talking and joking, Angel and Foster "made up our mind not to be imposed upon by another prisoner reporting us . . . so we made up our mind, that if he kept on, to hit him." After another report from the monitor, Foster and Angel hit Thompson, but for Foster and Angel this attack was justified in order to settle a matter between prisoners:

> Q. You spoke of yourself and the other inmate . . . having made an arrangement whereby you were going to defend each other?
> A. Yes. . . .
> Q. And that you did strike an officer?
> A. A prisoner.

The matter changed when a guard got involved in the incident, attempting to strike Foster in the head with his cane. At this point Angel took the pact one step further. Knowing disciplinary action would follow, he "throwed up my hands" and attempted to shield Foster "every time not to get a strike with the cane." His intent, he told investigators, was "to stop [the guard] doing any harm, or hitting him, or anything."[47]

---

[45] Patton Testimony, Investigation Transcript, 61–62, 68–69, 121–22 (quote), 563.
[46] Investigation Report, 10–11; Patton Testimony, Investigation Transcript, 13, 59.
[47] Harry Angel Testimony, Investigation Transcript, 281–83, 285–86.

The 1892 investigation revealed that abuse within and manipulation of the monitor system were rife. "I am told," a member of the Philadelphia press reported about the monitors, "that some of these men use this privilege as a means of levying a veritable blackmail and in squaring grudges for themselves and others." Regular guards and Superintendent Patton himself admitted that staff officers often did not witness infractions by inmates as monitors reported, further inflaming antagonisms between the inmates, guards, and monitors.[48] Eddie Conlan recounted for the investigating committee a typical situation. According to him, monitors falsely accused him of infractions dozens of times, resulting in beatings and solitary confinement:

> Q. And you say positively that for those 39 or 40 tickets you did not commit any offense?
> A. Yes sir. . . .
> Q. Was any of this ill will before they got to be monitors?
> A. Yes; they would know I would have tobacco, and I wouldn't give it to them.[49]

Harry Levis received a paddling when he accused a monitor of stealing from him. "I caught one going through my coat; and I told him never to do that, except Mr. Smith said so," he testified. When taken to the guard room to explain what happened, "Mr. Smith said, 'You[r] word aint worth two cents'; and he said 'I'll take the word of the monitor.'" According to John Marlin, he too was reported "unlawfully" by a monitor. "Yes sir; they accused us to get out themselves."[50]

Monitors also used their positions of authority to engage in sexual encounters with inmates and to buy the silence of others who witnessed these encounters. When asked to testify about any known "abuse by a

---

[48] "The Scenes of Punishment," *Philadelphia Inquirer*, Mar. 22, 1892. When asked what a guard would likely do about a reported infraction not witnessed by anyone but a monitor, Patton said, the "keeper would probably believe that the monitor was telling the truth, and endorse the ticket." Patton Testimony, Investigation Transcript, 63. Similar abuse has been found among convict trustees in the penal South. For recent examinations, see Heather Ann Thompson, "Blinded by a 'Barbaric' South: Prison Horrors, Inmate Abuse, and the Ironic History of American Penal Reform," in *The Myth of Southern Exceptionalism*, ed. Matthew D. Lassiter and Joseph Crispino (New York, 2010), 74–95; Robert Perkinson, *Texas Tough: The Rise of America's Prison Empire* (New York, 2010); Chase, "Civil Rights on the Cell Block."

[49] Conlan Testimony, Investigation Transcript, 720–22 (quote on 721); Patton Testimony, Investigation Transcript, 50.

[50] Levis Testimony, Investigation Transcript, 749; Marlin Testimony, Investigation Transcript, 896.

monitor," inmate Frank Cole told of an instance that occurred one night while he tended to another inmate who had bronchitis. Cole came upon a night watchman monitor, William Franks, having sex with inmate James Monnett, through the bars of his cell. "I went up and seen him with his behind through the door, and this fellow pushing him from behind." When caught, "They begged me, and this Franks gave me a half plug of tobacco not to say anything about that." Another inmate, who also saw the incident, reported it to then-superintendent McClaughry. Franks received a "reduction from monitor back to the grade again," but no corporal punishment according to the recollection of Superintendent Patton. When pressed why the administration did not "inflict severe punishment upon a monitor," Patton answered, "If Franks is the man, there is some question about, I knew; because, if the charge had been sustained, he would have been punished in some other way than by reducing him." Yet according to Cole, then-superintendent McClaughry only investigated the charges to the extent of asking Franks, "You didn't do this, did you?" When Franks answered, "No. That settled the whole damn business."[51]

Yet inmates who engaged in same-sex encounters with other inmates or whom prison officials deemed chronic masturbators were dealt with harshly. Some 3.5 percent of recorded infractions receiving paddlings or solitary confinement were those of attempted sodomy and licentious intercourse—attempted and actual acts of homosexual sex—and gross indecency or exposure of person—charges commonly related to masturbation. In the case of Roscoe Smith, an eighteen-year-old from Northumberland County serving a three-year sentence for larceny, punishments for attempted and actual intercourse were frequent and severe: six strikes with the paddle for attempted sex with inmate John Wesley, ten for sex with inmate Lewis Bauman, five days in solitary along with Alfred Young and William Wolf for going to one another's cells for "immoral purposes." Chronic masturbators had their penises "painted" by PIR's doctor with iodine to cause rawness and pain. "I would apply it daily," Dr. Miller reported to the 1892 investigating committee, "so that it would break the skin, and make it unpleasant to have an erection, until broken of this habit." Others had their hands bound by leather straps at the neck to prevent self-touching.[52]

---

[51] It remains an open question whether this sexual encounter, and others discussed below, were consensual or rape. Cole Testimony, Investigation Transcript, 754; Patton Testimony, Investigation Transcript, 70–72.

[52] David Miller Testimony, Investigation Transcript, 363–424 (quote on 387).

These sexual acts and official responses to them must be understood as part of the larger, ongoing struggle over power and agency between inmates and administrators at PIR. The policing of behavior extended to inmates' sexuality and agency over the body, defining as deviant and subject to punishment sexual acts not only perceived as outside the norms of acceptable sexual behavior but that were also framed as evidence of inmates' lack of self-control. PIR administrators associated the lack of impulse control, which supposedly underpinned incarcerated individuals' propensity to break the law, with free sexual activity, whether with the self or others. "Crime and this vice go together," ascertained Dr. Miller. Administrators therefore perceived sexual expression as a particularly egregious kind of rebellion in and of itself, not only against the rules of the institution but also against emergent middle-class notions of healthy sexual desire expressed within the context of heterosexual marriage, and against the state and society more broadly. As historian Anthony Rotundo argues, in the nineteenth century sexual desire "was seen as an especially powerful force in a young man, distracting him from his work, blinding him from his future duties as a breadwinner . . . a young man who surrendered to sexual desire also gave up his ability to carry out the man's role." It was, in short, unnatural, and according to Dr. Miller—in keeping with common medical thinking at the time—the root of myriad ailments from meningitis and tuberculosis to suicidal tendencies and insanity. Underlying inmate Charles Hoskinson's meningitis was "that he was addicted to self-abuse"; for William Dickerson, who died of consumption shortly after discharge from PIR, masturbation "had broken his constitution." It was the source of Samuel Levy's "pure deviltry," it gave Robert Bryant a "very dull and droopy look," and it generally made inmates "nervous, and . . . irritable, and they will show signs of temper on slight provocation," producing insanity if allowed to "go on to excess." R. W. McClaughry went so far as to tell the investigators that inmate testimony was not to be believed because of inmates' propensity to masturbate. "I am not the Doctor; but my experience of them is that their memory becomes impaired; they are unreliable as to statements of fact. They are victims to a certain extent of delusions, even when they are disposed to be good and well-behaved." While Miller characterized masturbation especially as "the one bane of this institution . . . It has given us more trouble than anything else," for inmates, this behavior was an expression of agency and power—of their masculinity—exerted within and against a punitive punishment regime. "I can do it in three ways" William Dickerson told

Dr. Miller upon threat of another iodine painting. "I can do it with my fist, or lying on my face in bed, and I can do it by getting it between by legs, and rubbing it, sir. . . . I have done it three times this morning already."[53]

Through the course of the 1892 investigation, testimony—especially that of Dr. Miller—revealed that the reformatory's administrators habitually failed to provide basic care for PIR inmates, while their use of physical punishments and the physical and mental deprivation suffered in solitary confinement sickened many and drove other inmates to act erratically, to succumb to mental illness, and in noted cases to attempt suicide. Inmate testimony and family testimony about inmates who died shortly after release from the reformatory—twenty in all, according to Senator Osbourn—cited inadequate medical attention, poor diet, abuse, and overall conditions at PIR as the sources of sickness. Yet prison officials were steadfast in their opinions that these were not caused by paddlings, solitary confinement, or general treatment in the prison but instead by heredity, preexisting conditions, or excessive masturbation. Eddie Conlan recalled that after a two-month stint in solitary, prison officials transferred William Chick, the inmate whose cell was next to his in their regular cell house, to the Norristown Asylum. Harry Anderson, who spent three months in solitary, began acting in a way that made prison officials think he was insane when returned to his regular cell. "I took the clothes off, and wouldn't wear them any more. I was dirty; I had worn them for three months," he explained. "I suppose they thought I was going to die in there." He too was transferred to Norristown. Though dismissed as a

---

[53] David Miller Testimony, Investigation Transcript, 386–88, 371, 405–9, 414, 420; Patton Testimony, Investigation Transcript, 94, 108–9; McClaughry Testimony, Investigation Transcript, 568; E. Anthony Rotundo, *American Manhood: Transformations in Masculinity from the Revolution to the Modern Era* (New York, 1993), 71–74. See also 119–22, 275. This discussion is informed by Michel Foucault's interpretation of sexuality, power, and discourse in *History of Sexuality*, vol. 1 (1978; repr., New York, 1990). On the development of the homosexual-heterosexual binary, class norms, and medicalization of defining sexual identity through the early twentieth century, see Chauncey, *Gay New York*. A growing body of scholarly literature considers the history of sexuality within gendered and racial frameworks, as well as within the context of policing bodies, sexual activity, and the state. See, for example, John D'Emilio, "Since Intimate Matters: Recent Developments in the History of Sexuality in the United States," *Journal of Women's History* 25, no. 4 (2013): 88–100; Regina Kunzel, *Criminal Intimacy: Prison and the Uneven History of Modern American Sexuality* (Chicago, 2010); Margot Canaday, *The Straight State: Sexuality and Citizenship in Twentieth-Century America* (Princeton, NJ, 2011); Russell Robinson, "Masculinity as Prison: Sexual Identity, Race, and Incarceration," *California Law Review* 99, no. 5 (2011): 1309–1408; and Lakisha Simmons, *Crescent City Girls: The Lives of Young Black Women in Segregated New Orleans* (Chapel Hill, NC, 2015), esp. chap. 5.

product of habitual masturbation, Charles Hoskinson, William Dicker-son, and Samuel Levy all attempted suicide after their stints in solitary.[54]

This vacuum of care drew prisoners into networks of reciprocity to provide for one another simple amenities of daily life and basic health care. These networks underpinned and further strengthened bonds of mutuality and solidarity among inmates within the institution. Ellen Keerse, the mother of two inmates, David and Hugh, both of whom had died by the time of the 1892 investigation, testified that care for her son David fell not to the prison doctor or hospital workers, but to his brother and other inmates in his cell house with whom David worked in the chair shop. "David is poorly," read a letter submitted into evidence, "He is very thin and it is difficult to get him to move bodily. . . . We cannot move him the least, without we put him in agony. He is very sick, and could not get along without the best medical care. . . . He is in a perfectly helpless condition." Asking investigators why he was treated in his cell and not at the reformatory hospital, Mrs. Keerse testified, "[H]is brother told me that he was not treated well. In letters he told me that [David] was in his cell, and he waited on him in the day; and there were other boys that came in at night and waited on him, and took his place."[55] After a paddling from Superintendent Patton that left cuts in his skin, Charles Nickoli received medical attention not from the doctor, who refused Nickoli's request for treatment, but from Eddie Conlan. "[H]e said he couldn't give me any [liniment] . . . when I got spanked," Nickoli recounted, but Eddie shared some he had previously received from the doctor to treat a sprained wrist.[56] Likewise, prisoners would steal food from the kitchen or secret food away from their own meals and slip it to

[54] Francis A. Osbourn Statement, Investigation Transcript, 760; Conlan Testimony, Investigation Transcript, 684, 689; Patton Testimony, Investigation Transcript, 35, 89; Anderson Testimony, Investigation Transcript, 800–803, 808; "The Inquiry at Huntingdon Next Tuesday," *Philadelphia Inquirer*, Mar. 20, 1892. See especially Senator Osbourn's line of questioning in David P. Miller Testimony, Investigation Transcript, 368–417; Susan McGinnis Testimony (on behalf of James McGinnis), Investigation Transcript; John S. Angle Testimony (on behalf of Philip Evans), Investigation Transcript; and Thomas Dickerson Testimony (on behalf of William Dickerson), Investigation Transcript. "Huntingdon and Home to Death: William Dickerson's Sad Story," *Philadelphia Inquirer*, Mar. 16, 1892; "Huntingdon Reformatory: Investigation of Charges of Cruelty," *New York Times*, Apr. 6, 1892; "Reformatory Abuses: The Investigation at Huntingdon at an End," *New York Times*, Apr. 7, 1892.

[55] Ellen Keerse Testimony, Investigation Transcript, 622–27. The letter written by Hugh Keerse appears on 622. David was originally diagnosed by Dr. Miller with St. Anthony's dance, what is today usually diagnosed as chorea, a neurological disorder that produces abnormal, involuntary movements. One common form of chorea is a complication of rheumatic fever.

[56] Charles Nickoli Testimony, Investigation Transcript, 319.

those on a bread and water diet in solitary confinement, an infraction punishable by the paddle or a stint in solitary. They "[w]ould get food slipped to them. We did not always find out who did that," Deputy Superintendent Smith testified about the men in solitary:

Q. From the other inmates you mean?
A. Yes, sir.[57]

Prison administrators were also negligent in their mission to provide reformatory inmates with vocational training and education while there. Yet testimony showed that many of the incarcerated men took the promise of work and the possibility of learning a trade seriously. The reformatory approach to criminal rehabilitation was heavily laden with middle-class notions of right thinking and right living, the rehabilitative nature of work, and the male breadwinner model of gender norms and respectability. Purposeful work was therefore meant to be a central component of the punishment-rehabilitation program of the reformatory prison system. But upon arrival at PIR, inmates discovered that, like formal classroom education, which first- and second-grade men could attend for an hour a night, neither was available to them on a consistent basis. Through 1889 and 1890, PIR established industrial shops for carpentry, shoemaking, tailoring, blacksmithing, chair making, brush making, and stone and brick masonry, a functioning farm of nearly seven hundred acres, and a forestry camp. But the vocational training program at PIR had foundered almost immediately, and prison administrators paid little attention to the educative aspects of work undertaken therein. "The rapid increase of inmates made it necessary to decide at once upon some industry which would furnish employment for a large number," PIR's administration reported, but adding, "we had no appropriation with which to purchase material which would be mainly wasted in endeavoring to teach trades to young idlers who had never worked, and had no idea of labor, or desire to learn how to perform it." Severe flooding in 1889 and a yearlong drought during 1890 essentially shut down the reformatory's farm and forestry camp. Between 1891 and 1892, PIR's Board of Managers listed in their biannual report that inmates were engaged in a wide range of trades, but a devastating fire in August 1892 destroyed several of the refor-

---

[57] Smith Testimony, Investigation Transcript, 480.

matory's key workshops, including the brush shop, repair shop, tin shop, paint shop, planing mill, and carpenter shop.[58]

In reality, by the time of the 1892 investigation, PIR's labor system—and its utility to impart vocational instruction—was in disarray. In addition to paltry appropriations from the state, and the infrastructure and administrative issues growing out of drought, flood, and fire at PIR between 1889 and 1892, as in other states organized labor lobbied aggressively for the passage of convict labor laws in Pennsylvania. Both the Knights of Labor and, later, the American Federation of Labor spearheaded state anti–prison labor campaigns with significant successes from the 1880s through the turn of the century. In 1883 the Pennsylvania legislature passed a limited prison contract labor ban and in 1891 made it illegal for inmates engaged in any kind of labor to work more than eight hours a day. Against this larger backdrop, the work done by inmates at PIR was therefore geared toward neither vocational training nor large-scale industry for profit making, but first and foremost for the maintenance of the institution and personal care of the inmates—cleaning, cooking, and baking, laundry and tailoring, hospital work, and infrastructure maintenance and repairs among them. Without this labor, Superintendent Patton asserted, the state would have to hire at least one hundred additional paid employees. Still, at the time of the investigation, up to one-fourth of the inmates at the reformatory were completely unemployed, with the remaining three-fourths employed only intermittently and for "short hours."[59]

For PIR inmates, however, work and learning a trade, even while incarcerated, were important to their self-definitions as men and even their

---

[58] Pennsylvania Industrial Reformatory, *Biennial Report of the Pennsylvania Industrial Reformatory at Huntingdon for 1889–90*; Pennsylvania Industrial Reformatory, *Biennial Report of the Board of Managers*. On opportunities for formal schooling at the reformatory, see Patton Testimony, Investigation Transcript, 138, 188; and J. H. Likens Testimony, Investigation Transcript, 440–42.

[59] Commonwealth of Pennsylvania, "Report of the Sub-Committee of the Board of Public Charities to the Board of Public Charities Relative to the Investigation of the Reformatory Held March 22, 23, 24, 1892 at Huntingdon and on April 5 and 6, 1892 at Philadelphia," June 1, 1892, 9, series 88, PIR Records, Pennsylvania State Archives; Smith Testimony, Investigation Transcript, 581; Patton Testimony, Investigation Transcript, 589–94. Organized labor's most significant achievement in the Pennsylvania prison labor fight came in 1897 with the passage of the Muehlbronner Act, which abolished the use of power machinery in the manufacture of prison goods and limited the number of inmates employed in any single trade within each prison. It stood until 1915, when Pennsylvania began moving toward a state-use system for the products of its prison industries. See McKelvey, "The Prison Labor Problem," 259.

notions of personhood. "I have not done any work for a year. I have laid in my cell like an animal," inmate Charles Meyers explained to the Board of Charities investigators. "They told me I could get some up here, and learn a trade here. I did come here to learn, and get a trade," he explained, but he got no work. "[B]eing a man," he continued, "I told [the superintendent] some three times,—I told him I didn't want to be a tough, or anything of the kind,—to send me to the Penitentiary, where I could work." For other inmates, the conditions in which they worked or the jobs prison officials expected them to do undermined their manhood as well. Work in the chair shop, John Ward said, was "work [that] was intended for children, and not for men."[60]

Inmates' associations of work with masculinity and networks of solidarity in the context of shared work experience paralleled language common to, and elements of shop-floor conduct among, nineteenth-century skilled male workers. While not necessarily craft workers themselves or undertaking skilled work at the reformatory, inmates there by virtue of their work backgrounds on the railroads and the docks, as apprentices to skilled trades, and in mills, foundries, mines, and industrial workplaces of all sorts would at the very least have been exposed to such gendered and class-based notions of identity and agency. This in turn informed their labor-management, inmate-guard relationships at PIR.[61] The generic offenses of "refusal to work" or "insubordination at work" in fact littered PIR's punishment ledgers, masking both inmate-guard conflicts, violence, and individual and collective acts of resistance to the reformatory's work-discipline regime, together accounting for some 7 percent of all infractions resulting in paddling or solitary confinement.[62] Some of these infractions were inadvertent, like when Eddie Conlan damaged a kitchen door by banging a cart into it. "Yes sir, I admitted it. . . . It was in the dark of the morning, and I couldn't see,—4 o'clock in the morning." Others were the result of power struggles between inmates, guards, and monitors that erupted in PIR's workspaces. "Yes, I was put in solitary, and remained in solitary 23 days on bread and water," Harry Angel recounted of his time

[60] Ward's statement was recounted by Charles Meyers. Charles Meyers Testimony, Investigation Transcript, 341.

[61] There is an extensive literature regarding notions of masculinity and class-based labor solidarity, especially studies that focus on particular industries. For a general introduction to these concepts, see David Montgomery, *Workers' Control in America* (1979; repr., New York, 1992), 9–31.

[62] This included two instances of taking or breaking tools. Record of Special Punishments, PIR Records, Pennsylvania State Archives.

working in the chair shop. "Of course I refused to work for him under considerations that that was my monitor."[63]

Institutional records further show that inmates also joined together in collective action. Eddie Conlan recounted attempts to rectify the freezing temperatures in the chair shop through a group complaint. "I had a bucket of water, and I had to put the sponge in the water," Conlan recounted, and "several of us told the guard of the shop . . . that the room was cold, that we couldn't work very well." Though the chair shop was not heated any better, in this instance the shop workers were not punished beyond a mark on their conduct records. But other inmates did not fare as well. Edward Creasy, Hiram Reed, and Thomas Hatfield each received six strikes with the paddle for starting "a revolt in the chair shop" in November 1889, Frank Ray received ten strikes in March 1890 for "circulating a note in the shop intended to stir up mutiny," and William Cassell received two strikes in May 1890 for "taking the lead in insubordination" and intentionally ruining bricks in the brickyard. "They drive you like a dog," John Miller testified of his work experiences at PIR, "and then pull out a pencil; and when you explain, they give you no show at all; and when you go to talk, they give you a lick in the nose."[64]

In the end, the 1892 investigation of the Pennsylvania Industrial Reformatory revealed that while there should have been vast differences in the experience of prisoners incarcerated under the old and the new systems, there were not. Yet the committee tasked by Pennsylvania's governor with investigating the charges against the reformatory recommended only minor changes to the prison administration and operations, and ultimately concluded that fault for failure in the system lay not with its design or implementation by administrators but with the inmates themselves. "[T]here are frequent cases of incipient revolt, combinations for insubordination and purpose to break the rules," committee members wrote in their final report. "[A] certain proportion of inmates appear naturally and extremely depraved and disposed to conduct themselves in a manner disgraceful to humanity and deserving of treatment as brutes rather than human beings."[65]

[63] Record of Special Punishments, PIR Records, Pennsylvania State Archives; Conlan Testimony, Investigation Transcript, 701; Harry Angel Testimony, Investigation Transcript, 284.

[64] Conlan Testimony, Investigation Transcript, 650–51; John Miller Testimony, Investigation Transcript, 225, 299. T. B. Patton specifically discussed the punishments of inmates Frank Gallagher, William Dickerson, and Harry Anderson for insubordination at or refusal to complete work in his testimony.

[65] Investigation Report, 8.

Following the close of the hearings about conditions at PIR, Senator Osbourn enumerated nine specific recommendations for reform and called for the removal of Deputy Superintendent George Smith, though noting, "whatever has been done has been chiefly through errors of judgement, and not willfully and maliciously." Ultimately, the investigation brought little change to the institution or to its management. The final report of the investigating Board of Public Charities committee recommended shorter terms of solitary confinement and better attention to inmates therein. It called for reform of the use of monitors "as far as practicable" and "found fault" with the reformatory's failure to record incidents where Deputy Superintendent Smith or other guards struck inmates. But in the end, the committee concluded "that so far as the Management of the Institution is concerned, it has been well meaning, honest, and competent." In spite of calls for his removal by Senator Osbourn, the committee said that Deputy Superintendent Smith was "peculiarly well fitted for the position he occupies" and "was shown to be considerate of every inmate of the Institution, giving them frequent advice regarding their conduct and expressing regret at the necessity of imposing punishment on any one. . . . He was personally courageous, prompt and effective in the performance of his duties." In the final account, blame for conditions at the prison rested largely with the inmates themselves, who were "not model children."[66]

Even the minor changes recommended by the committee to the operating procedures at PIR that would be implemented in the years following the investigation came too late for Eddie Conlan. Perhaps in an attempt to punish or silence him for instigating the investigation, perhaps in response to a final act of rule breaking or rebellion perpetrated by Eddie himself, on March 6, 1892, two weeks before testimony began at the formal inquiry, Edward Joseph Conlan Jr., PIR inmate number 159, was "[d]elivered to Court Officer R. O. Ott . . . for transfer to Eastern [State] Penitentiary."[67]

The investigation of the Pennsylvania Industrial Reformatory and similar, subsequent investigations at other reformatories in the country pro-

[66] Senator Osbourn Statement, Investigation Transcript, 897; Investigation Report, esp. 32–34. See also "The Reformatory Inquiry," *Philadelphia Inquirer*, Apr. 15, 1892; "Remedies at Last at Huntingdon," *Philadelphia Inquirer*, June 5, 1892; and "Plain Truths Concerning Huntingdon," *Philadelphia Inquirer*, June 6, 1892. "Suggestions for Reform," *Philadelphia Inquirer*, Apr. 8, 1892; "The Reformatory Reports," *Philadelphia Inquirer*, June 10, 1892.

[67] Edward Conlan (#159), Biographical Register.

vided overwhelming evidence that, like their antebellum penitentiary predecessors, turn-of-the-century reformatory prisons were rife with abuse, overcrowded, underfunded, understaffed, and often run by brutal and despotic prison administrators. Yet supporters of the new penology and state politicians continued to tout the promises and purported successes of the reformatory system for decades.[68] Rather than address the systemic, root causes of failure, reformers and policymakers alike largely ignored the flaws in the theories behind, financial appropriations for, and implementation of the reformatory approach to criminal incarceration. Instead, they found it easier to argue that blame for such conditions lay with inmate behavior rooted in and reinforced by inmate cultures that developed, in part, in response to the deficiencies and administrative lapses that existed at institutions including PIR. Such thinking circumscribed possibilities for broad institutional reform in the late nineteenth and early twentieth centuries and helped to further entrench and normalize punitive punishment regimes in America's prison system that prioritized discipline over rehabilitation.

Princeton University   BETH ENGLISH

---

[68] On other, similar investigations, see Pisciotta, *Benevolent Repression*, 33–59, 92–103.

"Shining A Light in a Dark House": Riots, Rebellion, and the Politics of Penal Reform in Pennsylvania

The degree of civilization in a society can be judged by entering its prisons.
—Fyodor Dostoyevsky, 1862

ABSTRACT: Since the late eighteenth century, Pennsylvania's penal reformers believed the primary goals of corrections were punishment and protection, ensured by custodial personnel who impose the strict discipline of people with histories of criminal behavior in an environment that restricts privacy and personal freedom. In 1953, correctional officers faced threats, assaults, and even being taken hostage during a riot at Western State Penitentiary in Pittsburgh, a facility with a long history of unrest. The Western uprising was historically significant because it led to a specially appointed commission of penologists and other professionals who investigated the riot and what caused it. More notably, in the spirit of Pennsylvania's earlier reformers, the commission also made numerous recommendations that dramatically transformed and improved the state correctional system and are still evident in 2019.

T HE TROUBLE STARTED just after dark, about 7:00 p.m. on a thirty-degree Sunday night on January 18, 1953, when a fire started by a lone inmate in the license tag factory quickly spread throughout three buildings in Pennsylvania's seventy-one-year-old Western State Penitentiary in Pittsburgh. A prison staff's worst imagined nightmare had become a terrifying reality.

Almost immediately, according to warden James W. Cloudy, formerly a Protestant minister, a spontaneous riot ensued when the prisoners began shouting profanities at the guards; they then fed the flames with chairs,

The author would like to thank the anonymous readers of this manuscript for their valuable, critical input and *PMHB*'s Christina Larocco for her patient and flexible guidance. He also is grateful to members of the administrative staff and especially communications director Susan McNaughton at the Department of Corrections in Camp Hill for providing access to DOC archives and other resources.

bedding, clothing, and any other flammable material within their reach. What they could not burn, such as metal furniture, light fixtures, and plumbing apparatus, they destroyed. Within minutes a city river patrol boat cruising offshore joined six hundred Pittsburgh police officers. Eventually Pennsylvania state troopers formed a tight ring around the prison walls as the inmates held five guards as hostages.[1]

Securing a maximum-security prison during a riot is difficult at best, but flames shooting into the frigid night air inside the penitentiary's heavy stone walls made reestablishing control over one thousand agitated incarcerated men nearly impossible. Firemen from Pittsburgh's Engine Company No. 30 labored to extinguish the flames under life-threatening conditions. One prisoner assaulted Captain George Klein, striking him in his right eye with a brick. When firefighters tried to extend hose nozzles through bars in the windows, several rioters threatened that "if you put those hoses in here . . . these guards are going on top of the fire." The mutineers showed compassion, however, when they released fifty-eight-year-old guard Francis Dougherty because of his age and because inmates said they respected him. Neither the fire nor the riot was premeditated, but those involved quickly seized the opportunity to show force. Anxious police and prison officials could only wonder if they had seen the worst.[2]

FALSE STARTS AND THE FAILURE OF REFORM

A prison uprising was not a new phenomenon in the 1950s. The first recorded American inmate riot occurred in 1774, in Simsbury, Connecticut. Since then, at least one prison disturbance had been reported nearly every year, and it is impossible to know precisely how many incidents were never publicized. In the mid-twentieth century, however, a sudden wave of inmate uprisings punctuated what criminologist Austin H. Mac-

[1] *The History of Western State Penitentiary*, 10, box 3, Record Group 15, Bureau of Correction, Pennsylvania Historical and Museum Commission, Harrisburg, Pennsylvania; "State Penitentiary for the Western District of Pennsylvania," n.d., Department of Corrections Archives, Camp Hill, PA [hereafter DOC Archives]; Charles H. Allard, "Rioters Fire Western Pen Buildings, Hold 4 Guards," *Pittsburgh Post-Gazette*, Jan. 19, 1953. The inmate who set the fire was later identified as twenty-four-year-old Richard Gorham, who was serving a fifteen- to twenty-year sentence for using a sawed-off shotgun to hold up six stores in the South Hills area. Vince Johnson, "Grand Jury to Probe Western Penitentiary Riot," *Pittsburgh Post-Gazette*, Jan. 22, 1953. The term "inmate" probably derives from the 1580s, when it described a person "allowed to live in a house rented by another." By the 1830s inmate was used to describe a person confined in an institution.

[2] Allard, "Rioters Fire Western Pen Buildings"; Judith R. Smith, *30th Anniversary Commemorative History: The Bureau of Corrections and Its Institutions* (Camp Hill, PA, 1983).

Cormick described as "the darkest years in modern penal history." In the period 1950–55, more than forty-seven prison riots erupted, and in one eighteen-month period, from April 1952 to October 1953, forty riots—more than had occurred in the previous twenty-five years—broke out at institutions throughout the nation. Occasionally, the riots were planned, but most of them were spontaneous, usually led by white inmates making demands to improve living conditions behind bars.[3]

Penologists struggled to identify a pattern that would explain the outbreak of riots. Most of them occurred outside the South, where prison farms relied on "a cadre of . . . prisoners to maintain order," and the brutality of convict labor made a riot almost as difficult as on a plantation. Other than this geographical exception, however, there were no consistent criteria. One unusual characteristic shared by almost all the riots was that they were not so much about escaping as they were to establish control of the cellblocks. According to MacCormick, "riots rocked institutions of every age, size, or type and quality," making it impossible to anticipate where the next disturbance might occur. Graterford, Pennsylvania's largest penitentiary, imposed a more repressive disciplinary code than did Western, but it did not experience a major riot.[4]

There were, however, several contributing factors to the many violent inmate uprisings in the post–World War II era. An abnormally antagonistic prison atmosphere, administrative indifference, enforced idleness, overcrowding, a politicized penal system, and injudicious use of probation and parole created an explosive inmate environment. Some penologists attributed the precipitous increase of inmate unrest on displaced soldiers returning home and lengthy, punitive drug sentences, which resulted in overcrowding and other deprivations. Within the prison population, a sharp rise in juvenile admissions, which had been climbing for several years, generated the greatest concern. Sensitive to the totalitarian struc-

[3] Steve D. Gillingham and Reid H. Montgomery Jr., "Prison Riots: A Corrections' Nightmare Since 1774," *The Prison Journal* 63, no. 1 (1983): 32; Bert Unseam and Peter Kimball, *States of Siege: U.S. Prison Riots, 1971–1986* (New York, 1989), 10; "Convict Riots Frequent in 1952," *Pittsburgh Post-Gazette*, Jan. 19, 1953; Mitchell P. Roth, *Crime and Punishment: A History of the Criminal Justice System* (Belmont, CA, 2011), 262; Austin H. MacCormick, "Behind the Prison Riots," *Annals of the American Academy of Political and Social Science* 293 (1954): 17; John Pallas and Bob Barber, "From Riot to Revolution," *Issues in Criminology* 7, no. 2 (1972); Ronald Berkman, *Opening the Gates: The Rise of the Prisoners' Movement* (Lexington, MA, 1979), 34–35.

[4] MacCormick, "Behind the Prison Riots," 17; Dan Berger and Toussaint Losier, *Rethinking the Prison Movement* (New York, 2018), 48; Larry E. Sullivan, *Forlorn Hope: The Prison Reform Movement* (Boston, 1990), 48–49; Marie Gottshalk, *The Prison and the Gallows: The Politics of Mass Incarceration in America* (New York, 2006), 171.

ture of prison life and the emphasis on punishment in the 1950s, most states endeavored to improve the prison environment by adopting Progressive Era reforms, especially the medical model that diagnosed inmates and prescribed a treatment much as a physician would treat a patient. Pennsylvania was one of several states that adopted the medical model, but it did not provide sufficient staffing or financial resources to support it.[5]

Even where these reforms were more vigorously supported, they usually failed to achieve the intended results. Classification and treatment programs were poorly designed, and the goals of custody and rehabilitation often conflicted. Poorly trained prison personnel, arbitrary rules of discipline, and too few psychiatrists and psychologists created what David J. Rothman called "places of pervasive brutality." This was the experience at Western.[6]

The first inmates—eleven men and one woman—arrived at Western State Penitentiary on July 1, 1826, before construction was completed. Principal keeper John Hannen and his staff of two assistants and two physicians were immediately beset with problems. Natural light was almost entirely shut out of the six-by-nine foot cells, and the only access to them was through heavy iron doors hung on walls three feet thick.[7]

Western was one of two penitentiaries—the other was Eastern State—commissioned for construction by the General Assembly in 1818 to alleviate the crowding at the Walnut Street Jail in Philadelphia and to implement the Quaker-inspired "Pennsylvania system." Unfortunately, Western's future would be one of false starts and a stormy evolution. Introduced in 1790 at the Walnut Street Jail, this innovative penal code promised to help inmates save themselves through remorse and reformation. At Western, inmates would achieve such reformation while being isolated from society and each other as they performed hard labor in soli-

[5] Edgardo Rotman, "The Failure of Reform, United States, 1865–1965," in *The Oxford History of the Prison: The Practice of Punishment in Western Society*, ed. Norval Morris and David J. Rothman (New York, 1995), 188–89; Rothman, *Conscience and Convenience: The Asylum and Its Alternatives in Progressive America* (Boston, 1980), 117–18, 133; Scott Christianson, *With Liberty For Some: 500 Years of Imprisonment in America* (Boston, 1998) 133–34.

[6] Rothman, *Conscience and Convenience*, 143–52; Smith, *30th Anniversary Commemorative History*, 18; Harry Elmer Barnes, *The Evolution of Penology in Pennsylvania* (Montclair, NJ, 1968) 196; *Ashe Report*, 6–7.

[7] Charles Shaler, Edward King, and T. I. Wharton, *Report on Punishments and Prison Discipline by the Commissioners Appointed to Review the Penal Code of Pennsylvania* (Philadelphia, 1828), 22.

tary confinement. Imposing the equivalent of "shining a light in a dark house," Quaker reformers believed, would restore "the calm contemplation of mind which brings on penitence," transforming the criminal.[8]

At least that was the plan. Influenced by Jeremy Bentham's panopticon, Western's 190 cells were arranged in a circular formation with a central observation post. But instead of providing open cells with natural light that would allow inmates to perform labor, the cells were too dark. Western's physical plant was inadequate; it was a massive complex penologist Harry Elmer Barnes described as "wholly unsuitable for any purpose except a fortress." As a member of the prison Board of Inspectors ruefully acknowledged, "It was unfortunate that the building was first put up and the system of punishment afterwards prescribed."[9]

Because the prison's design did not complement the Quaker philosophy, in 1833 the General Assembly approved a bill to demolish Western's original cells and replace them with cells more suitable for inmate labor. A "new" Western opened in 1837, but even in this redesigned construction, inspectors soon realized that inmates were not becoming penitent as reformers had anticipated. On the contrary, prolonged social isolation led to mental and emotional problems so severe that warden John Patterson petitioned Governor George Wolfe to renovate the facility so an inmate would be secluded at night but could perform labor in congregate workshops during the day, according to New York's "Auburn system," which was better suited to meet the demands of factory production. In 1869, Pennsylvania completely abandoned its system and transferred control of penal affairs, which had been under the direction of the Committee of Lunacy, to the Board of Charities.[10]

[8] Norman Johnston, *Crucible of Good Intentions: Eastern State Penitentiary* (Philadelphia, 1994), 31–35; Amos H. Mylin, *State Prisons, Hospitals, Soldiers' Homes and Orphan Schools Controlled by the Commonwealth of Pennsylvania*, vol. 2 (Harrisburg, 1897), 300.

[9] Michael Meranze, *Laboratories of Virtue: Punishment, Revolution, and Authority in Philadelphia, 1760–1835* (Chapel Hill, 1996), 71. William Strickland was Western's architect. *First Prisoners in the Western Penitentiary*, vol. 5, 726–27, 4th series, Papers of the Governors, Pennsylvania State Archives, Harrisburg, PA; Barnes, *The Evolution of Penology in Pennsylvania*, 139–40, 193–94; *State Penitentiary for the Western District of Pennsylvania*, 1, box 3, Record Group 15, Bureau of Corrections, Pennsylvania State Archives; Eugene E. Doll, "Trial and Error at Allegheny: The Western State Penitentiary, 1818–1838," *Pennsylvania Magazine of History and Biography* 81 (1957): 3–27.

[10] Adam Jay Hirsh, *The Rise of the Penitentiary: Prisons and Punishment in Early America* (New Haven, CT, 1991), 61–66; Barnes, *The Evolution of Penology in Pennsylvania*, 139–41; *History of Western State Penitentiary*, box 3, Record Group 15, Bureau of Correction, Pennsylvania Historical and Museum Commission; *Report of the Committee Appointed by Honorable Edward Martin to Survey the Penal and Correctional System of the Commonwealth of Pennsylvania*, July 1944, Department of Welfare, Pennsylvania State Archives (hereafter the *Ashe Report*). In March 1833, John Haviland, the

Despite extensive physical modifications, Western soon became too overcrowded to maintain security, necessitating yet another reconstruction, and in 1878 the legislature appropriated the site of the House of Refuge in Pittsburgh for a new penitentiary. When the prison's 1,160 cells opened in 1882, officials boasted that "the structure is as permanent as the hills." Costing $2 million and widely regarded as the most expensive prison built in the United States, it was relocated next to a suburban railroad station in Woods Run on the Ohio River, in part so prison inspectors could easily make a daily stop on their way to the downtown business district.

The new Western was state-of-the-art. Its amenities included running water, individual toilets in each of the seven by nine foot cells, individual heat and exhaust ventilation, and gang locks to open and close several cells simultaneously. It would be the first prison with electric lights in each cell. A thousand feet of river frontage might have made the prison grounds more aesthetically appealing, but it did not offset adverse natural and human-made conditions. Dampness and fog could be so dense that it was too dark for convicts to leave their cells before noon and so heavy that it held in nearby factory smoke.[11]

By 1892, Western again had become overcrowded and was derisively recognized as the "most expensive and pretentious prison building . . . in America." Worse, unforeseen environmental changes made Western's location unacceptable. On the Ohio in a dirty, industrial area where "the soot and dirt and smoke are often so thick that electric lights must be burned all day long," Western was in a flood plain where the river frequently spilled over its banks. In 1884, 1902, 1907, and 1936, floods inundated the prison yard; often times many of Western's cell blocks were under several feet of water.[12]

Realizing the penitentiary was no longer sustainable, in March 1911

---

architect who designed the world-recognized Eastern State Penitentiary in Philadelphia, was contracted to rebuild Western.

[11] *The History of Western State Penitentiary*; Harry Elmer Barnes, "The Evolution of American Penology as Illustrated by the Western Penitentiary of Pennsylvania," *Western Pennsylvania Historical Magazine* 4 (1921): 193; Barnes, "The Historical Origins of the Prison System in America," *Journal of Criminal Law & Criminology* 12 (1921–22): 35–60; LeRoy B. DuPuy, "The Triumph of the 'Pennsylvania System' at the State's Penitentiary," *Pennsylvania History* 21 (1954): 128–44; *Ashe Report*, 6–7.

[12] *Ashe Report*, 29; Barnes, *The Evolution of Penology in Pennsylvania*, 196; "History of Western State Penitentiary," box 3, Record Group 15, Bureau of Correction, Pennsylvania Historical and Museum Commission.

the state legislature authorized a five thousand–acre rural site in Centre County for a new Western. Located in the geographic center of Pennsylvania, six miles north of State College at Rockview, the inspectors intended to replace the obsolete and inadequate Western State with a new prison farm and consolidate Western and Rockview under one warden.[13]

Although Rockview was a more modern prison, the state's penal operations suffered from ineffective leadership and inefficient organization. Political patronage also plagued the system. Because the governor appointed each prison's nine-member Board of Trustees, who in turn appointed as many as forty-five subordinate officers, favoritism was rampant, and legislation was too often influenced by political interests rather than the needs of the prisons. This dynamic caused Barnes to lament in 1927 that this "type of political prostitution" had relegated "the record of Pennsylvania [as] among the worst in the history of American penology."[14]

Western suffered from more than political and bureaucratic turmoil. The institution had a history of riots long before the uprising in 1953. The first large-scale inmate disturbance occurred in July 1921, when more than one thousand inmates rioted before prison guards and seventy-five Pittsburgh police officers armed with Winchester rifles and shotguns could restore order. Eight inmates were shot and four city policemen and firemen were wounded during the melee, which resulted in $750,000 in damages. In February 1924, two guards were killed trying to quell a "savage fight" that involved at least one hundred prisoners and quickly exploded into a full-scale riot. The causes of the riot would not have seemed to justify the violent behavior: some imprisoned men wanted more cigarettes, and female inmates demanded permission to use powder puffs.[15]

Acting to prevent future uprisings, Governor Gifford Pinchot appointed Stanley P. Ashe, a noted Pennsylvania educator and nationally recognized authority on penal affairs, as Western's new warden. During

[13] *The History of Western State Penitentiary.* Rockview accepted its first prisoner, a "colored man," in August 1912. Because the new penitentiary was designed to "jail convicts rather than promote their reformation," Barnes characterized it as a "penological white elephant." Barnes, *The Evolution of Penology in Pennsylvania*, 170–72, 181–82, 216–18, 220–21.

[14] *Report of the Committee Appointed by John S. Fine, Governor, to Investigate the Peno-Correctional System of the Commonwealth of Pennsylvania*, April 1953, 15, 35–36 (hereafter *Devers Report*); *Ashe Report*, 43; Barnes, *The Evolution of Penology in Pennsylvania*, 194–95, 403–5.

[15] *First Prisoners in Western Pennsylvania Penitentiary*, 726–27.

his tenure, Ashe introduced a graded school system, psychological counseling, improved medical care, and new athletic activities.[16]

Ashe's new reform policies notwithstanding, conditions were so deplorable at Western that in February 1927, secretary of welfare Dr. Ellen Potter described custodial management there as a "hardbacked type of utter restraint with shackles, dungeons, solitary and mental torture with depravity and deterioration of men." Consistent with the Progressives' demand for more democracy and good government, Dr. Potter, the lone female member in Governor Pinchot's cabinet, wanted to eliminate politics from penal administration, among other reforms. The Department of Welfare administered the Bureau of Penal Affairs and Prison Industries, but the real power was invested in the Boards of Trustees, who independently administered the prisons and appointed wardens and all custodial and civilian personnel. Potter was unsuccessful.[17]

A plethora of problems, either by commission or omission, produced a toxic environment for inmates and guards. Inmates had no opportunity to respond to write-ups for disciplinary infractions. At the same time, a contemporary report described Western as a "modified country club where there was no security program and serious malpractice within the prison." This "serious malpractice" included sexual "pervasion," which was not uncommon in penal institutions, but there was little effort to prevent it at Western. Late lock-ups allowed two hundred inmates to move freely inside the prison until 9:00 p.m., providing an opportunity to evade surveillance while causing resentment among inmates who had to be in their cells at 5:00. In November 1952, eight inmates escaped from Western.[18]

Perhaps in part for these reasons, the president of the Board of Inspectors at Western believed the 1953 uprising was simply inevitable. When reporters asked him about why the riot happened, he responded, "These things just happen. There's nothing you can do. They just seem to be happening in cycles across the country." Maybe the riots were cyclical, but few "things just happen" without explanation, and the riot at Western was neither mysterious nor inexplicable. Despite the introduction of diagnosis,

[16] "Ringleaders of 'Pen' Rebellion In Dungeons On Bread and Water Diet," *Indiana Evening Gazette*, July 20, 1921; Guy V. Miller, "Bloody Pen Riot of 1921 Recalled By Latest One," *Pittsburgh Post-Gazette*, Jan. 19, 1953, 14; and "1,000 Convicts Riot as Explosions Rock Western Penitentiary," *Indiana Evening Gazette*, Feb. 11, 1924.

[17] "Brief on the Subject of Parole," *The Prison Journal* 7, no. 1 (1927): 10–11. Potter proposed several other reforms, including the indeterminate sentence, a state parole board, and eliminating jury discretion in recommending the death penalty or life imprisonment.

[18] *Devers Report*, 41.

classification, and more tolerable physical conditions, penologists lamented that "prison was still dominated by the old 19th century concepts of monotony and repression." Indeed, in 1934 Department of Welfare officials investigating prison industries concluded that "idleness among prisoners is degenerating, causes unrest and rioting and tends to breed rather than reform criminals."[19]

If we are to believe one prisoner who shouted from a window that the riot started because "one of the guards went off his nut this afternoon and shot Frank Lovejoy [an inmate] in the foot," the inspectors and warden Claudy were right in characterizing the riot as "spontaneous." There was no evidence to confirm an inmate was shot, but there were identifiable, tangible conditions that caused the riot. A handwritten note a prisoner threw out a window read, "We prisoners want a more conservative handling of cases by the parole board." The note also listed "greater leniency on the commutation of cases by the parole board" and insisted that "an investigation be held among prisoners, not the administration." Living in overcrowded prisons lacking professional services while enduring a seemingly endless period of deteriorating idleness exacerbated restiveness among the incarcerated men. Problems that had been fomenting for years at Western—sentencing disparity, arbitrary work assignments, and inconsistent discipline—were becoming increasingly intolerable to inmates housed in a "mephitic climate of hate and turbulence." By 1953, Western was a cumulative product of its turbulent past: a riot waiting to happen.[20]

RESTORING ORDER

News of the Western disturbance quickly spread throughout Pittsburgh. Anxious residents living near the prison were concerned about their safety, but many of them reacted to the riot more as a curiosity rather than a threat to community security. Thousands of sightseers walked or drove as close to the penitentiary as police would allow to secure a better vantage point. Hundreds of automobiles lined the Ohio River Boulevard and were backed up on the McKees Rocks Bridge before police closed both arteries to traffic. State officials, who understandably wanted to pre-

[19] Negley K. Teeters, "The Dilemma of Prison Riots," *The Prison Journal* 33, no. 1 (1953): 14; Teeters, "State of Prisons in the United States: 1870–1970," *Federal Probation* 32 (1969): 22; *Report on Prison Industries* (Harrisburg, 1934), 5.

[20] "1,000 Rioting Convicts Fire Prison In Pittsburgh and Seize 5 Guards," *New York Times*, Jan. 19, 1953; *Devers Report*, 26, 43, 46.

vent a citywide panic, tried to reassure the public that the inmate revolt would not disrupt normal activities. Department of Revenue secretary Otto F. Messner reassured Pennsylvania motorists that even a prison takeover of the license shop would not interfere with operations in Western's Automobile Tag Department, which produced about fourteen thousand license plates a day.[21]

Approximately eight hours after the insurrection began at Western, inmates declared a state of war against the prison administration. Despite a potentially deadly confrontation with heavily armed law enforcement officers, the mutinous prisoners remained defiant and even seemed indifferent to the possibility they might be seriously wounded or killed. When Pennsylvania state police superintendent James W. Slusser assured the protestors that "there is no chance of escape" and warned them that "if you try it, we'll mow you down," one of the rioters defiantly yelled out, "Go to hell!" The captors displayed bravado, but they were at a decided disadvantage, armed only with "shivs," or homemade knives. If anyone was going to be "mowed down," it was more likely to be the incarcerated men, since police officers brandishing Browning submachine guns were preparing to move into the cell blocks.[22]

Hoping to prevent—or at least minimize—possible bloodshed, Republican governor John S. Fine instructed warden Claudy to order the police into the recreation hall rather than storm the cellblocks, which almost certainly would have caused heavy casualties. Minutes later, inmate representative Al Roman asked for a meeting on the afternoon of Monday, January 19, with a committee that included the local media. Known throughout the incarcerated population as a "talker," forty-year-old Roman had a criminal record dating back seventeen years and was serving a ten-year sentence for robbery and a parole violation. He proved over the course of the conflict to be an effective mediator.[23]

Early the next morning, Roman presented a list of thirteen demands to Fred Mathias, chief of Allegheny County detectives. Some of the grievances were perfunctory and typical of most penal institutions: "Food. Just bad," "Visits are too short," and "Wider variety of merchandise in commissary." Other issues, however, were more substantive, including "more

[21] William M. Rimmel, "Western Penn Riot Causes Traffic Jam," *Pittsburgh Post-Gazette,* Jan. 19, 1953; "Riot at Pen Won't Delay Auto Tags," *Pittsburgh Post-Gazette*, Jan. 20, 1953; Bureau of Correction, *Annual Report 1954* (Camp Hill, PA), 25.

[22] Allard, "Rioters Fire Western."

[23] "Pen Rioter Has Long Record," *Pittsburgh Post-Gazette*, Jan. 20, 1953.

leniency," "commutation of sentence," and, presaging a prisoners' rights movement, an inmate "representative on the parole board." Inmates also wanted more flexible state parole board procedures, a registered nurse in the cell block at all times, a law library, a study of possible excessive sentencing, and the right of a grand jury to visit the institution once a month.[24]

Allegheny County district attorney James F. Malone helped ease tensions when he agreed to conduct "a complete and impartial investigation of all your complaints," but he promised nothing until the "results of the investigation were complete." There would be no reprisals taken if the incarcerated men agreed to release the hostages and reestablish peace. Beyond that concession, there was little more the inmates could hope for if they believed Governor Fine, who declared unequivocally that "we are certainly not going to let prisoners dictate to us what shall be done."[25]

Roman was adamant that the inmates would not end the siege until he read Malone's terms in the *Post-Gazette*, which he did at 7:10 p.m. Five minutes after the inmates read about their stand-off, Malone announced that the remaining three guards held hostage had been released—a second guard was freed earlier after suffering a knife wound and cuts around his eyes—and that the penitentiary would be returned to state control.

After agreeing to conditions, guards returned the inmates to their severely damaged cells with doors so badly mangled they could not be used to confine inmates securely. The destruction was extensive. During the uprising, prisoners built fires against the doors, warping the metal in the locks and making it impossible to operate the mechanisms. Because the pole bar locking system and individual cell locks was jammed, warden Claudy and his staff used heavy chains to reinforce padlocks to secure the cell doors. Prisoners had destroyed so much of the plumbing system that they waded through water eight inches deep in some cell blocks. Though the damage was significant, no shots were fired during the approximately twenty-four-hour-long riot, which involved 1,127 inmates.[26]

[24] Vince Johnson and Mel Seidenberg, "Four Guard Hostages Freed Here," *Pittsburgh Post-Gazette*, Jan. 20, 1953; and "Warden Replies to Rioters' Complaints," *Pittsburgh Post-Gazette*, Jan. 21, 1953.

[25] "Rioting Prisoners Set Fire to State Pen, Nab Guards," *Bradford* (PA) *Era*, Jan. 19, 1953.

[26] On Tuesday, January 20, the *Post-Gazette* informed its readers how it "figured dramatically in efforts to restore peace to riot-torn Western Penitentiary." "Post-Gazette Helps Effort to Stop Riot," *Pittsburgh Post-Gazette*, Jan. 20, 1953; *The History of Western State Penitentiary*, 12; "Warden Replies to Rioters' Complaints"; Thomas J. Moran, "Malone Returning to Help Quell Riot," *Pittsburgh Post-Gazette*, Jan. 19, 1953; James W. Ross, "Governor's Call Breaks Tension at Pen," *Pittsburgh Post-Gazette*, Jan. 20, 1953; "Mass Prison Break Plot Bared," *Pittsburgh Post-Gazette*, Jan. 24, 1953.

Not until Saturday morning, January 24, after a shipment of nine hundred padlocks arrived, were armed state police officers and prison guards finally able to confine the incarcerated men in their cells. With the prison sufficiently secured for the first time since the riot began six days earlier, a search of each inmate produced two buckets of weapons, including an assortment of screwdrivers and pieces of pipes torn from the plumbing. Not confiscated in the shakedown was "a pile of knives" that inmates threw over the railings.[27]

The riot at Western had ended, but its estimated cost of $250,000 in damages might have been avoided if state officials and prison administrators had adopted preventive measures recommended after the November 1952 escape. District attorney Malone strongly urged then for the state to address potential security problems after inmates easily made their way out of the penitentiary. Local newspapers, elected officials, and Malone also harshly criticized the state welfare department for not tightening lax security measures that allowed inmates to requisition sheets without question and to make ropes "right from under the noses of the guards" to pull off the largest escape in the prison's history. One of the prisoners even managed to steal an electric-operated grinding and polishing carborundum wheel he used to manufacture shivs. Incarcerated men used material from the prison workshops to make crude knives, a table, and a crowbar, and they demanded that welfare secretary William C. Brown investigate the turbulent conditions at Western to determine what caused the riot.[28]

AFTERMATH

Problems at Western were not limited to the incarcerated population. An inexplicable lapse in communication was a critical factor in the Western riot. Warden Claudy could not account for why more than one hour passed from the time the guards were overpowered until one of the prisoners was spotted making his escape. Claudy also had no explanation for why prison officials waited three hours before sounding an escape alert.[29]

Chaotic conditions at Western were confirmed by prison employees who described a dangerous environment at the institution and low morale among the staff. One of five guards overpowered in the November escape,

[27] "Mass Prison Break Bared."

[28] Editorial, "What's Wrong at the Pen," *Pittsburgh Post-Gazette*, Jan. 20, 1953.

[29] "Pen Break Brings Probe Demand," *Pittsburgh Post-Gazette*, Jan. 19, 1953; "Mass Prison Break Plot Bared."

Kenneth E. Keay, resigned after the riot, claiming he "couldn't take it any longer" and that working in a constant state of "fear and tension" was not worth his $3,000 annual salary.[30]

Keay's complaint about an inadequate salary was not the only source of employee discontent at Western. According to officials, integrating long-term inmates who had been convicted of crimes involving violence and frequently suffered from mental and emotional disorders with incarcerated individuals who did not share this history made it more difficult to control the population. Ralph C. Busser Jr., the state chairman of the Pennsylvania Citizens' Association's Penal Affairs Division, lay much of the blame for the riot on prison policies, in which "sadistic criminals, the mentally ill, and first offenders [were] jammed together behind the same prison walls."[31]

As Busser was making his case for reforms at Western with the media, district attorney Malone told reporters about the "torture chamber" the November escapees and other incarcerated individuals called "the hole," a bare, dark dungeon half the size of an ordinary cell, with no windows, no furniture, and no plumbing. Prisoners sent to the hole, either for serious or minor infractions, were restricted to a diet of bread and water. Many state-level corrections officials were stunned, if not appalled, to learn that such inhumane treatment of prisoners was routinely administered at Western. Ironically, a year before the riot, secretary Brown praised officials at Western for providing "an outstanding example of what can be accomplished with proper administration and with trained, efficient personnel."[32]

A SECOND RIOT

Even inside prison walls, most individuals are not entirely shut off from the outside world. Western had not returned to normal operations when about 600 of the 775 inmates at Rockview, also under Claudy's supervision, seized six guards as hostages and took their revolvers. About 6:00 p.m., just after the dinner hour count, on Monday, January 19, inmates set fire to several mattresses and destroyed furniture and plumbing fixtures. Subfreezing temperatures deterred them from breaking windows. Forty

[30] "Average Wage Index, Calendar Years 1951–98," *OASDI Trustees Report*, DOC Archives.
[31] "Pen Break Brings Probe Demand," *Pittsburgh Post-Gazette*, Jan. 19, 1953.
[32] "Pen Break Brings Probe Demand."

state police troopers and seventy correctional officers were set to storm the prison before the protestors surrendered.[33]

Established as a Western "branch" institution in 1912, Rockview was not much better managed than Western. Work assignments were haphazard and determined arbitrarily by the deputy warden. These inconsistent regulations and loose security allowed some men to easily confiscate knives and other weapons. Rockview, a minimum-security facility, was administered by the same indifferent Board of Trustees and acting warden Myron M. Cobb, described as a "fine, lovable individual, but not trained in prison matters." No doubt the underlying causes of the second Western riot can be attributed to any of these policies.[34]

The riot was brief but unsettling; it demonstrated that serious security breaches were not unique to Western. At the very least, there was a breakdown in communication and/or security at Rockview. Sometimes called an "honor prison" housing mostly offenders not found guilty of crimes involving violence in a "Progressive classification" system, it was purposely located in a bucolic setting on five thousand acres in central Pennsylvania and designed as a facility where incarcerated individuals could engage in constructive agricultural activities. The riot at Rockview was another example of a lack of institutional control. Hours after the riot began, warden Cobb, "an aged man, hard of hearing," was not aware the riot had spread. Deputy warden Harrison R. (Buck) Johnston, however, apparently more attuned to the prison climate, insisted he knew better, declaring, "Damn right we had an idea [the riot] was going to happen. We took every precaution we could but it came anyway." Johnston added that he knew "for some time" trouble was brewing, and that he had received "a tip at noon that it was coming today [Monday]."[35]

Informed about the second disturbance, attorney general Robert E. Woodside and secretary Brown flew from Pittsburgh to Rockview on Governor Fine's plane to assess the situation. Fortunately, shortly after 9:00 p.m., on Tuesday, January 20, about 450 of the prisoners surrendered

[33] Guard Rankin Tate convinced his captors he was ill and was released. "Riot Breaks Out at Rockview," *Pittsburgh Post-Gazette*, Jan. 20, 1953; Frank M. Matthews, "450 Rioters Quit, Others Hold Guards," *Pittsburgh Post-Gazette*, Jan. 21, 1953; Smith, *30th Anniversary Commemorative History*, 2.

[34] Helen D. Pigeon et al., *Principles and Methods in Dealing with Offenders: A Manual for Pennsylvania Correctional and Penal Workers* (State College, PA, 1944), 93–94; *Devers Report*, 46–49, 51–55; Smith, *30th Anniversary Commemorative History*, 51.

[35] Pigeon, *Principles and Methods in Dealing With Offenders*, 93; "Rockview Officials Knew Riot coming; Did Little," *Pittsburgh Post-Gazette*, Jan. 20, 1953.

and agreed to return to their cells, although another group of 320 inmates refused to release the hostages. Late on Wednesday afternoon, officials decided to take action. Around 5:30 p.m., more than one hundred state police officers, "heavily armed" with tear gas and submachine guns, prepared to storm the cell blocks. Prisoners were armed only with eight .38 caliber revolvers and five hundred rounds of ammunition, but they had leverage with the six guards they had taken as hostages, one of whom made a likely coerced plea for police to "come to a decision and give these men a fair hearing. We are okay. No one has forced me to say anything." At 6:15 p.m., after two F-51 fighter planes and a C-47 transport plane periodically buzzed the prison at treetop level, the prisoners exited the cell block. Woodside, standing in for Governor Fine, who was attending the inauguration of President Dwight D. Eisenhower in Washington, DC, guaranteed only that there "would be no head-cracking by the State Police if the guards were immediately released." Pennsylvania's second riot within a week was over, but the two conflicts caused great concern, if not alarm, among legislators, prison officials, and the citizenry, especially those who resided in proximity of the two prisons.[36]

POLITICAL FALLOUT

Almost no one questioned the need for a full investigation into the conditions that contributed to the uprisings at Western and Rockview, but it was not certain who should conduct it. Warden Claudy ruled out an internal investigation because he believed an unwritten code of silence among the incarcerated men would not likely produce useful or candid testimony. State legislators agreed that an investigation was necessary, but it was not clear who had political jurisdiction or the legal authority to conduct it or what the scope of it should be. Some legislators wanted a more comprehensive review of the entire correctional system. State representative Nick Kornick (R-Fayette) introduced a bill to create a special committee that would make a "searching inquiry" of all state penitentiaries and report back to the state house of representatives. State senator

[36] Frank M. Matthews, "Rockview Rioters Give Up," *Pittsburgh Post-Gazette*, Jan. 23, 1953; "Statement Phoned by Woodside for Governor Fine's Approval," William B. Wheaton file, box 4, Record Group 206, Papers of Governor John S. Fine, Pennsylvania Historical and Museum Commission. For a scholarly, contemporary perspective on the Western and Rockview riots, see Teeters, "The Dilemma of Prison Riots."

John H. Dent (D-Westmoreland) wanted a legislative investigation, or at least to have a legislative representative on the governor's committee.[37]

Malone, who felt the state should have taken more vigorous action after the November escape attempt, criticized Brown on January 12, less than a week before the riot erupted at Western, for the Department of Welfare's indifference to public safety and lack of cooperation. Malone argued that because the state was reluctant or unwilling to open an investigation, and because the prison was in Allegheny County and the riot threatened the safety of many Pittsburgh residents, a local grand jury should investigate conditions at Western. Brown disagreed, arguing that since Western was a state institution, the commonwealth should lead any investigation.

When Malone announced he was considering calling a grand jury inquiry despite the secretary's resistance, Brown apologized for his "seeming neglect" in contacting the district attorney, but the bureaucratic turf war between state and local jurisdictions was evident. Even when Brown told the press two days after the Western riot that the welfare department would be conducting an immediate investigation of what caused the disturbance, attorney general Woodside's assessment that the situation at Western "is pretty well cleared up" was surprising.[38]

Malone's argument for grand jury involvement was supported by the *Post-Gazette*, which assured its readers that "he will do the sort of job the State failed to do following the escape of prisoners that last November 30." The newspaper criticized prison officials for "too much leniency and too little attention to security" while faulting the welfare department for forcing taxpayers to shoulder the expense of another costly investigation.[39]

On Monday, January 26, the day the grand jury was to begin its investigation "from top to bottom, convicts to warden," Woodside filed a petition in common pleas court to stop it, arguing that a local body does not have authority to investigate the management of a state agency. The state

[37] Thomas J. Moran, "Malone Returning to Help Quell Riots," *Pittsburgh Post-Gazette*, Jan. 19, 1953; Vince Johnson, "Malone to Ask Sweeping Grand Jury Prison Probe," *Pittsburgh Post-Gazette*, Jan. 21, 1953; "Probe Wanted of All State Penitentiaries," *Pittsburgh Post-Gazette*, Jan. 21, 1953; "Malone Fumes at Fine's Delay of Prison Probe," *Pittsburgh Sun-Telegraph*, Jan. 28, 1953; William B. Wheaton file, box 33, Pennsylvania Historical and Museum Commission; and William B. Wheaton file, box 4, Pennsylvania Historical and Museum Commission.

[38] Malone, a Republican, was district attorney from 1952–56. "State's Probe of Pen Break Hit By Malone," *Pittsburgh Post-Gazette*, Jan. 12, 1953; John E. Jones, "Welfare Official Pledges Complete Probe of Riot," *Pittsburgh Post-Gazette*, Jan. 20, 1953.

[39] Editorial, "A Welcome Prison Probe," *Pittsburgh Post-Gazette*, Jan. 21, 1953; Editorial, "Let Grand Jury Proceed With a Probe at Prison," *Pittsburgh Post-Gazette*, Jan. 26, 1953.

Supreme Court agreed, stating that the lower court had no power to order an investigation "into the conduct and management of the state penitentiary, and that any grand jury activity be limited to criminal acts committed within the county."[40]

INVESTIGATION

While county and state officials wrangled over who was empowered with the legal authority to investigate Pennsylvania's prison system, on January 27, 1953, Governor Fine announced the creation of a specially appointed five-person committee to make an

> immediate and exhaustive investigation of the Western State and Rockview outbreaks, as well as operations at other state penal and correctional institutions. . . . [to] . . . examine methods of instruction, discipline, detention, imprisonment, care and treatment of prisoners and the government or management of prisoners.[41]

The composition of the committee reflected the diverse backgrounds of its members. John C. Burke, warden of the Wisconsin State Prison at Waupun, was a "hands-on" administrator who frequently walked unescorted through the prison yards. Another progressive prison administrator, Joseph E. Ragen, was a reformer and warden for twenty-five years at the nation's largest prison at Stateville in Joliet, Illinois. Burton R. Laub, author of *Laub's Index in the Penal Code of 1939*, was a former Erie County district attorney and a common pleas court judge for eight years; and William P. Witherow was a Pittsburgh industrialist described as "long on facts and short on theory."[42]

Governor Fine selected Jacob L. Devers of York to chair the committee. Devers was from outside the corrections profession, but he possessed

[40] "Pennsylvania Grand Jury Denied the Right to Investigate Conditions Leading to Prison Riots," *Journal of Criminal Law, Criminology, and Police Science* 44 (1953): 351–52. Malone appealed to the state Supreme Court. "Fine Names 4 to Probe Pen Riot," *Pittsburgh Post-Gazette*, Jan. 26, 1953. Politics may have been a factor in the dispute between the commonwealth and the Allegheny County district attorney. In a letter to Governor Fine, a Malone supporter pointed out the "political differences between yourself and Mr. Malone" and that "Malone was nominated over your opposition and the opposition of the Republican Committee of Allegheny County." William B. Wheaton file, box 33, Pennsylvania Historical and Museum Commission.

[41] "Fine Names 4 to Probe Pen Riot," *Pittsburgh Post-Gazette*, Jan. 26, 1953.

[42] "Fine Names 4 to Probe Pen Riot." Witherow was president of Blaw Knox Company and a delegate to the Republican presidential convention in 1944. Vince Johnson, "Five-Man Board Begins Prison Probe Monday," *Pittsburgh Post-Gazette*, Jan. 31, 1953.

impressive credentials. During World War II, as a four-star general of American forces in the European theater, he was responsible for much of the planning and training for the allied invasion of Normandy in June 1944, and he was later promoted to Deputy Supreme Allied Commander in the Mediterranean theater.[43]

The Devers committee was faced with a formidable task, considering the broad scope and nature of the inquiry and the governor's explicit instruction to "conduct an in-depth evaluation of Pennsylvania's penal system." The committee's work was not limited to administrative policies. Fine wanted the investigators to move beyond procedural issues, "expecting it to investigate the official conduct of the trustees, wardens, superintendents, and all other State officers charged with the management of our State prisons and correctional institutions."[44]

Satisfied with the governor's creation of the Devers committee, state senator John M. Walker of Allegheny County announced that Republicans would withdraw their demand for a legislative inquiry. District attorney Malone, however, continued to oppose state involvement by submitting a brief on January 27, 1953, outlining his prerogative to conduct a grand jury investigation. Two days later, common pleas court judge Sara M. Soffel, Pennsylvania's first woman to reside over an Allegheny County criminal court, ruled that the governor's special committee did not interfere with or hinder a local probe and that the district attorney's office could conduct a grand jury investigation "of broad scope" into conditions at Western. In her decision the judge cited the Department of Welfare's failure to complete an investigation of conditions at Western after Malone warned about more unrest. She also was mindful of local sovereignty, noting that when criminals escape "with apparent ease from the penitentiary armed with deadly weapons, there is an immediate threat to the security of all citizens residing in the congested residential community that surrounds the prison." Woodside and the justice department immediately appealed Judge Soffel's decision to the state superior court, which unanimously ruled that a grand jury could investigate only criminal acts of inmates involved in the riot or escape. The governor's committee

---

[43] Vince Johnson, "Five-Man Board Begins Prison Probe Monday"; William B. Wheaton file, box 4, Historical and Museum Commission. Edward R. Cass, American Prison Association secretary and member of the Ashe committee, was a sixth member who served in an advisory capacity. *Devers Report*, 78. For more biographical information on Devers, see Jacob L. Devers Papers, York County Historical Center, York, PA.

[44] *Devers Report*, 2.

would be solely responsible for investigating the causes and disposition of the prison riots.[45]

The Devers committee inspected each of the state's seven penal institutions; conducted interviews with inmates, prison employees, and public officials; and examined records and documents pertinent to prison operations. In its final report, submitted in mid-April 1953 after a two-month investigation, the committee enumerated twenty-eight recommendations in eight categories. The only substantive issue on which Devers's findings differed from the Ashe report was on the disposition of the Eastern and Western Penitentiaries. Rather than close the facilities, the committee, anticipating "violent disagreement with our recommendation," advised that retaining and refurbishing the oldest facilities in the system would be more cost effective than replacing them.[46]

The committee attributed the riots to several problems common to incarceration, including complaints about food, overcrowding, and sexual tension. Other, less tangible factors, such as lack of administrative direction, staff indifference toward the inmates, and poor planning, required more comprehensive revisions. In the personnel category, the committee recommended salary upgrades and the classification of all positions below warden or superintendent to boost employee morale and to provide a more competitive and uniform salary structure. Guards, it determined, were underpaid and inadequately trained. To ensure a higher degree of professionalism, the committee suggested that prospective prison guards be sent to the state police training facility in Hershey because "proper correction involves the entire compass of human emotion, [and] custodial officers are literally sitting upon a powder keg."[47]

There were other, more serious problems that triggered the riots. What the committee discovered while conducting an onsite inspection of Western's cell blocks nearly defied belief, with inhumane conditions for misconduct that were more common in the nineteenth century than the twentieth. For many other minor offenses, inmates were held in a modified form of isolation in "basket cells" that were surrounded with an extra

[45] Vince Johnson, "Judge Likely to Start Studying Brief Today in Pen Probe Dispute," *Pittsburgh Post-Gazette*, Jan. 28, 1953; "DA Probe of Pen Approved," *Pittsburgh Post-Gazette*, Jan. 29, 1953; John E. Jones, "Malone Refuses GOP Bid to Run for Mayor," *Pittsburgh Post-Gazette*, Jan. 29, 1953; Vince Johnson, "Grand Jury Investigation of Western State Penitentiary," *Pittsburgh Post-Gazette*, Apr. 15, 1953; Superior Court of Pennsylvania, Appeal No. 44, April 15, 1953.

[46] Pennsylvania's seven penitentiaries were Western, Eastern, Rockview, Huntingdon, Camp Hill, Graterford, and Muncy. *Devers Report*, 21–22, 74.

[47] *Devers Report*, 18–20.

wall of wire mesh. More serious violators were confined in a "home block," or a group of four small cells in the basement. Because only two of the cells had toilet facilities, there was a "stench of urine on the floor," and dimly lighted corridors provided the only opportunity for prisoners to view their dreary surroundings. None of the cells had cots or other furniture. Prisoners were stripped before entering a cell to prevent them from harming themselves. Inmates requiring "major punishment" were sent to the "hole," a block of narrow cells also beneath the main building. Like the home block cells, the hole cells contained no furnishings and no toilet facilities. But the hole was even less tolerable. Two cell doors, one iron with small gratings, the other solid wood, shut out all light and air when closed. Oppressive heat and poor ventilation made breathing difficult and unhealthy in what the committee described as "medieval dungeons [that] can only produce harm." As the report concluded, "their very existence stands as an indictment against the prison administration."[48]

Despite these many problems, the Western riot might have been prevented had there not been what the committee determined was a "marked absence of security precautions." This was not a subjective criticism. In the six weeks between the November 30 escape and the January 18 riot, guards had conducted only one general shakedown of the cells, even though the inmates smuggled an eight-inch power drill out of the weave shop and held "about seven or eight bushels of knives and tools" at the time of the riot. It was hardly surprising the investigators found a "noticeable absence of rules and regulations for either guards or inmates" and "a general atmosphere of laxity at Western."[49]

The committee was particularly concerned about the Board of Trustees, members of which "have outside interests and . . . cannot acquire intelligent control." It was not at all confident that only one warden could effectively manage both Western and Rockview, which the committee believed was "virtually headless," mentioning by name acting warden Cobb as the "nominal head at Rockview, a fine, lovable individual but not trained in prison matters . . . who was by-passed by his inferiors."[50]

Even acknowledging these many deficiencies, penologists were perplexed that conditions could have been so bad at Western and Rockview after Progressive reforms emphasizing rehabilitation had been introduced.

[48] *Devers Report*, 44–46.
[49] *Devers Report*, 47–48.
[50] *Devers Report*, 52.

The Devers investigation uncovered numerous problems specific to Pennsylvania's institutions, but it was James V. Bennett, director of the Federal Bureau of Prisons, who identified several correctional paradoxes that compromised more effective incarceration. In his annual report, Bennett enumerated several contradictory functions of a penal system, noting that

> on the one hand, prisons are expected to punish; on the other, they are supposed to reform. They are built to be operated like vast impersonal machines, yet they are expected to fit men to live normal community lives. All too frequently restrictive laws force prisoners into idleness despite the fact that one of their primary objectives is to teach men how to earn an honest living. They refuse the prisoner a voice in self-government, but they expect him to become a thinking citizen in a democratic society.[51]

IMPACT AND REFORM

Appalled at Western's barbarous methods of discipline, the committee recommended shutting off the hole and the home block. Believing that a capricious, torturous disciplinary code and the use of isolation cells contributed to the riot, the committee called for more humane forms of discipline. To provide for more effective supervision of inmates, the committee recommended establishing two correctional diagnostic and classification centers, which the state officially opened on January 1, 1954. The first deputy commissioner for treatment, Dr. Kenneth E. Taylor, was responsible for classifying inmates as minimum-, medium-, or maximum-security risks based on individual case histories and diagnoses.[52]

In addition to recommendations for improving the staff and physical plant, the committee wanted "all supervision and control of correctional institutions transferred from the Department of Welfare to the Department of Justice." Actually, the committee wanted to do more than transfer correctional responsibilities from a department it noted "is now, and has been for years, in a state of stagnation insofar as prison administration is concerned and has become little more than a depository for papers." The Devers committee emphatically recommended the creation of "a Bureau of Correction in the Department of Justice headed by a Commissioner of Correction responsible to the Attorney General." To eliminate adminis-

[51] Larry E. Sullivan, *Forlorn Hope: The Prison Reform Movement* (Boston, 1990), 49.
[52] *Devers Report*, 45–46.

trative fragmentation, "all institutional Wardens, Superintendents and bureau personnel should be under the Commissioner."[53]

Accordingly, on July 29, 1953, Governor Fine signed Public Law 1428, creating a separate bureau of correction under the direction of the state attorney general in the Department of Justice. Fine nominated Arthur Prasse, then warden at Camp Hill, as its first commissioner. Each institution still maintained a board of trustees, but perhaps mindful of Barnes's concern about "political prostitution," they were stripped of any administrative authority. To deter inmates from taking hostages in future uprisings, Republican state representative Edwin M. Tompkins sponsored an unsuccessful bill in April to impose life imprisonment in solitary confinement and a $10,000 fine.[54]

Devers delivered the committee's final report to Governor Fine in early April 1953, but because it exposed the inhumane treatment of inmates and the deprivation of services and was sharply critical of longstanding BOC practices, Fine delayed its official release until after the May primary election. Once released, however, several reforms were introduced almost immediately. In addition to implementing administrative changes at Western, the BOC increased and reorganized the custodial personnel, built five handball courts, added new isolation cells, installed a twelve-foot cyclone fence, and provided a qualified medical team available at all times. Warden Claudy abruptly retired and was replaced by Pennsylvania State Police captain James F. Maroney, who was expected to improve the morale and restore discipline of the inmate population.[55]

Two months after the Devers report was made public, the American Prison Association (APA) released the findings of its nationwide investigation of prison riots. Believing that prison riots resulted from "costly and dramatic symptoms of faulty prison administration," the commission concluded that "the underlying causes of poor prison administration all stem from a lack of public understanding of the problem and from a consequent reluctance to provide adequate financial support and to keep politics out of management."[56]

The APA might have had the Pennsylvania legislature in mind when

[53] *Devers Report*, 8, 14.
[54] Editor, "Pennsylvania's Correctional System," *American Journal of Corrections* 16, no. 5 (1954): 7–8; "Highlights of Governor Fine's Budget," *Pittsburgh Post-Gazette*, Jan. 27, 1953; "Bill to Curb Riots Offered," *Pittsburgh Post-Gazette*, Apr. 14, 1953; "State Warned of Peril of Prison Riots," *Pittsburgh Post-Gazette*, Apr. 15, 1953.
[55] *The History of Western State Penitentiary*, Smith, *30th Anniversary Commemorative History*, 3.
[56] Editor, "Prison Riots and Disturbances," *Prison World* 15, no. 3 (1953): 10–11.

it commented in its summary that "functional apathy" among prison personnel was a major cause of prisoner unrest and that "inmate rebellions occur because penal institutions are habitually neglected by corrections officials and state legislatures." Specifically, the APA blue ribbon commission listed substandard personnel, overcrowding, sentencing and parole practices, and lack of professional leadership as fundamental deficiencies contributing to conflict, essentially the same problems the Devers committee identified.[57]

No doubt influenced by the Devers report and the APA study, in July 1953 an uncommonly unified state legislature enacted eighteen reform measures, including one to prevent future inmate disturbances by imposing more severe penalties for hostage-taking, assault, escape, and inciting to riot. Most of the legislation, however, incorporated the committee's suggestions to improve the state's penal system.

On August 31, 1953, attorney general Woodside swore in Prasse as the state's first head of the bureau of correction. In his new $14,000-a-year post, the fifty-year-old commissioner was responsible for approximately seven thousand incarcerated individuals in seven correctional institutions. Prasse toured each facility with a particular concern for harsh disciplinary measures. Restrictive diets for inmates held in the "hole" accomplished little in the way of rehabilitation, he argued, because "there was nothing corrective about that." He was succinct but compassionate when stating his penal philosophy: "I believe in kindness. It is our job to restore, to rehabilitate men. It is necessary to restrain men and to be firm, but I do not believe in brutality."[58]

Reflecting Prasse's preference to "correct and control without repression or sentimentality," the new BOC phased in a "new look" in correctional policy. Aimed at preventing further disturbances, the reorganized, reformed penal system replaced outmoded methods of dealing with "problem type" prisoners, expanded or added new industries at Western to minimize inmate "unemployment," and organized all the state's institutions under the same administration. Western and Rockview, both redesigned, were to function as separate institutions.[59]

---

[57] "Prison Riots and Disturbances," 10–11.

[58] Prasse began his career in corrections as an instructor at Morganza in 1925. In 1940 he was appointed superintendent of George Junior Republic, a correctional school for boys in Grove City. Ten years later he was named superintendent at Camp Hill. "A Modern Corrections Pioneer," *Correctional Newsfront*, Jan.–Mar. 1978, 1–2; Frank M. Matthews, "Prasse Takes Over as State Prisons' Boss," *Pittsburgh Post-Gazette*, Sept. 1, 1953.

[59] Bureau of Correction, *First Annual Report* (Camp Hill, PA, 1954), 5, 24.

In 1954 the APA changed its name to the American Correctional Association (ACA), incorporating a more positive, therapeutic image of prison. The new ACA also encouraged state penal systems to rename their prisons and penitentiaries as "correctional institutions," which Pennsylvania did. In 1955 Democratic governor George M. Leader abolished Pennsylvania's prison boards of trustees. Diagnostic centers were established, a classification system was introduced, and a training school opened at Hershey for the sixteen hundred guards employed at other SCIs. Adopting the "corrective" approach as prescribed by the ACA, all of Pennsylvania's penal institutions were designated as state correctional institutions in 1955. In the spirit of reform, and to soften the repressive image of incarceration, guards were designated as "correctional officers," punishment cells would be known as "adjustment centers," and wardens became "superintendents."[60]

The disastrous 1953 riots proved to be a watershed in Pennsylvania's penal system in other ways. In his *First Annual Report*, commissioner Prasse acknowledged that he and the bureau had inherited "a demoralized group of institutions and penal administrators." It was also evident to Prasse that these disturbances

> were just about the last straw for a group of conscientious and loyal career workers who felt, whether rightfully or wrongly, that they had long been neglected by both the Public and by State Officials, restricted by obsolete laws and regulations and left groping in the dark by the lack of a coordinated modern program of penal administration.[61]

PAST TO PRESENT

Before the Revolutionary War, Pennsylvania was widely recognized as a pioneer in penal philosophy. Prominent citizens of Philadelphia, such as Benjamin Franklin, Benjamin Rush, William Bradford, and Caleb Lownes, repudiated barbaric criminal codes, abolished the death penalty,

[60] In 1993, SCI Cambridge Springs, located about twenty miles south of Erie, was opened as Pennsylvania's second facility for women. Smith, *30th Anniversary Commemorative History*, 3, 4; *First Annual Report*, 8; *Month's End Net Population of the Bureau of Correction, 1940–1969* (Camp Hill, PA, 1970); Unseem and Kimball, *States of Siege*, 10.

[61] *First Annual Report*, 3; Smith, *30th Anniversary Commemorative History*; "A Modern Corrections Pioneer"; "Prison Affairs," William B. Wheaton file, box 4, Pennsylvania Historical and Museum Commission; Harrington Adams, Deputy Attorney General, to Duncan C. McCallum, secretary to the governor, Jan. 19, 1954, "Boards & Commissioners," box 3, Papers of Governor John S. Fine, Pennsylvania Historical and Museum Commission.

and formed the Philadelphia Society for Alleviating the Miseries of Public Prisons, convinced that offenders be afforded an opportunity to change their behavior through penitence, solitude, and the Bible rather than be "corrected" with corporal punishment. By the mid-twentieth century, however, legislative and bureaucratic complacency seriously tarnished Pennsylvania's reputation. Many of its policies had become antiquated, and there was no indication any substantive reforms were forthcoming. According to Harry Elmer Barnes, "Pennsylvania, which in the early part of the Nineteenth Century, blazed the torch in penal reform throughout the world, has lagged behind a number of states which in recent years have inaugurated courageous dynamic and progressive penal programs."[62]

In the early twentieth century, Pennsylvania's general assembly seemed to recognize the state's regression in correctional policy. In 1911, it appointed a commission "to investigate the prison system and the organization and management of correctional institutions," which concluded that "the greatest abuse of the prevailing system is the lack of imagination and understanding . . . which keep alive a severe and repressive discipline."[63]

Perhaps most surprising about the riot at Western is that it did not happen sooner. In 1921 the state's five prisons were transferred to the newly created Department of Welfare, where few personnel had experience managing penal institutions. In its cover letter to secretary of welfare Sophia M. R. O'Hara in 1944, the Ashe committee was well aware that "for many years nothing constructive either as to building or housing has been done within the Commonwealth." The committee justified the "enormous sum" of $18 million that it estimated would be necessary to meet its recommendations by averring, "the Commonwealth of Pennsylvania has to start practically from scratch if it is going to surpass, or even catch up with a number of States in the Union, it is not out of line."[64]

In 1944, Republican governor Edward Martin appointed warden Ashe to head a five-member commission in response to concerns about an anticipated rise in postwar crime. Its most notable recommendation was to close the Eastern and Western penitentiaries, establish a classification

---

[62] Barnes, *The Evolution of Penology in Pennsylvania*, 79–81, 220; Herman I. Pollack, "The Pennsylvania Correctional Program for Adult Offenders," *Temple Law Quarterly* 24 (1950): 27, 37.

[63] The commission also recommended that two members should be added to the Board of Charities, "at least one of whom should be a woman." "Report of Commission to Investigate Penal Systems," *The Journal of Prison Discipline and Philanthropy* 58 (1919): 19, 44.

[64] *Ashe Report*, 39.

center, and create a centralized bureau of correction. If implemented, these proposals might have prevented the inmate rebellion at Western, but available funds were diverted to the state's mental hospitals. None of the reforms were adopted. Legislators did not create a classification center, and they did not close Western. They did not even replace the roof that inmates crawled through during the riot.[65]

It was in this milieu that the Devers committee set into motion reforms representing a sharp departure from Pennsylvania's outdated custodial philosophy. Still, it was unrealistic to expect that one committee investigation could solve problems that had been festering for more than a century. In 1953, the real question was not if a riot would occur, but where? The Western and Rockview riots were analogous to fire bells in the night in exposing the inadequacies of Pennsylvania's outmoded and inefficient management style.

Conditions at Western improved, but it could not escape its ignominious history. In November 1965, an inmate fatally stabbed a guard in the back with a homemade knife and critically wounded a second guard. In December 1973, twenty-eight state troopers were called to Western when a guard was beaten to death with several chairs and florescent lamps while guarding prisoners in an exercise room. In January 1987, inmates took advantage of a fire to ransack prison offices and beat guards and fellow inmates for ten hours. In 1989, a United States district judge declared Western to be unsafe and unconstitutional. In January 1997, six inmates tunneled their way out of the prison beneath its forty-foot walls.[66]

On the administrative side, in 1984 the BOC was reorganized as the Department of Corrections (DOC) and elevated to cabinet-level status, headed by a secretary, rather than a commissioner. In 1995, the DOC renamed Western as SCI-Pittsburgh, which finally closed in January 2005 but reopened in June 2007 to accommodate a burgeoning inmate population. To replace Western, the DOC opened SCI-Fayette in neighboring Fayette County.

Despite numerous reforms and a physical makeover, ghosts from Western's tumultuous past emerged in 2011, when prisoner allegations sur-

---

[65] *Report of the Committee Appointed by the Honorable Edward Martin to Survey the Penal and Correctional System of the Commonwealth of Pennsylvania* (Harrisburg, 1944), 43.

[66] "Stabbing Death Motive Sought," *Pittsburgh Press*, Nov. 14, 1965; Robert McHugh, "Slaying at Pen Stirs Strike Talk," *Pittsburgh Post-Gazette*, Dec. 11, 1973; Matthew Brelis, "Arson, Chaos Fueled Western Pen Violence, *Pittsburgh Press*, Jan. 28, 1987; David M. Brown, "End of an Era for Historic Prison," *Pittsburgh Tribune*, Jan. 14, 2017.

faced that corrections officers inflicted verbal and sexual abuse on gay and transgender inmates and other inmates convicted of sexual offenses. Two hundred counts were filed against seven officers.[67]

In January 2017, Governor Tom Wolfe approved closing Western, in part because of a mounting state budget deficit and a declining inmate population. Ironically, the waterfront site on the Ohio River that was once deemed unhealthy and dangerous was now in demand by investors for profitable redevelopment projects. Rockview remains operational in 2019, more than a century after it opened in 1912.[68]

The riots at Western and Rockview were regrettable tragedies that threatened institutional and social control. The penal system embodies the policies and politics relative to societal expectations of our prisons. Concomitantly, they are vital, essential agents not only in the criminal justice system but, more critically, for their impact on human lives. Dostoyevsky was right about prisons being a barometer of societal compassion. The Devers investigators who transformed Pennsylvania's correctional institutions were modern-day reformers still "shining a light in a dark house."

Pennsylvania State University, Emeritus   JOHN C. MCWILLIAMS

[67] Karen Langley and Adam Smeltz, "Officials Envision New Life for Riverfront Site of SCI Pittsburgh," *Pittsburgh-Post Gazette*, Jan. 26, 2011.

[68] Karen Langley, "Pa. To Close Just One Prison—In Pittsburgh," *Pittsburgh-Post Gazette,* Jan. 26, 2017. One investor was Shell Chemical, which wanted to build a petrochemical complex in adjoining Beaver County. "Officials Envision New Life for Riverfront Site of SCI Pittsburgh." For Rockview inmate statistics, see Pennsylvania Department of Corrections, *Monthly Population Report*, July 31, 2019.

"Can't Jail the Revolution": Policing, Protest, and the MOVE Organization in Philadelphia's Carceral Landscape

ABSTRACT: This essay examines the anticarceral protest and lifestyle politics of the MOVE organization in 1970s Philadelphia. MOVE is a group
of mostly Black radical naturalists who formed a collective in West Philadelphia in 1972. Between 1972 and 1978, the organization engaged in
varying forms of anticarceral resistance and directly confronted the emerg-
ing carceral landscape in Philadelphia, characterized by not only prisons
but also police violence, housing segregation, surveillance, and counterinsurgency. This work offers an account of how MOVE members challenged racialized and gendered police violence, prisons, and housing
inequality during the early years of the group's existence in order to demon-
strate that the 1978 raid on their home in Powelton Village was part of the
city's systematic repression of Philadelphia Black radicalism. This work
charts MOVE's changing use of protest politics and unconventional lifestyle practices as tools for resistance. This article unearths early MOVE
philosophy and practice while exploring the conditions of racialized and
gendered police violence that led to the ongoing incarceration of the
MOVE 9 political prisoners.

AUGUST 2019 MARKS the forty-first year that the MOVE 9 have
been incarcerated in Pennsylvania. The MOVE 9 are nine Black
men and women who are first generation members of the MOVE
organization, a family of self-proclaimed revolutionaries and naturalists
who came together in Philadelphia around 1972. Six years into MOVE's
formal existence, on August 8, 1978, hundreds of Philadelphia police
staged an attack on members of the organization living communally in a
Victorian-style home at 309 North Thirty-Third Street. Within a few
hours of the predawn police raid, officers fired thousands of rounds of
ammunition, dispensed tear gas, and destroyed the home with water deluge guns and cranes. Afterward, twelve MOVE adults were beaten and
arrested after one police officer was fatally shot in the exchange of fire.

THE PENNSYLVANIA MAGAZINE OF HISTORY AND BIOGRAPHY
Vol. CXLIII, No. 3 (October 2019)

Nine of the twelve adults who were arrested in August 1978 were charged and convicted of murder, criminal conspiracy, and a series of related charges. Those nine MOVE people—Delbert, Janet, Eddie, Janine, Michael, Merle, Chuck, Debbie, and Phil Africa—each received sentences of thirty to one hundred years in prison.[1] In 1981, when the MOVE 9 were convicted, their criminal trial was the longest running trial in the history of the state of Pennsylvania.[2]

The spectacular nature of the lengthy judicial process, along with the heavy media coverage around the trial, deeply entrenched the appearance of MOVE's criminality and obscured almost a decade's worth of police violence and MOVE's active dissent. Understanding the events and patterns in the years prior to 1978 is crucial for contextualizing the conditions of incarceration for the MOVE 9 and the systemic nature of police violence carried out against MOVE members overall. This article explores the experiences of MOVE people nearly a decade before the more spectacular and culturally memorable police bombing of 1985.[3] I will focus instead on MOVE people's experiences during the 1970s, in the years leading up to the Powelton police raid and the subsequent incarceration of the MOVE 9. In doing so, I will chart a longer history of MOVE's political and radical presence in Philadelphia. I will explore their complex

[1] I will refer to members of the MOVE organization as "MOVE people," "MOVE members," or even "MOVE" and employ the pronouns "they/them/theirs" in order to describe the collective of self-identified individuals who became part of the organization. Since MOVE people took the surname "Africa," I will also refer to individuals by their first names throughout this work. The title of this article comes from the former chairman of the Illinois chapter of the Black Panther Party, Fred Hampton, who was murdered in his sleep by Chicago police in concert with the Federal Bureau of Investigation in December 1969. Hampton's slogan was "you can jail revolutionaries, but you can't jail the revolution."

[2] Appellate Brief from the office of District Attorney Edward G. Rendell to the Superior Court of Pennsylvania RE: Commonwealth v. Africa, Oct. 4, 1984, box 43, Philadelphia Special Investigation Commission Archive (PSIC), Acc. 669, Special Collections Research Center (SCRC), Temple University Libraries, Philadelphia, PA.

[3] In 1985, the Philadelphia police and fire departments, under the mayoral leadership of Wilson Goode, dropped a bomb on MOVE people living at the 6200 block of Osage Avenue. Eleven MOVE men, women, and children were murdered. The entire city block was burned down, and Black families living on that block were displaced. The works of many scholars and filmmakers focus on this moment in MOVE history, including but not limited to Louis Messiah and Toni Cade Bambara's film *The Bombing of Osage Avenue* (1986), Jason Osder's film *Let the Fire Burn* (2013), and Robin Wagner Pacifici's *Discourse and Destruction: The City of Philadelphia Versus MOVE* (1994). This emphasis on the events that occurred in 1985 is also reflected in the accessible archives of MOVE history at Temple University and the City Archives of Philadelphia. Thus this article relies largely on news media accounts from the 1970s, alongside some police accounts and other city agency documents from the above archives.

relation to and resistance against Philadelphia's carceral state, characterized by early examples of racialized law and order discourse, surveillance, and the pathologizing of Black family life.

MOVE people sustained a critique of the carceral state throughout the 1970s, in the midst of increased state repression of the organization. Their responses to state violence were multiple, founded in collective self-sufficiency, radical publication, and protest politics. MOVE people waged what might be considered indirect confrontation with the carceral state through their experiments with holistic lifestyle alternatives for displaced Black and poor people. Over time, they adapted their resistance modes in relation to racialized and gendered forms of police repression; those modes increasingly relied on the very same armed self-defense strategies they once repudiated. MOVE members reformulated their politics and practices based on the increasing vulnerability of their collective, particularly that of the women and mothers in their family. I will explore the criminalization of MOVE people, Black dissent, and Black family life— all of which were crucial to the early formation of mass incarceration and law and order politics nationally and within Philadelphia.

First, I examine the early philosophies of MOVE people and contextualize them within Philadelphia's carceral buildup, as it occurred largely in and around Black communities and local Black Power organizations. Ultimately, I will explore the *multiple* carceral technologies that the city mobilized against MOVE while also locating the various modes through which MOVE members resisted the city's racialized and gendered violence. I will explore how criminality, incarceration, and displacement, all of which MOVE people endured over time, were modes of social control to destabilize their social movement. It was and still is MOVE's anti-carceral politics, characterized by protest and rehabilitative family formation, that marked their members as targets within Philadelphia's criminal justice system throughout the organization's foundational years.

MOVE BACKGROUND AND BELIEFS

The MOVE organization was founded by a middle-aged handyman and Korean War veteran named Vincent Leaphart, who was born in the West Philadelphia neighborhood of Mantua. Leaphart renamed himself John Africa, and those who joined MOVE took the surname "Africa." In the years leading up to MOVE's official founding, John Africa dictated his philosophies to MOVE members.[4] John Africa's philosophies were transcribed into a book called *The Guidelines*.[5]

The foundations of MOVE's political and social practices were based in an ethics of care, respect for life, and a desire to return to the most natural and simple state of living possible. Members often described this ethics as a self-determined religion—one that scholars say was infused with African cosmological values of justice, practical wisdom, and improvisation.[6] MOVE considered the wellbeing of humans, animals, and the physical environment interrelated and interdependent. Beginning in June 1975, MOVE published a twice-weekly column in the historically Black *Philadelphia Tribune*, entitled "On the MOVE." John Africa's sister Louise Africa (also Louise James) mostly authored the column.[7] In October 1975, James wrote: "The purpose of the MOVE organization is health." MOVE attributed illness such as heart disease and other ailments to "a lifestyle that is malfunctioning."[8] Thus MOVE members limited their use of technology while turning toward collective self-care and away from a for-profit medical system. Most MOVE women gave birth at home, and MOVE children were breastfed. Members refused to use chemical soaps and products on their bodies and wore their hair in free-formed dreadlocks, unmanipulated and in a "natural state."[9] They gradually adopted raw food diets and worked to be free of drugs and alcohol. They also experimented with composting. One member explained, "we return to the earth what we got from it."[10]

MOVE members aimed to offer practical resolutions to systemic social problems by amending their daily home lives. They protested the Philadelphia Board of Education for teaching "subtraction, multiplication and

---

[4] MOVE's official home at 309 North Thirty-Third Street was deeded to Donald Glassey "for purposes of convenience" until MOVE fully established the organization. Petition for Supersedeas, p. 1, *City of Philadelphia v. Donald Glassey*, Court of Common Pleas, Civil Trial Division, box 51, folder 7, PSIC, SCRC.

[5] Louise James, *John Africa's Childhood Story . . . Untold until Today*, 2013, Charles L. Blockson Afro-American Collection, SCRC.

[6] J. M. Floyd Thomas, "The Burning of Rebellious Thoughts: MOVE as Revolutionary Black Humanism," *The Black Scholar* 32, no. 1 (2002): 12–13.

[7] Louise Africa would later identify by her legal name, Louise James, after parting with her regular role in the organization. I will identify her herein as Louise Africa, the name under which she penned MOVE's column.

[8] Louise Africa, "On the MOVE," *Philadelphia Tribune*, Oct. 17, 1975.

[9] "MOVE Called Misguided," *Philadelphia Evening Bulletin*, Apr. 17, 1975, *Philadelphia Evening Bulletin* clippings collection (PEBC), SCRC; James F. Clarity, "Armed Group Defies Police in Philadelphia," *New York Times*, June 16, 1977, PEBC, SCRC.

[10] Larry Eichel, "MOVE Members Speak Out—Loudly," *Philadelphia Inquirer*, Apr. 21, 1975.

'admitted division,'" referring to Philadelphia's continually segregated school system.[11] In response to these conditions, MOVE members homeschooled their children. They claimed that modern technology only duplicated nature such that "the electric lightbulb is nothing more than a failing expression of the sun."[12] MOVE insisted on this ecological imperative not only by protesting the Philadelphia Public Utility Commission's increasing electricity rates but also by living without electricity.[13]

MOVE people formed a collective chosen family. Some members lived communally at 309 North Thirty-Third Street, engaging in nonnormative domestic relations. Their home was stripped of many modern materialist trappings as well as attendant heteronormative family relations. Their group comprised several individual families combined with different partners living together and in close proximity to the main MOVE house. They sustained themselves unconventionally as kin by supporting one another beyond blood ties. Some early couples in MOVE were Debbie and Michael alongside Janine and her husband Phil. MOVE boasted members from a range of socioeconomic backgrounds and educational levels.[14]

A regular day's work reflected the group's communal sufficiency as well. Daily life included group physical fitness, running with their family and many rescued dogs, operating a car wash outside their home for income, and completing construction and other contracted jobs in the community. In addition to their demonstrations against city officials and agencies, they wrote and engaged with print, television, and radio media outlets to spread their philosophies.[15]

Despite aims of self-determination, MOVE became the object of police surveillance in the early 1970s. City law enforcement kept records of MOVE's aims, origins, members, and even modes of transport to and from protests. Surveillance records reduced MOVE's politics to being "reactionary and fascist." Of the group's estimated sixty-five members,

[11] Carole Rich, "Foes Call Phila. School Board 'Hustlers,'" *Philadelphia Bulletin*, Apr. 16, 1974, PEBC, SCRC.

[12] Robert Africa, "On the MOVE," *Philadelphia Tribune*, Aug. 5, 1975; Dan Barshay, "Running the Dogs II: MOVE in Its Own Words," Mar. 29, 1979, *Delphia: The Entertainment Magazine of the Temple University*, SCRC.

[13] Laura Murray, "Radical Group Stirs Up Dull Electric-Rate Hearing," *Philadelphia Evening Bulletin*, May 17, 1974, PEBC, SCRC.

[14] Claude Lewis, "MOVE Stirs Anger," *Philadelphia Bulletin*, Oct. 25, 1975, PEBC, SCRC; Eichel, "MOVE Members Speak Out—Loudly"; Leslie Bennetts, "She Says Natural Childbirth and Really Means It," *Philadelphia Sunday Bulletin*, Aug. 10, 1975, PEBC, SCRC.

[15] Louise Africa, "On the MOVE," *Philadelphia Tribune*, Oct. 21, 1975.

one who piqued the city's interest was Delbert Orr Africa, who became Minister of Defense of MOVE after coming to Philadelphia as a fugitive from Chicago, where he had a similar role in the Illinois chapter of the Black Panther Party. [16]

MOVE people's notion of revolution bridged seemingly disparate ecological and social issues in ways that many considered "misguided."[17] Delbert Africa described MOVE's revolutionary ideals: "We believe in divorcing ourselves from the references that taught us racism and hate," and he emphasized that "we are not violent."[18] In fact MOVE deemphasized guns altogether, as they did other forms of technology, and instead weaponized their collective ability to divest from exploitative systems. Nonviolence remained part of MOVE's philosophies for years, but the group revised their position toward armed self-defense in 1977 after years of police harassment. Theirs was revolutionary naturalism, combining environmentalism and self-governance with critiques of racist and capitalist exploitation of Black and poor people.

PHILADELPHIA'S CARCERAL LANDSCAPE

MOVE emerged in West Philadelphia, desiring to divest from oppressive social and economic systems just as local, state, and federal governments began entrenching carceral conditions and targeting Black people in major US cities. Less than a year after urban riots in Harlem and Rochester, New York, in 1964, President Lyndon B. Johnson initiated the War on Crime. The War on Crime would quell growing Black resistance and riots against the racialized oppression and de facto segregation after legalized desegregation. Johnson's Congress passed the Safe Streets Act (1968), which established the Law Enforcement Assistance Administration (LEAA). LEAA distributed federal funds to state and subsequently local police departments for "riot" control or to otherwise quell Black insurgency against police oppression. Police departments gained the capacity to enact military control over Black neighborhoods through the purchase of helicopters, tanks, riot gear, and surveillance technologies.[19]

---

[16] Civil Disobedience Police Unit Surveillance File on MOVE, p. 2, Apr. 22, 1974, box 51, folder 3, PSIC.

[17] "MOVE Called Misguided."

[18] Rich, "Foes Call Phila. School Board 'Hustlers.'"

[19] Naomi Murakawa, *The First Civil Right: How Liberals Built Prison America* (Oxford, 2014), 73; Elizabeth Hinton, *From the War on Poverty to the War on Crime: The Making of Mass Incarceration in America* (Cambridge, 2016), 89.

Johnson's administration extended the punitive capacities of the earlier initiated War on Poverty by shifting funding toward police and away from social welfare programming, which also acted as a tool of social control to "simultaneously empower but also increase supervision of vulnerable communities."[20] Johnson's War on Crime rested on the belief that criminality was an inherent product of Black culture and family life. He embraced the findings in social scientist Daniel Patrick Moynihan's infamous report, *The Negro Family: The Case for National Action*. The report argued that crime (including riots), unemployment, and poverty were a result of "unstable" Black family life, characterized by female-headed and fatherless households.[21] The findings in his report helped to deemphasize social welfare programs that might address structural inequality and instead furthered punitive policy against Black families. Thus lawmakers simultaneously criminalized both Black insurgency and Black and often urban family life through the race neutral language of "law and order."[22] Law and order policies led to militarized policing that suppressed Black insurgency and criminalized Black communities in general. Black resistance in the form of protest and other forms of non-normativity that disrupted the prescribed social order were systematically suppressed through law and order funds, technologies, and state actors.

MOVE challenged the state through their family dynamic. As an everyday practice, they openly refused the discourses and policies criminalizing Black families. Louise James described MOVE as "a powerful family of revolutionaries, strong in collective commitment . . . [to] the urgency of freedom."[23] The collective she described was not based in normative or nuclear norms of family but instead an experimental kinship formation of multiple families, thus challenging heteronormativity. In her column, Louise argued that MOVE "does away completely with so called relegated roles . . . it is not strange to see a MOVE woman washing cars, or chopping wood, or working by her man's side . . . and the fathers in MOVE spend as much time with their children, as do the mothers. Our children are with us at all times, engaging with us in whatever we do." Louise insisted that prisons were a major threat to MOVE and other families, causing the "pain of separation."[24] She also described MOVE's

[20] Hinton, 54.
[21] Hinton, 59, 74–75.
[22] Murakawa, *The First Civil Right*, 79–80.
[23] John Africa quoted in Louise James, "On the MOVE," *Philadelphia Tribune*, June 28, 1975.
[24] Louise Africa, "On the MOVE," *Philadelphia Tribune*, Dec. 6, 1975.

expanded care network, whereby children were ideally cared for by other MOVE members in the event of incarceration. MOVE's alternative kinship structure was not necessarily more or less functional or productive than other forms, but experimentation with alternative kinship was part of their anticarceral politics. They used family building as a tool to mitigate carceral conditions of separation even as Black families were being tied to criminality.

Still, law and order politics continued to expand and produce a carceral landscape in Philadelphia. Radical imprisoned intellectual George Jackson described the ways in which Black urban spaces became increasingly like prisons in the 1960s, due not only to law and order politics but also the continued containment of Black subjects in urban spaces of under- and unemployment, police violence, surveillance, and spatial segregation.[25] Thus the very notion of a *carceral landscape* marks the capacious effects of prisons such that US urban spaces—including Philadelphia—and the prisons throughout the nation are mutually constitutive of one another.

Most of the members of the MOVE 9 came of age in Philadelphia's postwar era, as the carceral landscape was being solidified. During this period, quality housing and jobs increasingly moved to Philadelphia's "suburban periphery," as did white people, leaving large populations of Black people confined in highly concentrated spaces of disinvestment.[26] Philadelphia, like many other postwar cities, experienced a loss of manufacturing jobs after World War II. Black Philadelphians were most affected and on multiple fronts. In addition to decades of discrimination in hiring, unions, and training opportunities, housing discrimination and redlining prevented Black workers from migrating with the flow of capital into neighboring suburbs.[27] Racialized exclusion from jobs continued into the 1970s, as construction jobs were created through federal urban

[25] See George Jackson, *Soledad Brother: The Prison Letters of George Jackson* (Chicago, 1970), 69–70, 146. Historians writing about Jackson draw on these claims. See Dan Berger, *Captive Nation: Black Prison Organizing in the Civil Rights Era* (Chapel Hill, NC, 2014), 51.

[26] The Black population in Philadelphia greatly increased after the start of the Great Migration in the early twentieth century. Philadelphia's Black population increased from 376,041 in 1950 to 653,791 in 1970. After World War II, Blacks were mainly concentrated in north central Philadelphia and West Philadelphia. By midcentury, 85 percent of the Black population increase in the Philadelphia area occurred within the city limits, while 96 percent of the white population growth was in the surrounding suburbs. See Matthew Countryman, *Up South: Civil Rights and Black Power in Philadelphia* (Philadelphia, 2006), 50–55.

[27] Guian A. McKee, *The Problem of Jobs: Liberalism, Race, and Deindustrialization in Philadelphia* (Chicago, 2008), 12–13.

renewal programs, which also operated out of closed and discriminatory recruiting.[28]

Urban renewal and slum clearance were the economic initiatives of the era, as the city sought to replace urban "blight" with newer public housing and commercial structures. In reality, though, the Philadelphia Redevelopment Authority spent the decade working with corporations to clear land in Center City and South Philadelphia for the construction of office buildings and revitalized housing for white people to return from suburbs.[29] City officials and planners displaced Black residents from what was once the Seventh Ward into North, West, and parts of South Philadelphia.[30] The already dense population of Black people in Philadelphia lived in substandard and even dilapidated older housing.[31] Racist violence, redlining, and city council blocks against integrated housing in the 1950s were used to maintained segregated public housing.[32] Meanwhile, in places like Philadelphia's Black Bottom, which bordered MOVE's Powelton neighborhood, the University of Pennsylvania displaced a predominantly Black, working-class community. For Black Philadelphians, the twentieth century was marked by conditions of forced movement and intense confinement in spaces of government divestment, both of which undergirded MOVE's repression and resistance in the city.

The War on Crime further empowered racist Philadelphia police. In 1972, the Pennsylvania State Advisory Committee to the United States Commission on Civil Rights compiled a report based on the problems of "police-community relations" in Philadelphia. The report found that Black Philadelphians faced racist policing practices, characterized by "indiscriminate arrests," "excessive use of force," problems with "police accountability," and "unequal police protection in minority communities."[33] During the 1960s, three times as many Black city residents were

[28] McKee, 213.

[29] Countryman, *Up South*, 70.

[30] Countryman, 51–52.

[31] Countryman, 53.

[32] Eric C. Schneider, Christopher Agee, and Themis Chronopoulos, "Dirty Work: Police and Community Relations and the Limits of Liberalism in Postwar Philadelphia," *Journal of Urban History*, May 1, 2017, https://doi.org/10.1177/0096144217705497. Redlining affected low-income, Black city residents most. Insurance companies refused policies to residents in mostly Black neighborhoods, including North, West, and South Philadelphia, which were racially coded as "congested" and "bad risk" areas. See also "Your Savings Here Finance Mortgages Elsewhere," *Philadelphia Inquirer*, Nov. 30, 1976.

[33] A Report to the United States Commission on Civil Rights by the Pennsylvania State Committee (An Official Advisory Committee to the Commission), *Police-Community Relations in Philadelphia*, p. 4, June 1972, box 1, Police Advisory Board Archive, Acc. 670, SCRC.

killed by police as white ones, and this amount almost doubled by 1970.[34] Philadelphia police officers—a cohort of mostly white ethnic (Irish Catholic) men—believed, like other blue-collar and/or ethnic whites in the city, that they were superior to Black residents. They exploited their power to control Black working-class competition.[35] Officers maintained white supremacy by surveilling Black homes, searching Black people who appeared idle on the streets, and even harassing interracial couples and groups similar to MOVE's own racially integrated collective.[36] Within communities of color, the state advisory committee found that the Philadelphia Police Department was a "paramilitary institution" with the aim of "containment and control rather than protection and service."[37] Police accountability was undermined by the city government and officials as well as through the dismantling of the Police Advisory Board for the civilian review of police discrimination.[38]

PHILADELPHIA'S COUNTERINSURGENCY APPARATUS

Rather than rectifying the causes of structural racism, such cities as Philadelphia intensified policing as a response to Black uprisings and radicalism in the 1960s and '70s. In the summer of 1964, Philadelphians—along with their counterparts in Rochester and Harlem, New York—rose up in response to the racial oppression in US cities. The North Philadelphia riot of 1964 was activated by an encounter between Philadelphia police and a Black couple.[39] Liberal and conservative officials, including

---

[34] *Police-Community Relations in Philadelphia*, 7.

[35] Schneider et al., "Dirty Work," 2.

[36] *Police-Community Relations in Philadelphia*, 13.

[37] *Police-Community Relations in Philadelphia*.

[38] Established by mayor Richardson Dilworth in 1958, the Police Advisory Board (PAB) was a civilian review board charged with recommending appropriate action to the city government based on citizen complaints of police brutality and discrimination. Court of Common Pleas judge Leo Weinrott dissolved the PAB in March 1967, siding with Fraternal Order of Police complaints that the board undermined the authority of police. The PAB won its appeal to the Pennsylvania Supreme Court, but Rizzo ally Mayor Tate refused to reinstate the board. See Schneider et al., "Dirty Work," 11–12.

[39] Timothy J. Lombardo, *Blue Collar Conservatism: Frank Rizzo's Philadelphia and Populist Politics* (Philadelphia, 2018), 49–51. On August 28, 1964, two police officers had an altercation with the couple, whose car stalled at the intersection of Twenty-Second Street and Columbia Avenue. When one white officer tried to remove a Black woman, Odessa Bradford, from her vehicle by force, a Black man emerged from the crowd of witnesses and struck the officer. Onlookers proceeded to throw bottles and bricks. A riot ensued and lasted nearly three days. Two people were killed and 339 wounded. Property damage was notable but mostly against non-Black businesses.

"tough cop" Frank Rizzo, called for law and order after the riot rather than understanding it as a call for social change.

Rizzo quickly parlayed his tough-on-crime status into the role of police commissioner and later mayor.[40] Rizzo built up a counterinsurgency apparatus by strengthening the city's Civil Disobedience Unit. The mission of the unit was to maintain "extensive surveillance on Civil Rights militants and other radical activists in the city" and "develop strategies for movement inspired violence."[41] The Civil Disobedience Unit, later named the Civil Affairs Unit, was led by George Fencl. The unit's tactics trained officers to gather intelligence about activist leaders by gaining their trust. The unit surveilled groups with photographs and video, manned demonstrations, and trailed protestors. Leftist groups were infiltrated by police officers and civilian spies. By the summer of 1967, the Civil Disobedience Unit had a large supply of informers paid by the Federal Bureau of Investigation.[42] According to Frank Donner, "collaboration between the FBI and the Philadelphia police in destructive counterintelligence initiatives against the Philadelphia Black activists was used as a model for the bureau's aggressive intelligence program COINTELPRO."[43] Fencl and Rizzo's Civil Disobedience Unit conducted a violent campaign against Philadelphia activist groups, including antiwar activists, the ACLU, and especially prominent, community-based Black Power groups. Philadelphia was ripe with Black resistance groups, including the Revolutionary Action Movement (RAM), the Black People's Unity Movement (BPUM), the Philadelphia chapter of the Student Nonviolent Coordinating Committee (SNCC), and the Black Panther Party. Each met repression through brutal beatings, surveillance, and police raids based on alleged bomb and police assassination plots.[44] Perhaps the most memora-

[40] Rizzo was appointed acting commissioner in 1967 and fully took on the office afterward from 1968 to 1971. He was elected mayor of Philadelphia in 1972 and remained in the office until 1980 after changing the city charter so he could serve two terms.

[41] Countryman, *Up South*, 215.

[42] Frank Donner, *Protectors of Privilege: Red Squads and Police Repression in Urban America* (Oakland, CA, 1990), 202–4.

[43] Donner, 205.

[44] RAM rejected nonviolence and advocated militant struggle against oppression. The FBI and the Civil Disobedience Unit coordinated several raids on RAM. See "The Dirty Work of Philly's Political Police: From COINTELPRO to Powelton Village," *Revolutionary Worker*, Jan. 14, 2001. Philadelphia was one of the first test cases for SNCC in a northern city in the 1960s. SNCC's southern activists came to Philadelphia to promote leadership from within the city's working-class, Black neighborhoods to build a grassroots movement against racism, poverty, and Philadelphia's Democratic machine. See Countryman, *Up South*, 208–13. The Philadelphia police conducted four bomb raids of the SNCC office in 1966. Officers found only a few sticks of dynamite, which they used as rationale to acquire warrants for SNCC leaders. See "Philadelphia SNCC Members in Cus-

ble of Rizzo's raids occurred at the Black Panther Party offices in Germantown and North and West Philadelphia on August 31, 1970. Fencl himself led the raid in North Philadelphia. Officers shot into the headquarters and later forced the Panthers to strip down to their underwear.[45] The day after the raid, Rizzo announced the hiring of 599 more policemen.[46]

MOVE'S ANTICARCERAL POLITICS
AND POLICE REPRESSION

MOVE's 1972 emergence came in the wake of the state-sanctioned violent repression of Black Power activists in Philadelphia and across the nation under a banner of maintaining law and order. MOVE members challenged the militarized policing in their city and the simultaneous buildup of Pennsylvania prisons through nonviolent protest.

Early on, MOVE's environmental and social protests used defiant rhetoric and even profanity. MOVE people suffered several arrests during their regular protests, which ranged from environmental activism, challenging elected officials, and petitioning the Philadelphia Board of Education.[47] MOVE challenged the city's educational and welfare institutions as funding for these programs declined in comparison to the growing investment in police.

MOVE people pushed the normative bounds of social protest through their language especially, even as Black insurgency was being suppressed. They indicted police for enacting and promoting systemic violence in Black communities. MOVE protested at a local gang violence symposium in 1974, "shouting profanity and denouncing its sponsors," while blaming the criminal justice system for gang warfare.[48] Some saw MOVE's use

tody," *Chicago Daily Defender*, Nov. 14, 1966. Established in 1965, BPUM established the goals of racial unity and community control over political and economic institutions operating in Black communities. See Countryman, *Up South*, 198. The Philadelphia Panthers sought "total eradication of exploitation in this country" and maintenance of "community control over the police." See "Police Call Them Outlaws But Panthers Say They're Revolutionaries," *Philadelphia Tribune,* Jan. 10, 1970.

[45] Police raided the Philadelphia Panther office just before the party's Revolutionary People's Constitutional Convention, to be held in Philadelphia from Sept 5–6, 1970. According to local residents, police fired the first shots. Laurence Geller, "Many Criticize Police Raid On Black Panthers' Center," *Philadelphia Tribune,* Sept. 1, 1970.

[46] "Rizzo Gets Mayor Tate's OK To Hire 599 More Policemen," *Philadelphia Tribune,* Sept. 1, 1970.

[47] Robert W. Kotzbauer, "'Counsel' Held in Assault at Court Protest," *Philadelphia Bulletin,* Nov. 8, 1974; Rich, "Foes Call Phila. School Board 'Hustlers.'"

[48] Sam W. Pressley, "Blacks and Whites Disrupt Gang-Violence Meeting," *Philadelphia Bulletin,* Feb. 19, 1974, PEBC, SCRC.

of profanity as harmless. Philadelphia common pleas court judge Judith Jamison described the rhetoric and language as "annoying but not dangerous."[49] Still, the courts and police in the Civil Disobedience Unit criminalized their use of profanity. Officers claimed their language constituted disorderly conduct.[50] MOVE people were legally ordered to refrain from using "vulgarity" in their speech or on protest signs.[51] Still, MOVE members said that only profanity could accurately capture the violence of the system and that their language was mild in comparison. They questioned, "what is more profane than jail, solitary confinement, the electric chair?"[52] MOVE members protested police brutality often and were known for calling police officers "thugs" and "hit men" and otherwise showing fearless irreverence.[53] In addition to challenging the criminal activity within the police department, MOVE's language challenged recognizable and even state-sanctioned modes of redress, particularly for Black subjects. In the face of increasingly brutal arrests after protests, MOVE was forced to turn their attention more actively to the issue of police violence.

They especially confronted the violence of the Sixteenth District police, based in Powelton Village. The Sixteenth District helped carry out the Black Panther raids and was known for "accidental hangings" of Black prisoners.[54] MOVE members were arrested for protesting Sixteenth District police harassment on several occasions in 1974 and 1975. On Saturday, June 14, 1975, about twenty-five MOVE members demonstrated at the station for nearly three hours. *Philadelphia Inquirer* reporter Bob Lancaster watched them picket and shout profanity at officers over a public address system. Although Lancaster described their rhetoric as "angry" and "defiant," he said, "people mainly went on about their business," though plainclothes Civil Disobedience Unit officers watched from nearby.[55] MOVE people later told Lancaster that as soon as he left the area, they were beaten and arrested behind the police station. MOVE reported that Rhonda Africa's head was bashed into a glass window of

---

[49] Eichel, "MOVE Members Speak Out—Loudly."

[50] Eichel.

[51] Court of Common Pleas Order, May 21, 1974, box 91, Friends Peace Committee Records, Quaker Meeting Records at Haverford College Quaker & Special Collections, Haverford, PA, and Friends Historical Library of Swarthmore College, Swarthmore, PA.

[52] Claude Lewis, "Claude Lewis—An Opinion: MOVE Stirs Anger," *Philadelphia Evening Bulletin,* Oct. 25, 1974.

[53] Eichel, "MOVE Members Speak Out—Loudly."

[54] Mumia Abu-Jamal, "The Power of Truth," ca. 1987, in *Writings on The Wall: Selected Prison Writings of Mumia Abu-Jamal*, ed. Johanna Fernandez (San Francisco, 2015), 26.

[55] Bob Lancaster, "MOVE Rally MOVEs Few," *Philadelphia Inquirer*, June 18, 1975.

the station's rear entrance. Although police denied the assault, Lancaster wrote that the glass was, in fact, shattered when he returned. MOVE people were taken to the House of Corrections.[56]

Police denied the brutality and claimed that Rhonda may have bumped her head in the arrest.[57] Still, it was known that police officers regularly used "alley court," punishment in the form of extralegal and covert beatings, especially if they believed the charges against someone would not hold up in court.[58] *Philadelphia Evening Bulletin* photographer Donald Camp's images of the broken glass at the Sixteenth District showed that it shattered out three rings deep—a clear indication of force and not an accidental head bump.[59] Along with the police department and Civil Disobedience Unit's history of racial violence, Camp's images contradicted police testimony related to the beatings.

MOVE people conducted a campaign against police in the spring of 1974 by protesting the Twenty-Second and Twenty-Third police districts. MOVE distributed fliers calling on the community to join them in a two-week long protest against the districts because they "repeatedly harassed Blacks on the streets, at their jobs [and] in their homes." MOVE urged Black Philadelphians to "stop complaining privately" about "the beatings, shootings, killings, pats on the asses of our women" and instead to protest openly and collectively.[60] MOVE worked to empower Black people to challenge racial and sexual harassment by taking to the streets and openly resisting police brutality.

While continuing to protest police conduct, MOVE used their regular column to testify to police back alley beatings. Louise Africa challenged the racialized violence that was part of every MOVE arrest by inverting the commonly levied charges of "disorderly conduct." Instead she indicted officers' physical and verbal abuse of MOVE men and women. The police, she noted, "called us niggers [but] arrest us for profanity."[61] The abuse continued into the jails, where MOVE people were often held without food or water. In some instances, law enforcement failed to deny

[56] Lancaster.

[57] "Did a Head Hit This Pane?" *Philadelphia Evening Bulletin*, June 16, 1975.

[58] Schneider et al., "Dirty Work," 9.

[59] Don Camp, photograph accompanying "Did a Head Hit This Pane?"

[60] MOVE Police Demonstration Flyer, "You Are Needed," May 1974, box 91, Friends Peace Committee Records, Quaker Meeting Records at Haverford College Quaker & Special Collections and Friends Historical Library of Swarthmore College.

[61] Louise Africa, "On the MOVE," *Philadelphia Tribune*, Aug. 2, 1975.

the accusations. According to a Sheriff Murray, "verbal abuse" was hard for his men to tolerate, so "they occasionally strike back."[62]

MOVE arrests at demonstrations became so common by 1975 that part of their regimen was to sit "all night at 8th and Race, keeping vigil" in support of family members going before judges.[63] By May 1976, MOVE people reported that they had been arrested over four hundred times and had paid over half a million dollars in bail fines and other fees for misdemeanor charges.[64] Most of the charges levied against MOVE people during their protests included riot, disorderly conduct, criminal conspiracy, and failure to disperse. Misdemeanor charges of this kind were part of a national pattern of charges used to repress members of the Left.[65] Within Philadelphia, disorderly conduct charges were used as cover charges to suppress complaints of police brutality.[66]

In spite of experiencing many arrests, MOVE people suffered few actual convictions early on, which was not surprising considering the culture of "cover charges" in the city. Inside the courtroom, MOVE people challenged the legal process by refusing to stand when the judge entered court, speaking out during court, representing themselves in the legal proceedings, and challenging police and other official witnesses.[67] Once MOVE people showed their irreverence for court proceedings, they frequently ended up in jail for contempt of court, with the original charges going unresolved. Civil Affairs Unit officers were often present during court and ready to carry out contempt arrests.[68]

In the spirit of Black Power radicalism, Delbert Africa and others acted as counsel in MOVE trials. MOVE disregarded the conventions of the legal process outright and even challenged the judges on their philosophies. Sue Africa spoke directly to judge Judith Jamison, claiming that "I have as much authority as you." Sue said, "all women are exploited . . . including you."[69] By talking back to the judge, Sue offered a systemic

---

[62] Eichel, "MOVE Members Speak Out—Loudly."

[63] Louise Africa, "On the MOVE," *Philadelphia Tribune,* Oct. 21, 1975.

[64] Linn Washington, "4 Black Judges," *Philadelphia Tribune,* May 15, 1976.

[65] Donner, *Protectors of Privilege,* 226.

[66] Schneider et al., "Dirty Work," 9. It was "standard police procedure to charge a person with resisting arrest or disorderly conduct wherever the person charges the police with brutality." These charges, known as "cover charges," gave the district attorney leeway for a plea bargain or for negotiating the dropping of charges in return for a complainant not seeking legal redress against an arresting officer.

[67] Eichel, "MOVE Members Speak Out—Loudly."

[68] Kotzbauer, "'Counsel' Held In Assault at Court Protest."

[69] Marilyn Schaefer, "Radical Group Keeps Officer On Stand," *Philadelphia Bulletin,* Nov. 13, 1974.

critique of how women of all classes occupied similarly degraded places in society. In doing so, Sue used the courtroom as a space to document MOVE philosophies on the court record. MOVE members all kept vigil in the courtrooms, even in the trials of teenage members, in which seats were usually reserved for the immediate family of the defendants. MOVE members thereby extended notions of kinship.[70] MOVE people appropriated the reality of their arrests for their protest politics and managed to stage the courtroom as a space of resistance—a space where their own voices and ideologies could and did stand in direct opposition to authorities who challenged their right to free speech. According to Bob Africa, MOVE members "looked forward to the trials," since their many arrests produced a "backlog" to clog the functions of the criminal justice system.[71]

In addition to using their protests to challenge the general policing conditions in the city, MOVE people also protested the violence against MOVE prisoners in particular and their forced medical treatment in the jails. In early July 1975, MOVE protested several times outside the home of prison superintendent Louis Aytch. The first time they called for prison reform, and in subsequent protests they petitioned the superintendent because MOVE men in jail were being "badly beaten by guards," to the point of losing dreadlocks and sustaining jaw injuries.[72] The prison superintendent denied the beatings. "We are professionals," he told the *Philadelphia Tribune*, asserting that MOVE members sustained injuries from an incident "amongst themselves or with other inmates." He also claimed to fear that MOVE might incite others to resist medical examination.[73]

The superintendent's language of "professionalism" reflected the discourse of race-neutral "law and order" and police "modernization," which disappeared racist carceral violence in the period. Still, MOVE men challenged the prison's imposition of bodily manipulation and control. MOVE members' principles were rooted in bodily autonomy, which they fought to maintain. They likely faced physical harm, considering the superintendent's coded explanation of events and the fact that the MOVE men took the risk of writing to their comrades on the outside to expose the brutality hidden behind prison walls.

MOVE members spent 1975 forcibly filling the prisons and jails and

[70] Schaefer.

[71] Eichel, "MOVE Members Speak Out—Loudly."

[72] Len Lear, "MOVE Pickets Home Of Prison Director," *Philadelphia Tribune*, July 12, 1975.

[73] Lear. See also "Four From MOVE Held In Protest," *Philadelphia Daily News*, July 11, 1975, box 43, PSIC, SCRC.

exposing the shrouded violence through hunger strikes. Hunger strikes were, according to Sue Africa, a way to show the public how brutal prison conditions were. In August 1975, Conrad and Beowolf Africa went on hunger strikes in the House of Correction—MOVE's "second home" in those days—to protest against Eddie Africa's forced transfers between Broadmeadows and Holmesburg prisons.[74] Prison officials at Broadmeadows forced Eddie into the back of a hot wagon while he was bound in leg irons and a ball and chain. Upon arriving at Holmesburg, they left him in the wagon for hours and then "turned right around and transferred him right back to Broadmeadows."[75] MOVE members on the outside of Philadelphia prisons used the press to project the experiences and resistance of MOVE people inside the prisons. In the wake of prison strikes across the country calling for prison reform and an end to racialized segregation and brutality, MOVE also thrust Philadelphia's prison system into view. They exposed intricate instances of control that otherwise disappeared behind what Marie Gottschalk calls the "iron curtain" shrouding routine prison violence.[76] After periods of hunger strikes, MOVE people often found that their charges were dropped.[77]

HOUSING AND POWELTON VILLAGE

During the height of MOVE's protests and confrontations with police and the Civil Disobedience Unit, their members were also battling the city over housing violations deployed as part of a carceral project of removing poor Black residents from Powelton Village. The city's legally documented contention with MOVE was over "gross violations of the Health, Housing, Fire, Zoning and Safety Code." Authorities filed a civil suit against MOVE on November 18, 1975, which later became the formal impetus for the city to confine MOVE through a surveillance and later a starvation blockade.[78] In the 1975 civil suit, judge Fred DiBona

[74] Len Lear, "3 MOVErs On Hunger Strike In Area Prisons," *Philadelphia Tribune*, Aug. 5, 1975; Margo Downing, "2 MOVE Members Go 28 Days Without Food, 15 Minus Water," *Philadelphia Tribune*, May 3, 1975.

[75] Lear.

[76] Marie Gottschalk, *The Prison and the Gallows: The Politics of Mass Incarceration* (Cambridge, 2006),183. Gottschalk also discusses the increase in prison riots in the 1960s and '70s. In 1967 there were only five prison riots in the United States. In 1972 there were forty-eight reported instances of prison revolt in the nation. Gottschalk, 179.

[77] John T. Gillespie, "MOVE Members Win Paroles," *Philadelphia Bulletin*, Apr. 30, 1975.

[78] Supreme Court of Pennsylvania, Eastern District, Concurring Opinion in *City of Philadelphia v. Donald Glassey*, filed Mar. 15, 1978, box 51, folder 7, PSIC, SCRC.

demanded that MOVE allow inspectors of the Department of Licenses and Inspections to enter their home at 309 North Thirty-Third Street. Judge DiBona's order also said for MOVE to cease operation of their "car wash and/or laundromat and/or food market and from permitting garbage and debris to be strewn on the exterior portion of the premises and finally from having uninoculated and unlicensed animals on their premises."[79] The language of the suit criminalized MOVE's ecological practices and ideologies. The suit provided state justification for the violence that was already being perpetrated against MOVE people. The order reveals how the carceral state developed as a spatial technology rooted in the organized control, removal, and incapacitation of Black people, especially those refusing white, middle-class values and norms.

MOVE did not claim to be operating within the zoning laws. They were in many ways, in open violation of any "system" mandates on how they lived their daily lives. MOVE members resisted the opposition of their white, middle-class neighbors, who had levied the zoning complaints in the first place. Neighbors were uncomfortable with MOVE's general lifestyle and took issue with the some twenty stray dogs that MOVE housed. Powelton residents testified to that effect at a zoning board meeting in 1975, where they decried the smell of animal feces. MOVE responded by directing their neighbors to concern themselves with "real pollution" from "cars, insecticides, food additives, police and the noise pollution of fire sirens."[80] MOVE was scorned for the smell of trash in their yard from a "pungent compost heap," as well as for the "bodily odors" that resulted from eschewing soap.[81] MOVE people did not shy from conflict or strife with neighbors. They intentionally transgressed the social codes of the middle-class and student-centered neighborhood and asserted their right to inhabit space with vigilance. Their vigilance would be met with state violence on a massive scale in August of 1978.

The upwardly mobile position of Powelton Village was key to MOVE's criminalization. Neighbor complaints contributed to a larger carceral project rooted in maintaining segregated space. In February 1977, Milton Karabell, the executive director of the West Philadelphia Corporation, a

[79] Court Order signed by Judge G. Fred DiBona, Court of Common Pleas Civil Trial Division, Nov. 1975, *City of Philadelphia v. Donald Glassey*, box 51, folder 7, PSIC, SCRC.

[80] John T. Gillespie, "MOVE Appeals To Zoning Board Over 20 Stray Dogs," *Philadelphia Evening Bulletin*, Apr. 25, 1975.

[81] Bennetts, "She Says Natural Childbirth and Really Means It."

major development corporation, wrote to Mayor Rizzo backing Powelton residents' complaints. He claimed that, until MOVE's arrival, new families relocating from the suburbs had "renewed" Powelton. MOVE's presence, according to Karabell, brought a "blighting influence." Developers used the state's impending violence as a tool to increase their profitability and criminalized MOVE in the process by mobilizing the state's language of "blight," which also invoked Moynihan's language of Blackness as "pathological."[82] Housing speculation and increasing development of Drexel University had a large part in MOVE's imminent displacement and incarceration. Black removal from desirable neighborhoods was a central tenet of the growing carceral state. Even though Powelton Village was hailed as home to the city's countercultural radicals at the time, it was also becoming the site of intensive urban redevelopment projects and university expansion in the 1960s and '70s.

Black residents had been fighting for their homes in Powelton against local universities even before MOVE emerged. In February 1970, Black Powelton residents of the West Powelton Concerned Community Council conducted one of several sit-ins to protest the destruction of their homes at Thirty-Third and Arch Streets for the construction of a Drexel University dormitory. The judge on the case called for law and order and prohibited demonstrations on Drexel property, effectively criminalizing Black residents' resistance to displacement.[83] The residents charged that Drexel was collaborating with the West Philadelphia Corporation and the Philadelphia Redevelopment Authority to declare East Powelton a "slum" so they could use public urban renewal funds to secure residents' properties for Drexel.[84] The residents were correct. In the 1950s, the idea of a "University City," a modern complex devoted to learning and research, took root in Philadelphia. The University of Pennsylvania and Drexel Institute of Technology, along with neighboring institutions, agreed to organize and share the initial financial burden of the West Philadelphia Corporation. The corporation worked in concert with public officials and the Redevelopment Authority to acquire property and funds to implement

[82] Letter from Milton Karabell, executive director of the West Philadelphia Corporation, to Mayor Frank Rizzo, Feb. 10, 1977, box 51, folder 7, PSIC, SCRC.
[83] Len Lear, "Minister Arrested with Other Drexel Area Demonstrators," *Philadelphia Tribune*, Feb. 10, 1970; Lear, "Police Have Guard Dogs Removed From Drexel Area," *Philadelphia Tribune*, Feb. 7, 1970. Black residents of Powelton and Mantua held a sleep-in to protect their homes from demolition and Drexel University expansion.
[84] Lear, "Minister Arrested."

the University City concept.[85] The systematic displacement of Black people and MOVE in particular became inevitable, since they were not part of the vision developed by universities, the government, and private corporations. MOVE was undoubtedly targeted for protesting housing conditions as well, not only by refusing to open their home for inspection or to move from their home, but also by protesting the Redevelopment Housing Authority for razing properties in preparation for Drexel's expansion. MOVE called for Powelton to be reserved for poor Black families instead of for absentee white developers and owners.[86]

VIOLENCE AGAINST MOVE WOMEN

At the nexus of the issues of housing and domesticity came the issue of protecting Black mothers and motherhood within the MOVE family. As the city mobilized to make Powelton suitable for white, middle-class domestic life, the displacement and criminalization of MOVE was furthered through police violence against women in the group. MOVE women's place in the carceral state, vexed as it was by Moynihan's demonization of "Black matriarchs," became increasingly marked by violence. Black women in MOVE experienced the particular effects of the carceral state's role in degrading and separating Black families.

In July 1975, Valerie Africa was arrested along with other MOVE women and charged with obstruction of justice while protesting for "prison reform" at the home of the superintendent.[87] According to the Stenton Child Center's synopsis of the police report, Valerie had her seventeen-month-old daughter in hand when she was arrested, and she refused to give her child to police.[88] Valerie's baby was examined at Philadelphia General Hospital, then taken to Stenton Child Center by police on July 10, 1975. The baby was later placed in foster care in Rittenhouse Square. According to the Department of Welfare commissioner, a representative from the American Civil Liberties Union petitioned for Valerie's daughter to be returned to MOVE headquarters and cared for by other MOVE adults, but the appeal was refused unless the home could be

---

[85] Leon S. Rosenthal, *A History of Philadelphia's University City* (1963; repr., Philadelphia, 1998), pt. 9.

[86] Fred Hamilton, "Powelton Groups Clash over Houses," *Philadelphia Daily News*, Jan. 29, 1974.

[87] "Four From MOVE Held in Protest."

[88] Department of Public Welfare Case Record for Child, Life Africa, Mother, Valerie Africa and Father, Steve Africa, July 11–14, 1975, box 43, folder 7, PSIC, SCRC.

"investigated" to ensure safety. The home was later inspected, though it did not result in Valerie's daughter's prompt return. The Department of Public Welfare wrote, "MOVE may not be totally societally acceptable but it does not appear that the children are neglected."[89]

In the aftermath, Valerie and other MOVE people challenged the legality of the separation by calling the press. The *Philadelphia Daily News* reported that Valerie's seventeen-month-old daughter was held for forty-eight hours after Valerie's release from the House of Correction.[90] Louise also described Valerie's arrest: "when she tried to keep them from taking her child she was tripped and punched. They threw her literally into the lock-up, and took her child."[91] Valerie's experience, Louise further noted, was shared by other MOVE women whose children were also "arrested" and handled with force right alongside their mothers, who were often beaten by prison matrons.[92]

MOVE women like Valerie, along with other Black women and mothers in this period, were punished not only by police but also by city welfare agencies. The city welfare department enacted surveillance and social control by visiting MOVE's home, effectively demonizing MOVE's non-nuclear, non-normative family while simultaneously marking white and upwardly mobile Rittenhouse Square as the standard. During the 1960s and '70s, the carceral state was reinforced by social welfare programs and agencies that policed hegemonic values and used punitive, moralistic measures to control socially marginalized communities.[93] According to criminal justice scholar Beth Richie, welfare reform inscribed poverty as an issue of individual responsibility and subsequently left Black women to receive support services that still sanctioned, surveilled, and policed their social and family lives. Black women especially lost "rights to privacy" as they were "forced to make information public," which often left them "vulnerable to moral judgements and criminal sanctions."[94] Welfare insti-

---

[89] Report of the Department of Welfare Commissioner Joseph Wnukowski, July 14, 1975, Dept. of Human Services documents, box 43, SCRC. The question of MOVE children's welfare circulated throughout the 1970s and well into the 1980s, in spite of instances like this one involving Valerie's child, who was determined to be in good health. This question was posed as a response to MOVE's lifestyle, diet, and homeschooling. See, for example, "VA MOVErs Held On Child Neglect Charges," *Philadelphia Bulletin*, Jan. 16, 1980.

[90] "City Kept Tot Mother Charges," *Philadelphia Daily News,* July 15, 1975.

[91] Louise Africa, "On the MOVE," *Philadelphia Tribune*, Dec. 9, 1975.

[92] Africa.

[93] Beth Richie, *Arrested Justice: Black Women, Violence, and America's Prison Nation* (New York, 2012), 106–7.

[94] Richie, 112–13.

tutions were indeed a particular source of violence for MOVE women. Instead of being a system of support, these institutions disrupted MOVE's family life as a punitive measure and thus extended the work of the local police. In its report—already biased since it was a synopsis of the police record—the Philadelphia Department of Welfare omitted the fact that Valerie was brutalized. An ostensible institution of social welfare and protection thereby acted as an extension of Philadelphia's carceral apparatus, denying the legitimacy of MOVE people's kinship bonds by refusing to return the child to a home full of adults capable of offering care. It sanctioned MOVE's nonbiological familial bonds and denied Valerie's right to motherhood as a Black woman.

These systematic intrusions on MOVE family life came to a head when Janine Africa's baby, Life, was murdered. The death of Life Africa ignited a turning point for MOVE people. On March 8, 1976, Janine Africa gave birth to her and Phil Africa's son, whom she named Life Africa. Like other MOVE children, Life Africa was born at home, entering the world through what MOVE considered the most "instinctual" way, without doctors or medication.[95] As Life Africa was approaching three weeks old, there was cause for more celebration. In the early morning hours on Sunday, March 28, seven MOVE people were released from the House of Correction.[96] Upon their release, MOVE people celebrated in the front yard of their home. Neighbors recalled vibrant sounds of joy. One neighbor remembered hearing MOVE "talking and laughing amongst themselves like always—just being happy."[97] Janine recalled that MOVE people were in high spirits while greeting family members home from prison.[98]

The police halted the celebration, and violence ensued, resulting in the injury and arrest of several MOVE members and the death of Life Africa. What happened in between the arrival of freed MOVE people, the violent disruption by the police, and later the death of Life Africa was highly contested. According to Janine, police gave diverging reasons for the officers' presence. They first claimed that a resident had reported a fight in the area but later said they were responding to a noise complaint. Janine

[95] Bennetts, "She Says Natural Childbirth. And Really Means It"; Louise Africa, "On the MOVE," *Philadelphia Tribune*, Mar. 16, 1976.

[96] *25 YEARS ON THE MOVE* (Philadelphia, 1996), 13, box 1, folder 158.N, MOVE Collection, Charles L. Blockson Afro-American Collection, SCRC.

[97] Louise Africa, "On the MOVE," *Philadelphia Tribune*, Apr. 17, 1976.

[98] A. Brahmin Ahmaddiya, "In Their Own Words: Memories and Pain," in "MOVE," special issue, *Philadelphia Tribune*, May 14, 1993.

remembered that they arrived with their lights off. When MOVE questioned their presence, Janine recalled, police "started swinging their Blackjacks and everything. I happened to be in front of my husband, and to get to him they just took me and slammed me to the ground . . . kicked and stomped me. I had my baby in my arms and with that pressure, the baby's skull was crushed on the sidewalk."[99] Knowing that MOVE's naturalist beliefs excluded autopsies, police denied the baby's existence altogether.[100] Still, Janine remembered that police saw the child during their surveillance detail of MOVE's house while she sat on the front porch. Civil affairs officers also inquired about the child's whereabouts in the aftermath, according to their surveillance detail report.[101]

Louise Africa collected the statements of neighborhood eyewitnesses. None of the neighbors remembered hearing police sirens. They said police "came in quiet." The only sounds the neighbors remembered were those of screams and barking dogs. Gregory Richardson said police beat MOVE people "unmercifully with nightsticks . . . on the feet, legs, across the back . . . I just knew one or two of them would be killed." One female neighbor, Beverly Glover, said there were screams "like someone was being raped."[102] MOVE never did produce a body but instead challenged the city on their own terms, hosting a dinner at their home for local media and officials to bear witness over the baby's body. Councilman Lucien Blackwell called for a full investigation after visiting MOVE's home, but the organization refused to produce Life's body, and the city refused to investigate.[103]

The police likely knew that MOVE would not produce the baby's body or have legal documentation of his birth, making the officer's denial of his existence convenient. In spite of their surveillance of MOVE people, police still invoked their power to quite literally disappear the suffering of a Black mother and child and of MOVE people altogether. Janine's loss reflects the particular effects of the carceral state on Black women, as we are placed in ever closer proximity to the premature deaths of our children, partners, and of course ourselves. The violence Janine endured was legiti-

[99] Ahmaddiya.
[100] Linn Washington, "Full Investigation of MOVE Baby's Death Is Demanded By Councilman," *Philadelphia Tribune*, Apr. 13, 1976.
[101] Washington; Information Report RE: Arrest of MOVE Organization Members, Civil Affairs Unit, Wednesday March 28, 1976, private collection of Michael Davis Africa Jr.
[102] Louise Africa, "On the MOVE," *Philadelphia Tribune*, Apr. 17, 1976.
[103] Washington, "Full Investigation of MOVE Baby's Death is Demanded By Councilman"; "DA Refuses Action On MOVE Claim," *Philadelphia Evening Bulletin*, Apr. 13, 1976.

mated but rendered invisible at once. The city denied her motherhood, and she was effectively punished for claiming the status of mother at all, especially while also being Black and revolutionary, both of which were already condemned categories. As historian Kali Gross writes, Black women "are not entitled to the law's protection, though they [cannot] escape its punishment." [104] Instead, Black women have had to create avenues of justice for ourselves. MOVE people did just this when they channeled their experiences of family loss into a politics of armed self-defense. The death of Janine's baby initiated a series of events that shifted the course of MOVE people's lives and ideologies and led to the city's intensified show of force, not only in the form of surveillance but also the biological warfare of a starvation blockade and later the Powelton raid.

MOVE'S TURNING POINT

The Civil Disobedience Unit maintained its existing surveillance detail around MOVE's home in the aftermath of Janine's loss. Supposedly, the detail was in response to threats from MOVE people about bombing the Sixteenth District. Of course, the claim of bomb threats was an ongoing tactic for the unit to destabilize Black resistance. The unit spent full days from March to August 1976 watching MOVE people's daily lives, washing cars, selling papers, and walking dogs.[105] The MOVE family was being surveilled by police well before the city officially inaugurated and documented their twenty-four-hour surveillance of MOVE in 1977 as part of the common pleas court eviction order. Officers on duty saw "no unusual activity," even though MOVE was unloading ten long wooden boards from a bus to the front of their home.

These boards likely supported the platform that MOVE people eventually built in front of their home for their May 1977 porch protest, which was also their first show of armed self-defense. On May 20, 1977, MOVE

[104] Kali Gross, "African American Women, Mass Incarceration, and the Politics of Reform," *Journal of American History* 201 (2015): 25–26.

[105] Information Report, Civil Affairs Unit, Wednesday April 14, 1976, private collection of Michael Davis Africa Jr. The Civil Affairs Unit information reports detail police surveillance outside the MOVE organization's home at 309 North Thirty-Third Street. Logging activity across twenty-four-hour surveillance details, the reports also include incremental descriptions of officers' observations during their surveillance duty. Each individual report is typewritten and hand initialed in the top right corner. This particular set of reports is 126 pages in length. It begins with a report on Sunday, March 28, 1976, and ends on Thursday, August 19, 1976. I have not been able to obtain these documents through Temple University or the Philadelphia City Archives because these institutions do not hold the records.

people mounted the platform dressed uniformly in khaki jumpsuits, holding shotguns and protesting in their megaphone, calling for the release of their political prisoners and an end to police use of force.[106] Following MOVE's platform protest, Mayor Rizzo explicitly ordered twenty-four-hour surveillance of their home.[107] This surveillance blockade lasted for nearly a year, into March of 1978. MOVE people maintained their position of armed self-defense in the presence of open police monitoring. Rizzo's public call for a twenty-four-hour surveillance blockade effectively spectacularized the surveillance of MOVE while obscuring the fact that covert surveillance of the group had been in place since at least 1974—prior to the guns and even to DiBona's zoning order. Meanwhile, warrants were issued for MOVE people who took arms during the May 20 demonstration.[108] The city's use of increasing militaristic and carceral force against MOVE was reaching its climax.

Rizzo pushed to intensify the siege around MOVE's home and starve their members out. On March 16, 1978, a court-ordered starvation blockade was erected around MOVE's home. Hundreds of police sealed off a four-block radius in the Powelton area and manned sharpshooter posts around the neighborhood. They prevented all food and water from going into MOVE's home in spite of the men, women, and young children inside. The starvation blockade was granted even against the better judgment of some members of the Pennsylvania Supreme Court.[109] Several negotiators worked to mediate between MOVE and city officials, including Black activist Walter Palmer.[110] Powelton residents and community groups protested the blockade and the police presence in Powelton for much of the year.[111] MOVE people, along with their neighbors, were held captive in their own community.

[106] Frank Heik et al., "A Standoff in West Philadelphia: It's MOVE vs. the Police," *Philadelphia Inquirer*, May 21, 1977.

[107] Dick Cooper, "Standoff: MOVE, Police Sit and Stare," *Philadelphia Inquirer*, Nov. 21, 1977.

[108] Ray Holton and Robert Terry, "At Catastrophe's Brink in Powelton," *Philadelphia Inquirer*, Mar. 19, 1978.

[109] Pennsylvania Supreme Court justice Robert Nix Jr., who was Black, questioned the legality and "justifiability" of the blockade in his concurring opinion to dismiss MOVE's application for stay and petition for writ of prohibition against the trial court's order of the blockade. Supreme Court of Pennsylvania Eastern District "Order" No. 36 E. E. Miscellaneous Docket 1978, *City of Philadelphia v. Donald Glassey*, Mar. 15, 1978, PSIC, SCRC.

[110] Palmer was among the leadership of the BPUM, one of the first Black Power organizations in the city, established in 1965. He was also a member of the Citywide Community Coalition For Human Rights, a neighborhood group that helped MOVE negotiate with the city. See Hizkias Assefa, *The MOVE Crisis in Philadelphia: Extremist Groups and Conflict Resolution* (Pittsburgh, 1990).

[111] One thousand "anti-blockade, anti-Rizzo demonstrators" rallied all night at City Hall in protests organized by the Citywide Black Community Coalition for Human Rights. See Karen Datko,

The city legitimated its already existent police and civil affairs campaign of domestic terror against MOVE through the civil courts with zoning laws. Along with MOVE arrests, zoning laws became the basis for openly carrying out and intensifying the surveillance of and biological warfare against MOVE. The city even used neighbor complaints to effect its violent campaign. Neighbors were, in fact, dissatisfied with some of MOVE's practices, especially in the close proximity of the small Powelton city blocks. However, there were more neighbors, many of whom brought food and water to support MOVE, who were willing to come to agreement without the presence of police occupation.[112] Some neighbors were "roughed up and detained" for so much as talking to MOVE members. Police violence and surveillance of MOVE trickled down to other Powelton residents, who were required to show identification to enter their neighborhood and even faced random searches, fines, and harassment.[113]

The blockade culminated in May 1978 with a ten-point, ninety-day agreement between MOVE and the city. MOVE prisoners would be released on their own recognizance (ROR) if they agreed to first turn over their arms, allow the city to inspect their home, and ultimately vacate the home within ninety days. After the city searched the home and confiscated all weapons, MOVE's prisoners were released.[114] The city's willingness to replace incarceration with displacement suggests that officials saw MOVE as more of a threat to housing development than to public safety. This also reveals the political nature of MOVE people's incarceration today. Displacement and forced movement became a stand-in for MOVE's incarceration and one of many ways to destabilize MOVE's presence and maintain control over the ideological and spatial limits imposed on Black, insurgent bodies.

After ninety days, though, both sides challenged the agreement, which ultimately became ineffective. According to MOVE members, since the city continued to find reasons to summon MOVE into court for misde-

---

"Sympathizers March on City Hall," *Philadelphia Tribune*, Apr. 8, 1978. On April 16, fifty individuals protested the blockade, and nineteen people in the crowd were taken into police custody for trying to bring food to MOVE people. "MOVE Member Defects," *Philadelphia Inquirer*, Apr. 17, 1978.

[112] Of the five groups in the neighborhood that emerged during the years of the Powelton siege, four were either pro-MOVE or willing to negotiate so MOVE could remain. Assefa, *The MOVE Crisis in Philadelphia*, 29–33; Robert Terry, "MOVE Supporters Rally in West Phila," *Philadelphia Inquirer*, July 10, 1977; "Neighbors of MOVE Want Police to Go," *Philadelphia Inquirer*, July 1, 1977.

[113] Linn Washington, "Police Apply Repressive Tactics Against MOVE," *Philadelphia Tribune*, June 21, 1977.

[114] "Jailed Members Released, MOVE Surrendering Guns," *Philadelphia Bulletin*, May 9, 1978.

meanors, continuing the criminalization of MOVE during the ninety-day pact, the agreement was void.[115] The city maintained that MOVE had violated the terms by failing to vacate. When the ninety days expired in early August 1978 with MOVE still occupying North Thirty-Third Street, police proceeded to raid the home.

AUGUST 8, 1978

The police raid began at approximately 6:00 a.m. The street was packed with at least five hundred police officers, firemen, a bulldozer, reporters, photographers, and dogcatchers. MOVE people were barricaded in the basement as police surrounded the home. After the bulldozer destroyed the fence and platform around MOVE's home, a crane smashed in windows, and firefighter deluge guns poured high-pressure water into the home, officers entered the home and began sawing through the floors. The attack evidenced the military power and federal dollars that were endowed to local police departments through the War on Crime.[116] Eventually shots were exchanged. Police officers and members of the *Philadelphia Inquirer* staff maintained that MOVE fired the initial shot that morning and fatally injured one officer, James Ramp.[117] Still, many neighbors, and even journalist Linn Washington, have insisted that the shot was friendly fire that came from behind Ramp.[118] The only uncontestable detail of the day was the brutal beating of Delbert Africa, which was captured on camera. Officers dragged Delbert by his hair, kicking and beating him while he was on the ground surrendering.[119] The police brutality MOVE had charged police with for years was finally captured on video and in photographs.

By 12:20 p.m., MOVE's home was leveled by the city. The district

[115] Pamela Smith, "MOVE Declares City Breaking Its Agreement," *Philadelphia Tribune*, June 23, 1978.

[116] Murray Dubin, "MOVE Routed in Gun Battle with Police," *Philadelphia Inquirer*, Aug. 9, 1978; Pamela Smith, "Bulldozers Fail to Destroy Spirit of MOVE after Demolishing Compound," *Philadelphia Tribune*, Aug. 11, 1978.

[117] Dubin.

[118] Some reporters claimed that the shots came from a sniper in a neighboring house, "but police discounted the story." See Gregory Jaynes, "Officer is Killed as Philadelphia Radicals Are Evicted," *New York Times*, Aug. 11, 1978; see Linn Washington's interview in the documentary *MOVE!* directed by Ben Garry and Ryan McKenna (Cohort Media, 2004); Elmer Smith, "2 More Testify that MOVE Didn't Fire First," *Philadelphia Bulletin*, Apr. 16, 1980.

[119] Christopher M. Hepp, "MOVE Beating Trial Ends in Acquittal by Order of Judge," *Philadelphia Evening Bulletin*, Feb. 8, 1981, PEBC, SCRC.

attorney and city officials maintained that MOVE's home was bulldozed because MOVE might reoccupy.[120] Yet the city accepted bids for a demolition contract on August 2, 1978, only a day after the ninety-day agreement expired.[121] The city's quickness to secure economic gain from the destruction of MOVE's home and family demonstrates the profit-driven nature of the city's removal of MOVE. Nine years later, Drexel constructed an apartment building on the site.

The trial for the MOVE 9, including pretrial hearings, lasted until May 6, 1980, then extended into the next year when sentencing occurred on August 4, 1981.[122] Nine MOVE adults were sentenced to thirty to one hundred years in prison for charges of third degree murder and other assault charges related to the death of police officer James Ramp.[123] MOVE people defended themselves in court with court-appointed lawyers as co-counsel.

The city's decision to level MOVE's home, obscuring the scene and any viable evidence, was a highly contested issue during the trial. The city used police testimony and video in the stead of physical evidence, with the former especially prominent. Police officers, including Charles Stewart, claimed in their testimonies to have seen gunfire and flashes coming from the MOVE basement. Upon cross-examination from MOVE member Michael Africa, though, Stewart's testimony showed inaccuracies.[124] Overall, the leveling of the home left open the question of whether the city had suppressed evidence that would have made for a fair trial for MOVE.

Questions remained about the autopsy report of James Ramp having been tampered with as well.[125] MOVE people maintained that officer Ramp could have been shot by friendly fire; some officers, including Ramp, were at street level, while other officers fired from balconies

---

[120] A. Geiselman, "MOVE Site Razing No Cover-up," *Philadelphia Evening Bulletin*, Jan. 9, 1980, PEBC, SCRC.

[121] Appellate Brief from the Office of District Attorney Edward G. Rendell to the Superior Court of Pennsylvania RE: Commonwealth v. Africa.

[122] Joyce Gemperlein, "9 in MOVE Get 30 Years for Killing," *Philadelphia Inquirer*, Aug. 5, 1981, PEBC, SCRC. Two other adults in the house who were supporters were convicted of lesser charges, and another supporter was arrested but not charged.

[123] Gemperlein.

[124] A. W. Geiselman Jr., "Diagram on MOVE Has Error," *Philadelphia Evening Bulletin*, Jan. 18, 1980, PEBC, SCRC.

[125] Brief by the Inter-American Commission of Human Rights in the Matter of Ramona Africa v. United States of America, the State of Pennsylvania, by Teri B. Himebaugh, Esq., p. 24, PSIC, SCRC.

above.[126] Witnesses speculated that the officer could have been shot by a third party person who was seen being arrested for being armed in the area. [127]

Ultimately, the MOVE 9 were sentenced in absentia, which was characteristic of their trial, during which MOVE people were regularly ejected from court. They were sometime bound and gagged for flagrant protests against the legal proceedings.[128] At the end of the trial, their lawyers questioned the legitimacy of the judge's "across the board" sentences for all nine defendants in light of the one murder in question.[129] The sentencing judge, Edwin S. Malmed, justified the identical sentences by noting that the MOVE 9 had "repeatedly shouted they were a family . . . Therefore, I have treated them as a family with equal guilt shared for all."[130] Judge Malmed's statement revealed the arbitrary discretion and even bias inherent in his sentence.

THE MOVE 9

Janet, Janine, Debbie, Merle, Chuck, Eddie, Michael, Phil, and Delbert were the nine members of the MOVE family who were imprisoned in 1978. Until recent years, they all lived as political prisoners who were incarcerated for confronting the criminal justice system. Throughout their years in prison, they faced persecution in many forms—through solitary confinement, forced medical interventions, and prison officials' threats to cut their hair.[131] Still, the MOVE 9 sustained their prison resistance. They continued using hunger strikes and prison uprisings to challenge

[126] A. W. Geiselman Jr., "2 MOVE Defendants Ejected for 2nd Time Today," *Philadelphia Evening Bulletin*, Jan. 8, 1980, PEBC, SCRC.

[127] Brief by the Inter-American Commission of Human Rights in the Matter of Ramona Africa v. United States of America, the State of Pennsylvania, 29.

[128] Dave Racher, "9 MOVErs Get 30 Year-Terms In Shootout," *Philadelphia Daily News*, Aug. 4, 1981, PEBC, SCRC; Elmer Smith, "5 MOVE Members Bound, Gagged," May 17, 1979, *Philadelphia Evening Bulletin*, PEBC, SCRC. MOVE members' "disruptions" consisted of refusing to stand for a judge's entry, using profanity, or charging the judge, police, and prosecutor with colluding with Mayor Rizzo.

[129] Gemperlein, "9 In MOVE Get 30 Years for Killing."

[130] Racher, "9 MOVErs Get 30 Year-Terms In Shootout."

[131] Ahmaddiya, "In Their Own Words." Debbie and Merle were held in solitary confinement for three years for refusing prison medical exams. See Wayne Browne, "MOVE Takes Case to Public," *Philadelphia Tribune*, Aug. 11, 1992; prison physician Dr. Ernest Williams noted that prisons were forcibly drawing blood and threatening to snip the dreadlocks of MOVE members for "health reasons." Pamela Smith, "Prison Physician in Disagreement with 'Administrative Policies,'" *Philadelphia Tribune*, Dec. 5, 1978.

everyday prison oppression and gender violence.[132] They also maintained their anticarceral writings, including an independent news organ, *First Day*, which published the writings of the MOVE 9 and other political prisoners through the 1990s.[133]

Mostly in their late teens and twenties when they went to prison, the surviving members of the MOVE 9 are in their sixties and seventies today. Two members of the MOVE 9 have passed away since 1978. Merle Africa died in 1998 and Phil Africa in 2015, both under suspicious circumstances.[134] Over a decade after serving their minimum thirty-year sentence, several MOVE people have finally been released. Childhood sweethearts Michael and Debbie Africa were released in 2018. Eddie, Janet, and Janine Africa were released in 2019. They are now living with the demands of parole, which restrict their movement out of Pennsylvania and require them to find jobs even as they are scarcely able to navigate the challenges of reentry or the new digital landscape. The freedom of Chuck and Delbert Africa remains elusive; to date the courts have continually denied them parole in spite of the fact that they are both battling for their physical health, with Chuck Africa living with cancer. Both men are still imprisoned at SCI Dallas. They are among a lineage of other twentieth-century Black radicals continuing their freedom struggle from behind bars, displaced from fellow organizers. We must bring their experiences out of obscurity not only to honor that long struggle but also to better understand mass incarceration and its foundations in the confinement of late twentieth-century freedom fighters. Far from a new or passing phenomenon, mass incarceration is deeply embedded in our daily lives, violently organizing where and who we are and displacing the possibilities for dispossessed peoples to live freely.

University of Pennsylvania   TAJAH EBRAM

---

[132] In December 1981, MOVE men at Holmesburg rioted alongside other prisoners after realizing that a group of women at the House of Correction, including one MOVE woman, were brutalized by matrons. Violence ensued after guards used fire hoses to extract men who had refused to leave their cells. "Cops Got Late Call For Melee: Inmates Said to Protest Treatment of Women," *Philadelphia Bulletin*, Dec. 4, 1981.

[133] *First Day*, Mar. 1994, Ramona Africa Papers, Amistad Research Center, Tulane University, New Orleans, LA.

[134] Sam Roberts, "Phil Africa, of Black-Liberation Group Move, Long in Prison, Dies at 59," *New York Times*, Jan. 15, 2015.

A Hidden Gem Becomes a Fertile Mining Ground: Historic Prison Admission Books and Data-Driven Digital Projects

THE LIBRARY OF THE AMERICAN PHILOSOPHICAL SOCIETY holds three admission books that provide a personal biography of each inmate at the Eastern State Penitentiary. The books, covering the years 1830–50 (with a gap in the 1840s), contain information about each prisoner, including their name, age, the crimes for which they had been convicted, their sentence, and often a note on when they were freed (or died). Also included, though less consistently, is gender, race, and religious affiliation. Additionally, the penitentiary's moral instructor, a religious authority figure, recorded a paragraph-length note on each inmate detailing their religious education and other biographical details (fig. 1).

Donated to the APS Library between 2000 and 2002, the admission books complement and extend a larger collection of material related to the Eastern State Penitentiary. Within this collection is a wide variety of treasures. One such treasure is a set of correspondence from a prisoner in the penitentiary, Elizabeth Velora Elwell, addressed to another inmate. According to the collection's finding aid, the letters "suggest that Elwell carried a passionate love for a fellow prisoner at Eastern State, Albert Green Jackson, with hints that they may have met clandestinely on more than one occasion. It appears that the two had plans to marry when their terms expired."[1] The collection also contains a number of other volumes that detail the bureaucratic functioning of the penitentiary, including the daily rations and the overseer's roll.[2]

Even within this collection of gems, the admission books command

---

[1] See series 3: Elizabeth Velora Elwell letters of the State Penitentiary for the Eastern District of Pennsylvania Records, American Philosophical Society. Quote taken from the series' background note. For more on Elwell, see Rebecca Capobianco, "'She is the beauty of this place': Elizabeth Velora Elwell and the Role of Prisoner Participation and Deviance at Eastern State Penitentiary," *Pennsylvania Magazine of History and Biography* 142 (2018): 83–106.

[2] These volumes, along with the admission books, are in series 1 of the collection.

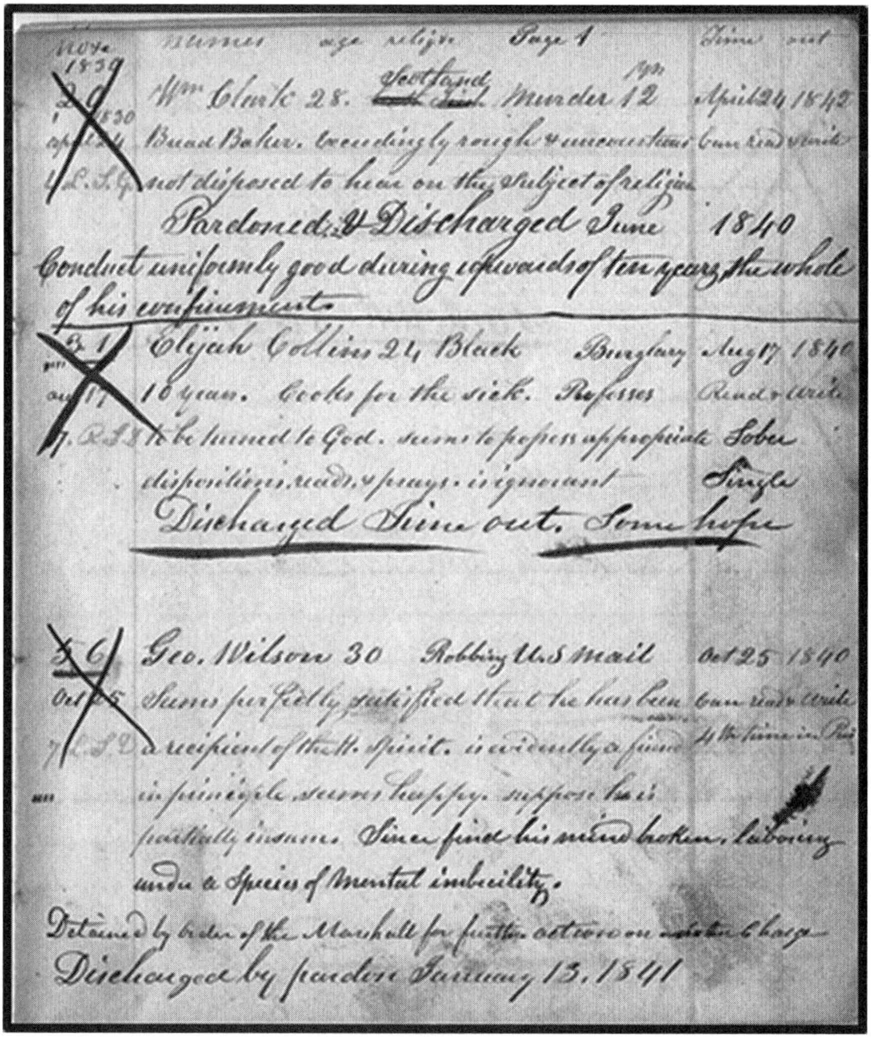
Nos. 1839 Names age religion Page 1 Time out

20 Wm Clark 28. Scotland Murder 12 yrs April 24 1842
Bread Baker. exceedingly rough & unconcerned can read & write
not disposed to hear on the subject of religion
Pardoned & Discharged June 1840
Conduct uniformly good during upwards of ten years the whole of his confinement.

31 Elijah Collins 24 Black Burglary Aug 17 1840
10 years. Cooks for the sick. Professes Read & write
to be turned to God. seems to possess appropriate Sober
dispositions, reads, & prays. ignorant Single
Discharged Time out. Some hope

56 Geo. Wilson 30 Robbing U.S. Mail Oct 25 1840
Seems perfectly satisfied that he has been can read & write
a recipient of the H. Spirit. is evidently a firm 4th time in Pris
in principle. seems happy. suppose he is
partially insane. Since find his mind broken, laboring
under a Species of Mental imbecility.
Detained by order of the Marshall for further action on another charge
Discharged by pardon January 13, 1841

Fig. 1: Sample page from Admission Book A, showing typical entries including name, age, offense, and note by the moral instructor.

special attention. The mix of biographical information, demographics, and moral commentary provides both a glimpse into the population of the penitentiary and into the beliefs that guided the institution. When digitized and transformed into a dataset, the admission books became a particularly fertile mining ground for historical insights.

In 2015, the APS Library digitized the admission books. Then, in 2016 and 2017, the library transcribed the content into spreadsheets. The library published the data in a variety of outlets and encouraged scholars to use the data for a wide range of projects.[3] In late 2017, the APS Library published a digital project based on the historic prison dataset. The project, "Eastern Apps: Visualizing Historic Prison Data," presents a suite of apps that allows users to generate interactive visualizations as a means of exploring the data through text-mining techniques and statistical analysis.[4]

The first app analyzes word frequency in the moral instructor's notes. This app constructs corpora based on user input and presents both word clouds and word frequency graphs (figs. 2 and 3). Additionally, users can explore specific words and phrases in context (figs. 4 and 5). The repetition of words by the moral instructor, and variation in usage over the years, reveals patterns in the individual descriptions of inmates.

The second app graphs sentencing length and maps sentencing location based on selected variables that include gender, age, place of birth, ethnicity, literacy, marital status, sobriety, charge, number of previous convictions, and admission year.[5] Modifying these variables updates both the map and the graph (fig. 6). The map produced by this app shows courts where inmates were sentenced and displays the average sentence length. The outer circle (styled red in the online version) corresponds to the average sentence length; the inner circle (styled blue in the online version) corresponds to the number of cases from that area (fig. 7). The graph shows variation in sentence length. The x-axis corresponds to the length of the sentence in months; the y-axis corresponds to the number of inmates who received a sentence of that length.

[3] In addition to the APS Digital Library (http://diglib.amphilsoc.org/), the datasets were published through the *Magazine of Early American Datasets* (https://repository.upenn.edu/mead/) and the APS Library Github page (https://github.com/AmericanPhilosophicalSociety/Historic-Prison-Data).

[4] Eastern Apps: Visualizing Historic Prison Data, http://diglib.amphilsoc.org/labs/eastern-apps/.

[5] In most cases, gender is not listed by the moral instructor. For the purposes of this analysis, gender is assumed based on pronouns used and first names. The authors acknowledge these assumptions can be problematic and that the nuance of gender and gender expression is not likely to be reflected in official prison records.

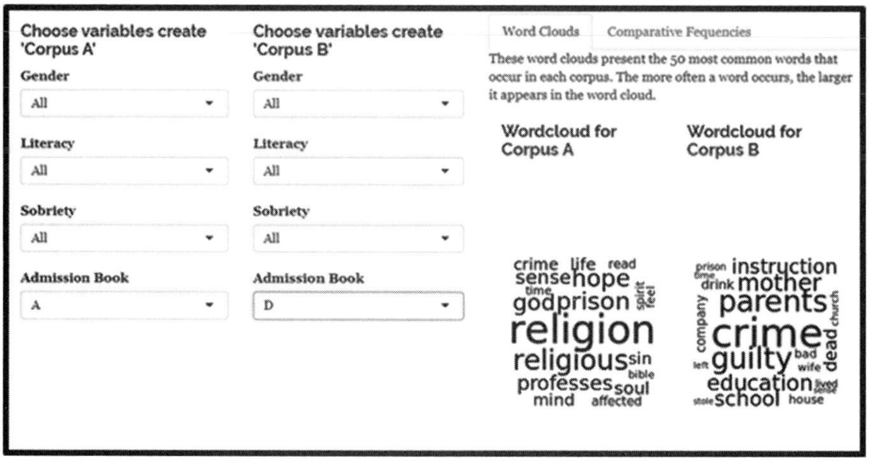

Fig. 2: Word clouds created from two corpora, showing list of variables. In this example, all variables are the same except for the admission book. The selection produces word clouds that reveal the most common words used in the first (1830–39) and last (1845–50) admission book.

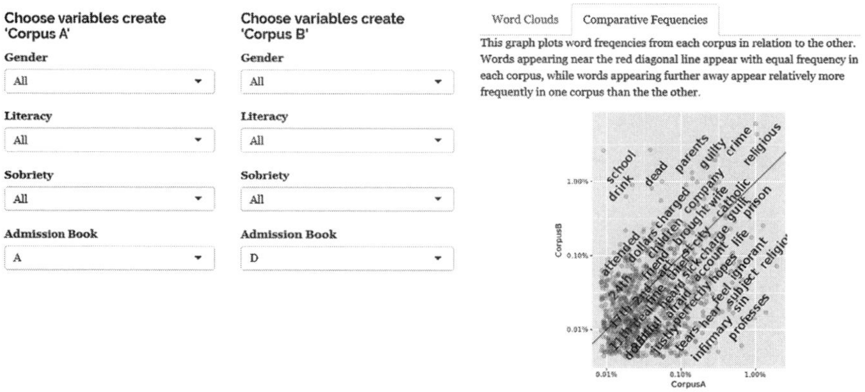

Fig. 3: Comparative word frequency based on two corpora. Using the same selection as fig. 2, the resulting graph shows that such words as "professes" and "sin" appear more prominently in Admission Book A (1830–39), while such words as "school" appear more frequently in Admission Book D (1845–50).

Enter a keyword:

sin

| Keywords in Context | Word Frequency over Time |

Here is the keyword as it appears in the descriptions recorded by the Moral Instructor.

Corpus A

pre	keyword	post	AdmissionDate	PrisonerNumber	FirstName	LastName	Source
No true sense of the evil of	sin	.	1/16/1836	559	Edward	Carnes	Admission Book A Admission Book A
obtained a joyful hope . Relapsed into	sin	, lost all his enjoyment . Has	4/9/1836	584	Augustus	Latimer	Admission Book A Admission Book A
his enjoyment . Has kept from that	sin	more than a year , but has	4/9/1836	584	Augustus	Latimer	Admission Book A Admission Book A
Seems unacquainted with the guilt of	sin	, but heard with some interest and	4/18/1836	588	Israel	Smith	Admission Book A Admission Book A
mind . Overwhelmed with a sense of	sin	, he cried out . Visited and	6/30/1836	603	John	Brown	Admission Book A Admission Book A
had deep conviction of the evil of	sin	which have resulted in conversion . Seems	8/10/1836	617	George	Carver	Admission Book A Admission Book A
learn if one . So old in	sin	and so vile and ignorant may hope	8/11/1836	618	David	Lindsay	Admission Book A Admission Book A
hope for pardon , no sense of	sin	, nor fear for its desert .	10/6/1836	648	John M.	Williams	Admission Book A Admission Book A
[searct]] vice was a	sin	against God ~ was softened greatly when	5/25/1839	1107	Moses	Hutson	Admission Book A Admission Book A

Corpus B

pre	keyword	post	PrisonerNumber	FirstName	LastName	Source
was tempted and he stole but his	sin	is forgiven and he is happy in	2476	Joseph	Greon	Admission Book D
is guilty of almost every kind of	sin	. (" almost everything bad "	2524	Charlotte	McKraig	Admission Book D
robbed him . Young but hardened in	sin	. Crime at 20 . Cause licentiousness	2544	Ellen	Bayley	Admission Book D

Fig. 4: Searching for keywords in context reveals that the word "sin" appears in such phrases as "no true sense of the sin," "seems unacquainted with the guilt of sin," and "no sense of sin." This suggests that the moral instructor's observations focused on whether inmates knew that their crimes constituted a sin.

Enter a keyword:

school

| Keywords in Context | Word Frequency over Time |

Here is the keyword as it appears in the descriptions recorded by the Moral Instructor.

Corpus A

pre	keyword	post	AdmissionDate	PrisonerNumber	FirstName	LastN.
seems as usual unhappy . Never at	school	utterly ignorant early habits idle and depraved	7/22/1839	1122	William	Presto

Corpus B

pre	keyword	post	PrisonerNumber	FirstName	LastName
. No religious instruction . No Sunday	school	. Crime at 35 . Cause Licentiousness	1941	Letitia	Jackson
. No religious instruction . No Sunday	school	. A stranger to early moral influence	1943	William	Smith
. No religious instruction . No Sunday	school	. Crime at 40 . Drink the	1946	Matthew	Hay
. No religious instruction . No Sunday	school	. Crime at 21 . Cause drink	1947	Moses	Snyder

Fig. 5: Searching for the word "school" in context reveals that in Admission Book D the word sin appears regularly in phrases such as "no Sunday school," often alongside the phrase "no religious instruction." This suggests that the moral instructor was still concerned with the sins committed by inmates, but the inquiry shifted to determining whether an inmate received an education that would make them aware of their sin.

The third app graphs and maps demographic data about the inmates. Based on a single variable, length of sentence in months, the graph compiles basic demographic data about the inmates. For example, for all records (zero to 252 months), the graph shows the variation in gender, ethnicity/race, marital status, and sobriety, among other categories (fig. 8). The map shows the location of sentencing. Over thirty court locations appear, with the size of the circle indicating the number of cases from each location (fig. 9). Analysis of this data shows that for the records with the longest sentences (140 to 252 months), the prisoners were most commonly convicted of burglary, followed by murder. These lengthy sentences came from only three courts: Philadelphia County, Lancaster County, and Montgomery County (fig. 10).

These finding are not conclusive and are not meant to be. The apps were designed to provide an easy and engaging way for researchers to

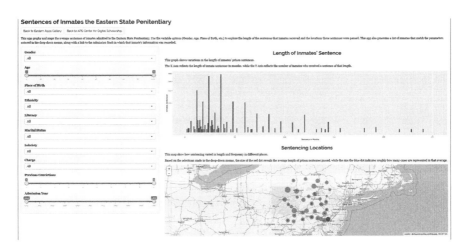

Fig. 6: Demographic data by length of sentence. This example shows all options. By changing the "Length of Sentence in Months" slider at the top, the graphs regenerate to show new data.

interact with the information contained in the admission books in the hope that the resulting patterns and correlations might spark further research. The apps cannot explain why inmates sentenced at the three previously mentioned courthouses received the longest sentences. However, identifying this trend in the data provides a starting point for a potential research project.

The admission books created by the Eastern State Penitentiary and held at the Library of the American Philosophical Society are hidden gems of great interest to a wide variety of researchers. By digitizing this material and reformatting the contents into data for computational analysis, the APS Library has made the admission books into a fertile mining ground for the discovery of additional gems.

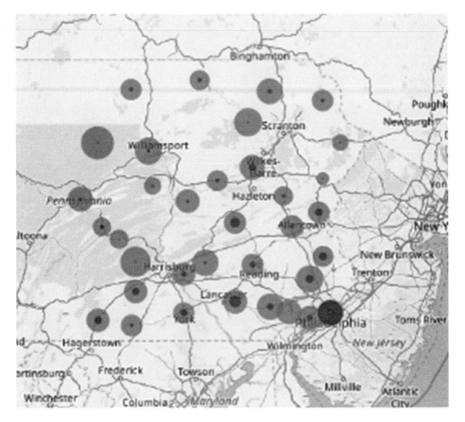

Fig. 7: A graph of offenses and sentencing locations, based on the length chosen. This example shows all options. By changing the "Length of Sentence in Months" slider at the top, the graphs regenerate to show new data.

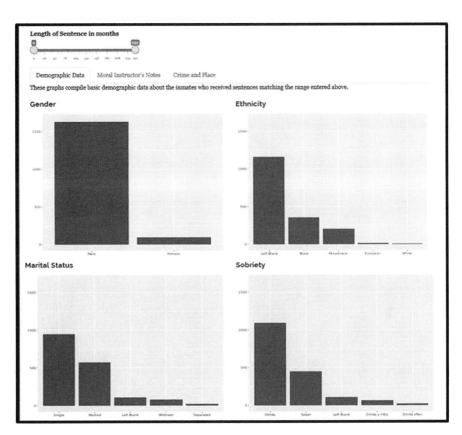

Fig. 8: Demographic data by length of sentence. This example shows all options. By changing the "Length of Sentence in Months" slider at the top, the graphs regenerate to show new data.

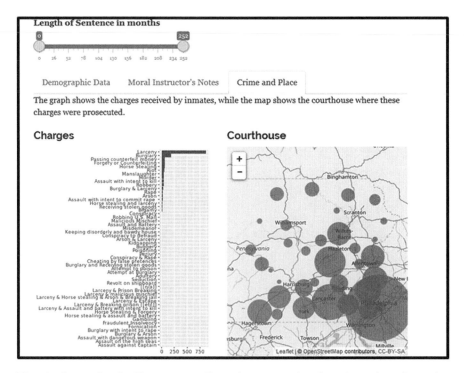

Fig. 9: A graph of offenses as well as the sentencing locations, based on the length criteria chosen. This example shows all options. By changing the "Length of Sentence in Months" slider at the top, the graphs regenerate to show new data.

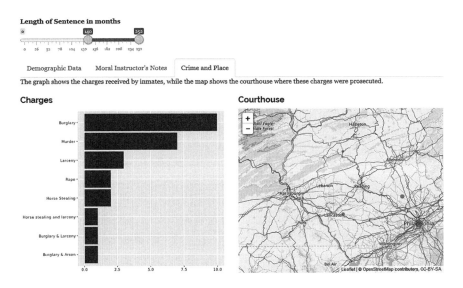

Fig. 10: List of charges and location of sentencing for the longest sentences (140–252 months).

Louisiana State University
Kingston, Ontario

S. L. Ziegler
Steve Marti

Prison Life at Eastern State Penitentiary as Seen through Pardon Records

T HE US CONSTITUTION AUTHORIZES the president of the United
States to "grant Reprieves and Pardons for Offences against the
United States, except in cases of Impeachment."[1] Today, many
Americans assume that this power is often wielded for partisan or personal reasons.[2] Throughout American history, however, ordinary prisoners and their families wrote directly to presidents seeking clemency. This
correspondence, which is organized into case files for each individual convicted of a crime, is housed in Record Group 204 (Records of the Office
of the Pardon Attorney) at the National Archives at College Park, Maryland. Materials in these historic case files offer remarkable windows into
the lives of prison inmates and their families, revealing new perspectives
on the experiences of ordinary Americans who suffered during the separation caused by incarceration.

Case files in RG 204, which span the years 1853 to 1946, typically
begin with an application for presidential clemency, written either by a
prisoner, a spouse or parent, the prisoner's attorney, or someone closely
acquainted with the situation. The size and scope of case files vary widely,
with some including a single document and others containing more than
a decade's worth of paperwork (in some cases, inmates petitioned multiple
presidents for pardon). Case files often include letters of recommendation
or protest, correspondence from politicians or lawyers who had partici-
pated in the imprisoned person's trial, statements from judges and prosecutors regarding the facts of the case, affidavits from prison wardens and
physicians regarding the applicant's behavior and health, trial transcripts,
briefs, and the reports and recommendations of the pardon attorney and
attorney general. Case files also often include statements regarding the
petitioner's character written by friends, neighbors, family members, for-

---

[1] U.S. Const., art. 2, sec. 2 (1787).

[2] See, for example, Jessica Reaves, "Pardongate Play-by-Play," *Time*, Feb. 27, 2001; and Matt
Ford, "The Problem with Trump's Pardons: How the President is Using His Executive Power to
Protect Himself," *New Republic*, June 1, 2018.

THE PENNSYLVANIA MAGAZINE OF HISTORY AND BIOGRAPHY
Vol. CXLIII, No. 3 (October 2019)

mer employers, or prison officials. Researchers can locate specific cases, or cases from particular jurisdictions, using the dockets, record books, lists, and indexes in RG 204.[3]

Historians have underutilized pardon case files, which are ripe for more scholarly attention. Records from the Civil War era in particular offer spectacular perspectives on the social history of the war and the effects of the conflict upon individuals and families on the home front.[4] Pardon records reveal a new view of the suffering that thousands of families in the North endured. The absence of so many men from their homes magnified financial burdens, and wives, mothers, fathers, and children adopted desperate measures to find necessary income while a loved one (usually the breadwinner) was stuck behind bars. Pardon records thus reveal the physical, mental, fiscal, and emotional toll of incarceration on those who remained outside of the prison gate.

Requests for pardon also lend insight into nineteenth-century Americans' understandings of civic responsibility and individual rights. As the Union war effort evolved into a struggle against slavery, incarcerated Northerners wrestled with their own place as unfree members of a free society—one in which they had lost not only their personal autonomy but also their citizenship rights. Often, prisoners situated their appeals for freedom in terms of their willingness to fight for the Union. In some cases, veterans who had served in the armed forces informed President Lincoln about what they had already done on behalf of the nation.

This article uses Civil War-era pardon requests from prisoners at Eastern State Penitentiary in Philadelphia to offer examples of the types of insights that historians can glean from these records. Franklin M. Read's file, for example, is instructive. On August 27, 1861, Read was convicted of embezzling $2 from a letter. According to news reports, he worked as a clerk at the post office in Philadelphia for twenty-four years, and "it was thought that he has for several years been tampering with the mails."[5] Secretary of the Interior Caleb B. Smith assured the Read family that a pardon would be granted within a year of Franklin's conviction, but a year passed, and no action had been taken. Franklin's wife, Elizabeth Read,

---

[3] For additional guidance in how to conduct archival research in legal and judicial history, see Jonathan W. White, *Guide to Research in Federal Judicial History* (Washington, DC, 2010).

[4] For analysis rooted in pardon records from the Civil War era, see Jonathan W. White, "The Presidential Pardon Records of the Lincoln Administration," *Journal of the Abraham Lincoln Association* 39 (2018): 55–65.

[5] *Clearfield* (PA) *Raftman's Journal*, Sept. 4, 1861.

wrote to several members of the Lincoln administration to follow up on Smith's promise. Writing in a state of utter despair, Elizabeth explained that she was unable to provide for her six children and that she relied on charity from friends and neighbors for survival. "For the last few months we have been compelled to subsist principally on dry bread and tea, meat or vegetables being impossible for us to obtain, except [when] sent to us by some kind friend," she wrote. The Read family was now indebted to several local merchants, she explained, "with no prospect of paying them." She worried that at any "moment we may all be turned in the street." In a letter to Secretary Smith, Franklin confirmed his wife's inability to make a living and claimed that she had been unable to work for twenty years because "the end of her fingers are almost eaten off, so much so, that it is with the greatest difficulty she can dress her children." He also informed the secretary that Elizabeth had resorted to selling their furniture to make ends meet.[6]

Pardon files like Read's can also take readers inside the walls of the penitentiary, giving them a rare glimpse of those few fleeting, intimate moments when prisoners got to see their loved ones. In one letter, Franklin described a visit he received from his family, which ended in "one fond embrace and all eyes filled with tears at our very sad fate." He informed Secretary Smith that his children asked him when he would come home and told him "how they wished that they could get in my cell to hug and kiss me, it is enough to break ones heart." On other occasions, Read's children asked if he would be home by Christmas or the Fourth of July. For two years, Elizabeth pleaded with officials in Washington to bring her husband home and restore the "happy family we once were." "Do for Gods sake act quickly," she implored, "and save us from utter destruction." For some unknown reason, Lincoln never chose to act in this case. Franklin M. Read served four years of his ten-year sentence and was pardoned by President Andrew Johnson on November 20, 1865.[7]

Another wife appealed to Lincoln as a merciful and forgiving president in an attempt to persuade him to pardon her husband. Mary E. Armstrong's "unfortunate husband," Christopher Armstrong, a fifty-year-old shoemaker, was sentenced to three years of solitary confinement on

---

[6] Elizabeth Read to Edward Bates, June 16 and Dec. 15, 1862, Dec. 3, 1863, and Feb. 16, 1864, Franklin Read to Caleb B. Smith, Dec. 8, 1862, and May 19, 1865, all in pardon case file A-408, RG 204, entry 1a (pardon case files, 1853–1946), National Archives at College Park (subsequent notes will simply list the pardon case file number).

[7] Elizabeth Read to Caleb Smith, Aug. 21, 1863, pardon case file A-408.

August 23, 1862, for sending forged applications for land warrants to the pension office in Washington. Armstrong left behind his wife, three children, and his seventy-five-year-old father-in-law, who relied on him for support. In late 1863, Mary sent two desperate letters to Lincoln. She explained that the only help she had after her husband's arrest was a seventeen-year-old boy, but he had enlisted twice and was now serving in the Invalid Corps. Now she had no one to help her take care of her family. Mary begged for "mercy from a forgiving God" and advised Lincoln that "we should be willing to show mercy to our fellow beings." She claimed that her husband's crime had not injured the government and reminded the president that "to err is humane [*sic*], to forgive divine." Mary believed that the fourteen months Christopher had already spent in prison "surely ought to be sufficient to satisfy justice it looks like a lifetime to me." More than a year later, Lincoln finally pardoned Armstrong on February 15, 1865, just six months before he was scheduled to be released.[8]

Letters from mothers and fathers also reveal insights into the suffering that families experienced during incarceration. Martha Dunkle, a seventy-three-year-old mother who had survived a stroke that "rendered [her] very helpless," pleaded with Lincoln for the release of her son, James, who was sentenced to five years at Eastern State for forging papers to defraud the US government. "I am very poor and deppendent . . . on my son . . . for support and comfort in my affliction," she wrote to the president. She worried that with her days "nearly numbered," she would live out the remainder of her life in poverty and misery without her son.[9] As in many others, Lincoln chose not to act in this case; however, President Andrew Johnson pardoned Dunkle in June 1867 after he had served four years and eight months of his five-year sentence.[10]

As can be seen in these few short accounts, imprisonment brought disaster and desperation to many households in the mid-nineteenth century. The records of the pardon attorney are a virtually untapped resource

[8] Mary E. Armstrong to Lincoln, Oct. 29 and Dec. 10, 1863, both in pardon case file A-538; *Philadelphia Public Ledger*, Nov. 3, 1862.

[9] Martha M. Dunkle to Lincoln, Feb. 26, 1863, pardon case file A-468. In 1860, James, a former Democrat, had written to Lincoln saying that if Lincoln sent him $2,500, James would stump in the state of Pennsylvania and carry it for the Republicans. See James M. Dunkle to Lincoln, July 16, 1860, Abraham Lincoln Papers, Manuscript Division, Library of Congress, Washington, DC.

[10] Warden's Daily Journals, vol. 2 (1856–1877), roll 6608, Nov. 25, 1887, series 15.50, Records of the Department of Justice, Eastern State Penitentiary, Prison Administration Records, Pennsylvania State Archives, Harrisburg, PA (copy provided by Annie Anderson and Erica Harman of Eastern State).

that offer extraordinary insights into social and political history. Some pardon case files reveal great detail about the mental health struggles of convicts.[11] In other instances, such as those in which prisoners offered their services to the Union army or navy in exchange for a pardon, the case files reveal much about Americans' understandings of civic responsibility.[12] Still others give insights into race relations, such as one case in 1864 in which a group of white Philadelphians wrote to Lincoln on behalf of a black inmate at Eastern State, describing his "reputation" as "a person of good moral character and a peaceful and law abiding citizen."[13] Taken together, pardon case files provide new perspectives on the experiences of prisoners and their families that are not usually present in other archival materials. These records can help historians sketch out a broader and more inclusive history of Pennsylvania and beyond from the mid-nineteenth century to the mid-twentieth.

Christopher Newport University   JONATHAN W. WHITE
                                                    TAYLOR BAGWELL

[11] See, for example, Taylor Bagwell, "Samuel Young: 'An Aberration of Mind,'" Feb. 7, 2019, Eastern State Penitentiary blog, https://www.easternstate.org/about-eastern-state/blog/samuel -young-aberration-mind.

[12] For the stories of two Eastern State prisoners who tried to make such bargains, see Hannah Broughton, "Treacherous Language While in a Passion," *Civil War Navy* 7 (2019): 66–68; and Taylor Bagwell, "A Letter to Lincoln," Oct. 9, 2018, Eastern State Penitentiary blog, https://www.eastern state.org/about-eastern-state/blog/letter-lincoln.

[13] B. F. Reimer and others to Lincoln, n.d. [Sept. 1864], pardon case file A-548. In another case, Lincoln chose not to pardon a black servant of his former political rival. See William M. Palmer, "Unpardoned by Lincoln: Stephen A. Douglas's House Servant," *Lincoln Forum Bulletin* 43 (2018): 4.

Working at the Margins:
Unearthing and Interpreting New
Research at Eastern State Penitentiary

PHILADELPHIA'S EASTERN STATE PENITENTIARY was the world's first true penitentiary, a building designed to inspire *penitence*—or true regret—in the hearts of its inhabitants. It pioneered the practice of solitary confinement, and its influence spanned penal philosophy and design. An architectural marvel, the penitentiary had advanced plumbing, heating, and ventilation systems, and it inspired the floorplans of more than three hundred prisons around the world. Open from 1829–1971, the prison was abandoned for twenty years before becoming a museum and historic site. Today, the site connects the past to the present and offers dialogue-based tours and exhibits about American criminal justice.

The staff at Eastern State Penitentiary is constantly learning new information about the nearly two hundred-year-old-building and the people who lived and worked in it. Archival digs at the Philadelphia City Archives, the Pennsylvania State Archives, and the Historical Society of Pennsylvania have revealed that both prisoners and administrators left paper trails extending throughout the region. These records illuminate the day-to-day realities of incarceration throughout the nineteenth and twentieth centuries for the eighty thousand individuals imprisoned at Eastern State. Documents address both pre- and post-incarceration lives, revealing the circumstances that brought some individuals into crime, what they confessed to prison officials and moral instructors upon arriving at the penitentiary, and the alleged indignities they faced from prosecutors and judges. The records tell of criminal trials, county prison terms, and parole proceedings. In my role as a researcher and public historian at Eastern State, I locate and write about these records, helping to develop exhibits, audio stops, signage, and tour guide training materials. In recent years, my coworkers and I have developed new interpretation on a number of minority populations, including young people, LGBTQ individuals, and people sentenced to Eastern State for acts that have been decriminalized in modern America (abortion, vagrancy, and drug- and alcohol-related crimes). Our goal has been to reveal previously hidden histories and expand the historiography of the penitentiary. Newly unearthed records about two prisoners, Isaac Hall and Charlotte Hilton, instruct us in the anxieties and insecurities penitentiary officials expressed about race, gender, and rehabilitation. The records reveal cultural norms and biases, reminding us of the paternalism and watchfulness always present in penal facilities.

Incarcerated in 1881, Isaac Hall was one of at least 484 people imprisoned at Eastern State for sodomy—a nebulous term criminalizing certain sexual acts, often between members of the same sex. Next to Hall's name on every court and prison document, in perfect cursive handwriting, is the alias "Lady Washington." Hall was either a trailblazing female impersonator, or Hall occupied, in whatever way 1880s Philadelphia allowed, something of a proto-transgender identity. Hall's alias, according to the *Philadelphia Inquirer*, "was obtained by personating lady characters at different times." The newspaper noted that Hall's alias "had much to do with the heavy sentence," but Lady Washington was likely more than just an alias.[1] It seems probable that Hall's set of behaviors—the gender contravention and performance—prompted the harsh sentence of $100 and eight years of solitary confinement for what records indicate was consensual sex with a male partner. The person arrested with Hall, a man named H. C. Campbell, pled guilty to a sodomy charge and was discharged by the court.[2] Hall, meanwhile, was tried, convicted, and sentenced within eighteen hours of the alleged incident. The conviction rested on the testimony of one witness.[3]

Hall served six years and six months of the eight-year sentence before being released early for good behavior, as Pennsylvania's commutation law allowed. Upon discharge, warden Michael Cassidy observed that Hall "was convicted in Philad. of sodomy & buggery. [Hall] was known in the locality where he resided as Lady Washington and is no doubt of the kind who are addicted to that crime."[4] Compared to the insults Cassidy regularly slung at other prisoners—he repeatedly referred to them as "worthless creatures" and "lazy, good-for-nothing vagabonds" during his twenty

[1] "Seeking Pardons," *Philadelphia Inquirer*, Apr. 18, 1882.
[2] "Seeking Pardons"; Dockets and Bills of Indictment for Isaac Hall and H. C. Campbell, May 1881, Clerk of Quarter Sessions, RG 21, Philadelphia City Archives, Philadelphia, PA.
[3] "Seeking Pardons."
[4] Michael Cassidy, Warden's Daily Journals, vol. 5 (1886–1888), Nov. 25, 1887, series 15.50, Records of the Department of Justice, Eastern State Penitentiary, Prison Administration Records, Pennsylvania State Archives, Harrisburg, PA.

years as warden—his assessment of Hall was in line with, and perhaps more benevolent than, his typical appraisals. Still, Cassidy's language reveals how non-normative sexual identities and acts were framed in the popular imagination of the era as addictions or compulsions.

After working as a music teacher, Hall died of a stroke in 1902 at the age of fifty-six or fifty-eight. Curiously, on one of Hall's burial records, the space next to "Wife's Name" was left blank, and an indecipherable scribble was written next to "Husband's Name." It is unlikely that the scribble indicated a partner, as the same record indicates that Hall never married.[5] I have spent the past several years compiling records about Hall, whose story reads as tragic and entirely mysterious to me still. By writing "Lady Washington" on every record of Hall's, were officials, in a round-about way, affirming Hall's gender? Court and prison administrators, tasked with adjudicating and imprisoning their fellow citizens, created documentation about this person where none might have ever existed. By policing Hall's gender and sexual acts—unethical by today's standards—they created a record of a singular Philadelphian whom I get to study and reclaim 138 years later (a gift to any historian trying to locate and document LGBTQ individuals, so invisibilized before the twentieth century). This spring, our team added a new stop to the penitentiary's audio tour that explores Hall's life and times.

In addition to revealing the hidden corners of LGBTQ life at the prison, we have begun to study and discuss the persistent racial disparities in the American prison system, evident today and throughout history. In service of this, we have been attempting a more robust excavation of the experiences of formerly enslaved people at the penitentiary. One person who survived the institution of slavery only to encounter the institution of prison was Charlotte Hilton. She arrived at the penitentiary in 1843 with a larceny sentence. For stealing eleven plates, valued at five cents each and totaling fifty-five cents (about $15 in today's dollars), Hilton and her two accomplices earned three years each in prison.[6] Officials recorded

[5] "First-Class Pianist Desires Engagements for Private Parties, Sociables or Dancing School" (classified advertisement), *Philadelphia Inquirer*, Nov. 14, 1897; James Gopsill, *Gopsill's Philadelphia City Directory for 1890* (Philadelphia, 1891); Death and Burial record for Isaac K. Hall, Historic Pennsylvania Church and Town Records, Historical Society of Pennsylvania, accessed on Ancestry.com; Death Certificate for Isaac Hall, June 11, 1902, Philadelphia City Death Certificates, 1803–1915, Philadelphia City Archives and Historical Society of Pennsylvania, accessed on FamilySearch.org.

[6] Bill of Indictment for Charlotte Hilton, May 1843, Clerk of Quarter Sessions, RG 21, Philadelphia City Archives; George Thompson, Warden's Daily Journals, vol. 1 (1829–1855), May 9, 1843, Pennsylvania State Archives.

the following on her admission register: "Charlotte Hilton 40 [years old] M[ulatto] Maryland . . . A Slave, husband purchased her freedom."[7] On another intake record, a different official confirmed that she had been enslaved, that her husband was living in New York and working as a barber, and that they had five children.[8]

Hilton would have been housed in the prison's women's quarters, possibly in Cellblock 1 or 2. While we have no records noting how she spent her time in prison, Hilton must have earned the respect of officials, who secured her a job upon her release—a rare occurrence. On May 9, 1846, three years to the day after she had arrived, Hilton left the penitentiary. Warden Thomas Scattergood wrote that "No. 1669 (Hilton) was sent in the wagon to a very respectable family where she is engaged at service. The benevolent head of which I have no doubt [will] do all in her power to strengthen the good resolutions that have been form'd whilst the object of her care was a sojourner with us."[9]

A brief note ends Hilton's admission register, possibly added the day she was released. An official wrote: "Very penitent now but tis the rod brings the tears. Hopes for reform."[10] The precise nature of this "rod" is unclear, as Eastern State did not use corporal punishments. Similarly, how Hilton fared at the (likely white) respectable family's home remains unknown. An 1855 census of Orange County, New York, shows Hilton, then in her fifties, reunited with her family, including her son and three grandchildren ages eight and under—one of them also named Charlotte. The final record we have for Hilton, from 1880, shows the eighty-one-year-old living on Baxter Street in Lower Manhattan. Though widowed and no longer living with any relatives, Hilton shared a building— possibly a tenement—with black, white, and biracial individuals from the West Indies, Italy, Ireland, and various corners of the United States.[11] At Eastern State, we encourage visitors to consider questions such as the following: Did Hilton share her stories of incarceration and enslavement

---

[7] Admission record for Charlotte Hilton, vol. B: Admissions (1839–1843), May 9, 1843, State Penitentiary for the Eastern District of Pennsylvania Records, American Philosophical Society (APS), Philadelphia, PA.

[8] Reception record for Charlotte Hilton, May 9, 1843, Convict Reception Registers, series 15.56, Records of the Department of Justice, Eastern State Penitentiary, Prison Administration Records, Pennsylvania State Archives.

[9] Thomas Scattergood, Warden's Daily Journals, vol. 1 (1829–1855), May 9, 1846, Pennsylvania State Archives.

[10] Admission record for Charlotte Hilton, APS.

[11] New York State Census, 1855, United States Federal Census, 1880, accessed on Ancestry.com.

with her neighbors? What kind of life, beyond her census-designated occupation of "keeping house," had she crafted for herself?

Like Hilton, most of Eastern State's population of formerly enslaved people came from Maryland and Virginia, though some had roots in the Carolinas, Louisiana, and Alabama, and some arrived at the prison by way of Indiana, New York, and Delaware. There are others, such as eleven-year-old Mary Ash, whose origins straddle pre- and post-emancipation life in America. Born in North Carolina around 1865, the biracial Ash is one of the youngest prisoners we have ever documented. Incarcerated for arson, Ash died at the prison of tuberculosis at age thirteen.[12] She was one of many prisoners of color who entered the prison in a more physically and socially vulnerable position than their white counterparts.[13] Of the thirty-five prisoners whom we know were formerly enslaved, seven died at the prison—a 20 percent mortality rate.[14] In 1843, when Charlotte Hilton and at least one other formerly enslaved person arrived to serve sentences, the mortality rate among white prisoners was 1.85 percent and among black prisoners 6.63 percent. Outside the walls in Philadelphia, the mortality rate among white people was 1.82 percent and among black people 2.49 percent.[15]

Researching these topics reveals how much—and sometimes, how little—our laws have changed. Despite major advances toward equality, LGBTQ people and people of color (and, of course, those who fit into both categories) continue to face barriers to jobs, housing discrimination, lack of political representation, lower health outcomes, greater incidences of mental health issues, family rejection, exclusion from institutions and tenuous social acceptance, "bathroom bills," and profiling. Isaac Hall was born at roughly the same time that Charlotte Hilton left the penitentiary. Their lives likely never intersected, and yet their narratives are woven together by us, the custodians of their records and their stories. They are the actual and spiritual forebears of people who still experience unequal

[12] Eastern State Penitentiary Death Ledger, Collection of Eastern State Penitentiary Historic Site; Death Certificate for Mary Ash, Jan. 16, 1878, Philadelphia City Death Certificates, 1803–1915, Philadelphia City Archives and Historical Society of Pennsylvania, accessed on FamilySearch.org.

[13] Edward S. Abdy, *Journal of A Residence and Tour in the United States of North America, from April, 1833, to October, 1834*, vol. 3 (London, 1835).

[14] Eastern State Penitentiary Historic Site staff have used multiple sources to identify formerly enslaved individuals and those who died at the prison, including intake and discharge records and the penitentiary's death ledger.

[15] *15th Annual Report of the Inspectors of the Eastern State Penitentiary of Pennsylvania* (Philadelphia, 1844).

outcomes before the law and in society at large. They show us lives lived on the margins and the effects of the normalizing, authoritarian forces they encountered. And while they may never have had much social capital or felt particularly powerful, both Hall and Hilton show us the human capacity for resilience and rebirth.

Eastern State Penitentiary   ANNIE ANDERSON

Illustrating Progressive-Era Reform in Pennsylvania: The Anna Wharton Morris Papers

"As we stood out on the pavement in the cool air, the smell that came from the jail door really frightened me." Anna Wharton Morris gamely entered the jail at Scranton, Pennsylvania, on October 22, 1915. What she found inside confirmed her fears: a "young man lying on his bunk, blood-spattered & feverish, but receiving no attention. Each cell had a <u>double bed</u> for <u>two</u> prisoners; <u>horrible!!</u>"[1]

One of the most active Progressive-era prison reformers in the state of Pennsylvania, Anna Wharton Morris (1868–1957) was described by a contemporary newspaper article as a "tall, forceful woman" who was "keenly interested" in prison reform and well-informed, articulate, and outspoken on the issue.[2] Hailing from Philadelphia's social and cultural elite, she seems an unlikely person to have had an intimate knowledge of prisons. Her father, Joseph Wharton, was the prominent industrialist who founded the Wharton School at the University of Pennsylvania. Her husband, Harrison S. Morris, was an author, magazine editor, and managing director at the Pennsylvania Academy of Fine Arts. She traveled to Europe, won horticultural awards, and rubbed shoulders with such artists as Violet Oakley. However, she was also an active member of the Religious Society of Friends (Quakers), a sect noted for its members' engagement in social reform movements and a history of imprisonment for their religious convictions.[3] Much of Morris's early prison work was done within the context of Quaker communities.[4]

---

[1] Anna Wharton Morris, "Journal of Prison Work," p. 4, series 6, Anna Wharton Morris Papers (RG 5/106), Friends Historical Library of Swarthmore College (FHL), Swarthmore, PA.

[2] Rudolph W. Chamberlain described Anna Wharton Morris as the "Quaker leader of prison reform in Pennsylvania" in *There Is No Truce: A Life of Thomas Mott Osborne* (New York, 1935), 398. Laura Lee, "Politics Blamed for Prison Evils: Mrs. Harrison S. Morris Believes It's a Duty to Prepare Inmates for Useful Life, Would Teach Officials," *Philadelphia Evening Bulletin*, n.d., series 6, Anna Wharton Morris Papers, FHL.

[3] Anna Wharton Morris's great-grandfather, Samuel Rowland Fisher, was imprisoned during the Revolutionary War. She published his journals of his experiences in the *Pennsylvania Magazine of History and Biography* 41 (1917).

[4] "Journal of Prison Work," p. 3, Anna Wharton Morris Papers, FHL.

Morris served in leadership roles for such organizations as the National Society of Penal Information, Pennsylvania Prison Society, Pennsylvania Committee on Penal Affairs, Prison Reform Committee of the Public Charities Association of Philadelphia, and the Thomas Mott Osborne Memorial Fund.[5] In about a twenty-year period, she spent nearly $100,000 on prison work.[6] She published articles and letters and spoke on prison issues on dozens of occasions.[7] Thomas Mott Osborne, one of the most influential prison reformers of the twentieth century, told her in 1921, "You are the only person I can trust in [Pennsylvania]!"[8]

The Anna Wharton Morris Papers at the Friends Historical Library of Swarthmore College is a wellspring of uncommonly well-organized sources on the Progressive-era prison reform movement. Morris kept diaries throughout most of her life, with mentions of prisons helpfully indexed and extracted into a "Journal of Prison Work" covering the first two decades of her efforts. The "Journal of Prison Work" features a list of nearly fifty prisons and jails Morris visited, with reports on the physical facilities as well as comments on the demeanor of guards, administrators, and inmates. Her visits were concentrated in Philadelphia but ranged across the country from San Quentin (California) to Sing Sing (New York) and beyond. These first-hand observations offer glimpses into a wide variety of carceral institutions.

Morris was also a prolific letter-writer, and her prison-related missives are conveniently sorted together. She corresponded with a vast network ranging from local activists and nationally significant reformers to current inmates. Her letters are rich in discussions of goals and strategy. Her most extensive correspondence was with Thomas Mott Osborne, a renowned prison activist from New York who counted Morris as a fierce supporter, key collaborator, and trusted confidant.[9]

A highlight of the collection is a series of fourteen cartoons drawn by Eastern State Penitentiary inmate Frederick Funk while incarcerated in the 1920s (cover image, figs. 1–2).[10] There are drawings illustrating the unsanitary and cruel conditions of prison life, as well as incisive political cartoons dramatizing the investigations into warden Robert J. McKenty. These

[5] "Journal of Prison Work," p. 3, Anna Wharton Morris Papers, FHL.
[6] Morris spent $94,504.04 between 1916 and 1937. "Journal of Prison Work," inside cover, Anna Wharton Morris Papers, FHL.
[7] "Journal of Prison Work," p. 3, Anna Wharton Morris Papers, FHL.
[8] "Journal of Prison Work," p. 12, Anna Wharton Morris Papers, FHL.
[9] Chamberlain, *There Is No Truce*, 398.
[10] Convicts and Ex-convicts file in Prison Reform Correspondence, series 6, Anna Wharton Morris Papers, FHL.

Fig. 1: Frederick Funk, "Boast-full Bob's Defiance," ca. 1920, Convicts and Ex-convicts correspondence, Anna Wharton Morris Papers, SFHL-RG5-106, Friends Historical Library of Swarthmore College (FHL).

Fig. 2: Frederick Funk "He is no doctor. He is a 'Nut' Doctor," ca. 1920, Convicts and Ex-convicts correspondence, Anna Wharton Morris Papers, FHL.

remarkable documents provide a unique view on prison reform from the perspective of someone with an intimate understanding of its implications.

The Anna Wharton Morris Papers comprises an extraordinary resource for understanding the Progressive prison reform movement in Pennsylvania. Despite its richness, the collection has scarcely been cited by scholars. The underuse of this incredible source material reminds one of Morris's words in a 1915 pamphlet: "Let us abandon the outworn method of secrecy in prison affairs! Let us take every opportunity to bring them and to keep them openly before the public, so that all may understand the vast waste of human material that has been practiced."[11]

Friends Historical Library   CELIA CAUST-ELLENBOGEN
of Swarthmore College

[11] Anna Wharton Morris, *The New Idea in Prison Reform*, Friends' Social Service Series Bulletin No. 14, 10mo 1915, Other Writings and Material on Prison Reform, series 6, Anna Wharton Morris Papers, FHL.

Tales from behind the Wall: ACT UP/Philadelphia and HIV in Prisons

URING THE 1990s, the AIDS Coalition to Unleash Power (ACT UP)/Philadelphia became increasingly involved in the fight against HIV/AIDS in poor communities of color, even as chapters of the group declined nationwide. The Philadelphia chapter became concerned with intersections between HIV and incarceration, taking up the case of Greg Smith, a black gay man in New Jersey, "serving what may be a life sentence, solely for being HIV positive."[1] Smith's story highlights two points of intersection between HIV and incarceration: the criminalization of people with HIV and the lack of adequate medical care in prison for people with HIV. ACT UP/Philadelphia's involvement in Smith's case points to the group's interest in addressing the twin epidemics of HIV and mass incarceration.[2]

In June 1989, Smith was serving a five-year sentence for burglary in Camden County Jail, just across the Delaware River from Philadelphia. After falling in his cell, Smith was taken to the county hospital for treatment. When a technician refused to take an x-ray of his back, Smith became angry and allegedly bit a guard on the hand while being subdued.

---

[1] ACT UP/Philadelphia's web page from that period is no longer live but is still accessible through the Internet Archive's Wayback Machine (https://archive.org/web/), a database of cached web pages. Here viewers can browse through defunct pages or trace changes to a single page over time. For this reason, it may be especially useful to those researching activist cultures of the 1990s, including resistance to mass incarceration. ACT UP/Philadelphia, "Prisoners with AIDS Are under Attack," cached by Internet Archive Dec. 24, 2002, http://web.archive.org/web/20021224223521/http://www.critpath.org/actup/Project%202.htm.

[2] See Jordan Andrews, "The Current State of Public and Private Prison Healthcare," Penn Wharton Public Policy Initative, Feb. 24, 2017, http://publicpolicy.wharton.upenn.edu/live/news/1736-the-current-state-of-public-and-private-prison; Sarah E. Wakeman and Josiah D. Rich, "HIV Treatment in US Prisons," *HIV Therapy* 4 (2010): 505–10; The Center for HIV Law and Policy, *HIV Criminalization in the United States: A Sourcebook on State and Federal HIV Criminal Law and Practice* (New York, 2017), https://www.hivlawandpolicy.org/sourcebook; Beth Schwartzapfel, "Why Some Prisoners with HIV Get Better Treatment Than Others," The Marshall Project, Mar. 29, 2016, https://www.themarshallproject.org/2016/03/29/why-some-prisoners-with-hiv-get-better-treatment-than-others; and Ernest Drucker, *A Plague of Prisons: The Epidemiology of Mass Incarceration in America* (New York, 2011).

THE PENNSYLVANIA MAGAZINE OF HISTORY AND BIOGRAPHY
Vol. CXLIII, No. 3 (October 2019)

The state charged Smith with attempted murder, arguing that, though the virus is not transmitted through saliva, his HIV constituted a murder weapon. At trial, prosecutor Harold Kasselman's argument turned on Smith's alleged intent to kill. Kasselman claimed that after biting the guard Smith had shouted, "Now die, you pig!" While AIDS advocates protested that the state had singled out Smith because of his race and HIV status, Kasselman painted Smith as a "selfish, malicious, three-time felony loser." After an all-white jury convicted Smith, Judge John Mariano sentenced him to twenty-five years in prison.[3]

On its website, ACT UP/Philadelphia gave Smith a chance to tell his side of the story. He wrote, "At the time of the incident I was handcuffed and shackled, suffering with a back injury and facing two armed guards. . . . [J]ust how many 'weapons of choice' does a shackled person have, anyway?" Smith protested the poor care that inmates with AIDS received, linking inmates' substandard treatment to Governor Christine Todd Whitman's efforts to privatize prison medical care by outsourcing it to Correctional Medical Services (CMS). Smith claimed that because CMS had the inmates' HIV medications shipped from Oklahoma, the prescriptions often arrived late or not at all. HIV drug regimens require strict adherence to be effective, so unreliable delivery meant that "this company is killing the inmates."[4]

ACT UP/Philadelphia hoped that publishing Smith's account would arouse sympathy and action for those living with HIV behind bars. The group described Smith as a "tireless advocate for prisoners with HIV/AIDS," which made him a target for "unlawful segregation and discrimination" by prison staff. ACT UP/Philadelphia encouraged readers to correspond with Smith, donate money for food and incidentals, and publicize health care issues within New Jersey prisons, such as the "law requir[ing] prisoners to pay for a portion of their health care costs . . . discourag[ing] preventative care." This treatment, the group argued, constituted "criminal neglect."[5]

When Smith died in prison in late 2003, ACT UP/Philadelphia made sure that he would not be forgotten. In January 2004, members staged a political funeral at Judge Mariano's home in Haddonfield, a wealthy New

---

[3] Kasselman quoted in Mary S. Petty, "Social Responses to HIV: Fearing the Outlaw," *Sexuality Research & Social Policy* 2, no. 2 (2005): 76–88; Joseph F. Sullivan, "AIDS-Infected Prisoner Receives 25 Years for Biting a Jail Guard," *New York Times*, May 19, 1990.
[4] ACT UP/Philadelphia, "Prisoners with AIDS."
[5] ACT UP/Philadelphia, "Prisoners with AIDS."

Jersey suburb just outside the city. Arriving early on a Tuesday morning, activists chanted, "Murderer!" while carrying a black casket to Mariano's front yard. Waheedah Shabazz-El, a new ACT UP member who had herself recently been incarcerated, recalled that, "We all went out there and turned his town upside down, put flyers on the neighbors' cars, and knocked on the neighbors' doors, and woke everybody up. 'Did you know there's a murderer that lives across the street in that house?'"[6]

ACT UP/Philadelphia's advocacy on Smith's behalf highlights the city's radical tradition, as the group remained vibrant by organizing those who had been disfranchised. This story also highlights the activity of Philadelphia's grassroots politics within the larger region, as members took on the New Jersey state prison system. ACT UP/Philadelphia not only drew attention to the injustice of a system that targeted people with HIV for punishment and then denied them medical treatment behind bars but also presented the "criminal neglect" of people with HIV in prisons as the result of neoliberal policies that enriched corporations at inmates' expense. These connections between the carceral state, public health, and the political economy in the midst of a declining welfare state deserve further attention from historians.

The publication of Smith's account on the ACT UP/Philadelphia website points to the importance of the internet in political organizing during the 1990s, as well as the challenge that this new technology poses to historians. A new generation of researchers will have to grapple with defunct websites and old email lists, not to mention social media and mobile apps, both as digital ephemera and as tools for sharing information and mobilizing likeminded people. To this end, archives and cultural institutions must think about what to preserve from the torrent of data that we now collectively produce every day and how best to preserve it. The answers to those questions will shape what future historians will be able to say and know about power and politics in the first decades of the information age.

Florida International University   DAN ROYLES

---

[6] Joseph A. Gambardello, "Activists Protest at Judge's Home," *Philadelphia Inquirer*, Jan. 30, 2004; Waheedah Shabazz-El, interview with the author, June 5, 2012.

Preserving the Recent Past of Prisons

O N A HOT SUMMER DAY in 2018, Tyler Stump, an accessioning and outreach archivist at the Pennsylvania State Archives, traveled to the State Correctional Institution at Camp Hill (SCI-Camp Hill) to gather historical documents from Pennsylvania's Department of Corrections. Instead of going to an office building, he went to an old horse barn, a surplus space that held over a thousand boxes. Stump dug through the boxes for noteworthy archival materials alongside his intern, Department of Corrections staff, two guards, and several imprisoned people. They struck gold when they found the Press Secretary Papers, an extensive collection that documented the prison system from 1970 to 2010.[1] The discovery and preservation of these materials reflects an important first step for the Pennsylvania State Archives because, until recently, the agency has had few items about the prison system from the 1980s to today. This silence in the records is deafening because the late twentieth century ushered in a new era of mass incarceration in Pennsylvania and across the country, as the number of people in prisons skyrocketed during these decades.[2] Historical records like the ones found in the old barn are invaluable to chronicling the rise of mass incarceration in the United States.

In Pennsylvania, the rates of imprisonment began to rise in the wake of Governor Dick Thornburgh's 1981 War on Crime legislation, which established a host of mandatory minimum sentences that lengthened the amount of time that people spent in prison. The number of people in the state's prisons rose from 7,989 in 1980 to 48,828 in 2010—almost sixfold in only four decades.[3] Incarceration became a hallmark of Pennsylvania's government and American society, as the United States imprisoned people at a higher rate than any other country in the world.[4] Unfortunately,

Thank you to Kate McDannold for her research assistance on this essay.

[1] Tyler Stump, interview with the author, Feb. 19, 2019.

[2] Heather Ann Thompson, "Why Mass Incarceration Matters: Rethinking Crisis, Decline, and Transformation in Postwar American History," *Journal of American History* 97 (2010): 703–34.

[3] Lee T. Bernard II, Ted E. Shumaker, John H. Mease, *Statistical Report, 1980–1986* (Camp Hill, PA, 1986), 17; Dean Lategan, Stacey O'Neill, and Angelo Santore, *Annual Statistical Report 2010* (Camp Hill, PA, 2010), 21.

[4] Peter Wagner and Wendy Sawyer, *States of Incarceration: The Global Context 2018* (Northampton, MA, 2018), https://www.prisonpolicy.org/global/2018.html.

few archives have documented this history. Until recently, the Pennsylvania State Archives, which collects documents from state agencies like the Department of Corrections, had only two boxes of materials from this era, comprising Record Group 58.[5] Pennsylvania and its state archives was not alone. Other states such as California, Illinois, and New York similarly had few records about their prison systems from these decades.[6] Prisons, with their barbed wire and guard towers, are often impenetrable to the public, and the lack of archives further obscures their place in our society.

In the past few years, the Pennsylvania State Archives has worked with the Department of Corrections to fill this gap in the historical record. In 2015, David Carmichael, the state archivist of Pennsylvania, made it a priority to collect critical materials from state agencies, including the Department of Corrections. The state archives hired Tyler Stump, who has worked to build relationships with Department of Corrections staff and improve records management procedures. As a result, Stump preserved the press secretary's records as well as materials at SCI-Camp Hill, SCI-Graterford, SCI-Huntingdon, the women's prison SCI-Muncy, and SCI-Waymart.[7]

This effort has uncovered hidden gems for researchers of modern prisons. The press secretary's collection, which had lain dormant in the old barn, contains documents, audiocassettes, videos, and photographs from 1970 to 2010 that document major events in the state's prison system. The state archives has also acquired materials about the 1989 riot at SCI-Camp Hill; news clippings about landmark legislation, including Megan's Law; and documents about day-to-day life at SCI-Graterford, such as logbooks and memoirs by people imprisoned there. Finally, the state archives has received twenty boxes of material about SCI-Muncy that

[5] The Pennsylvania Department of Corrections formed in 1984 after Governor Dick Thornburgh removed the Bureau of Correction from the state's Department of Justice. This administrative change had a powerful effect on document collection. While the Department of Justice had sent a large quantity of corrections materials to the Pennsylvania State Archives prior to 1984, the Department of Corrections did not, leading to a drop-off in materials after that date.

[6] The New York State Archives' Records of the Department of Correctional Services has four thousand cubic feet of records from before 1980; the Illinois State Archives' Department of Corrections Record Group lists only records dating up to 1978, except for the Centralia prison warden's files (1979–99); and the California State Archives Department of Corrections records has no materials after 1982. See "Prisons and Inmates," New York State Archives, accessed Mar. 6, 2019, http://www.archives.nysed.gov/research/prisons-and-inmates; Illinois State Archives, "Descriptive Guide to the Holdings of the Illinois State Archives," accessed March 6, 2019, http://ilsos.libraryhost.com; and California State Archives, "Inventory of the Department of Corrections," accessed March 6, 2019, http://pdf.oac.cdlib.org/pdf/csa/deptcorr.pdf.

[7] Tyler Stump, interview with the author.

date from 1920 to 1989—a major addition to the previously sparse collection about the women's prison. The archives staff is currently processing these materials and working to make nonrestricted records available to researchers. The effort to preserve the records of the modern prison system in Pennsylvania seems almost Sisyphean, as the Department of Corrections generated millions of documents during these years and continues to produce new records from the twenty-five correctional institutions that it runs. Still, the Pennsylvania State Archives has taken a crucial first step to preserve this history. In doing so, it has offered us a new opportunity to better understand the making of the modern prison system.

The University of North Carolina at Greensboro   ANNE E. PARSONS

THE

Pennsylvania Magazine

OF HISTORY AND BIOGRAPHY

VOLUME CXLIII

1300 LOCUST STREET, PHILADELPHIA, PA 19107
2019

CONTENTS

NOTES AND DOCUMENTS

STAFF

Charles T. Cullen, *President & CEO*

LIBRARY AND COLLECTIONS

Lee Arnold, *Senior Director of the Library &*
Collections

Archives

Cary Hutto, *Director of Archives*

Conservation

Tara O'Brien, *Director of Preservation &*
Conservation Services
Kate Devlin, *Project Conservation Technician*
Sophie Strachan, *Project Conservation*
Technician

Cataloging

Anthony DiGiovanni, *Copy Cataloger*

Research Services

David Haugaard, *Director of Research Services*
Sarah Heim, *Assistant Director of Research*
Services
Daniel Rolph, *Historian & Head of Reference*
Services
Steve Smith, *Public Services Librarian & Stacks*
Manager
Ronald Medford, *Senior Research Services*
Associate

INFORMATION TECHNOLOGY

Caroline Hayden, *Director of Digital Services*
Kat Antonelli, *InHOR Project Manager*
Andrew Williams, *InHOR Project Technician*
Bee A. Martin, *Drexel Intern*

PROGRAMS AND SERVICES

Beth Twiss Houting, *Senior Director of*
Programs & Services

Publications and Scholarly Programs

Christina Larocco, *Editor of* PMHB *& Scholarly*
Programs Manager
Kate Tyler-Wall, *Managing Editor of* JER

Public Programs

Jessica Dubbs, *Visitor Services Coordinator*
Margaret Maxey, *Visitor Services Coordinator*

DEVELOPMENT

Jon-Chris Hatalski, *Acting Head of*
Development & Director of Institutional Giving
Monica Fonorow, *Associate Director of*
Communications
Sarah Ruesch, *Development and Programs Associate*
Patrick Glennon, *Interim Staffing Content Writer*

FINANCE AND OPERATIONS

Lee Arnold, *Chief Operating Officer*
Dennis Williams, *Chief Financial Officer*
Joaquin Moreland-sender, *Business Operations*
Manager
Marc Glassman, *Facilities Director*
Naeem Saleem, *Maintenance Technician*

as of August 2019